Prashantham's monograph is a must read for all international new venture (INV) scholars as his rich analysis and interesting case examples expand INV scholarly thinking to examine the interface of INVs with multinational enterprises (MNE) and is certain to stimulate research on the MNE–INV engagement. Likewise, IB scholars will find the network opportunities with INVs fascinating and vital in today's global world.

Patricia P. McDougall-Covin, William L. Professor of Entrepreneurship, Kelley School of Business, Indiana University, USA

A highly stimulating, thought-provoking and timely volume by a leading scholar in the field, this research-based volume focuses upon the dynamic interactions between MNEs and international new ventures through business network relationships. It synthesizes existing innovative research and highlights new important and exciting research opportunities at the interface between global strategy and strategic entrepreneurship.

Stephen Young, Emeritus Professor, University of Glasgow, UK

This timely book explores the real and potential synergies that exist for both international new ventures and MNEs in the context of business networks. Although international entrepreneurship researchers have long known that piggy-backing on an MNE can help slingshot an international new venture into foreign markets, Prashantham discusses the relationship more deeply. Importantly, he also reminds us of the benefits to the MNE. As such, this volume will be of interest to researchers in both international entrepreneurship and international business.

Nicole Coviello, Professor, Wilfrid Laurier University, Canada

Professor Shameen Prashantham has written an innovative and very informative book on born global firms, networks and MNEs. The book provides excellent background on international entrepreneurship and highlights the critical role that large multinational enterprises play in the emergence and development of young venture firms in international business. It is an excellent resource for scholars with a research focus in international entrepreneurship and international business.

Gary Knight, Professor, Willamette University, USA

Prashantham synthesizes over a decade of field research in Bangalore, supplemented by case-studies in settings spanning Beijing, Cambridge and Scotland to consider how new ventures "dance with gorillas" – that is, engage with large multinationals – as a pathway to international markets; this is a novel and promising line of inquiry. I commend this distinctive contribution from an emergent international business scholar to researchers with an interest in born globals and international new ventures, as well as those studying entrepreneurship in global firms.

Julian Birkinshaw, Professor, London Business School, UK

Born Globals, Networks, and the Large Multinational Enterprise

Focusing on international entrepreneurship, this research book explores the accelerated internationalization of young firms. Known variously as international new ventures (INVs) or "born globals," such firms have come to be viewed as legitimate actors on the global stage alongside large multinational enterprises (MNEs). However, the current approach taken by scholars – studying large MNEs and born globals separately – is questionable.

This book explores the crucial MNE/INV interface – a fascinating, yet under-researched relationship in international entrepreneurship. Drawing upon a decade of case-based research, the author argues that the MNE influence on born globals must be considered more carefully and suggests how new ventures can leverage MNE networks in the pursuit of their rapid internationalization. Furthermore, it demonstrates that, as firms enhance their levels of innovation, new pathways emerge via multinational corporation networks, a phenomenon vividly demonstrated in the emerging economy context of the Bangalore software industry.

This innovative research text will be of interest to academics, researchers, and advanced students with an interest in international entrepreneurship and business, strategy, innovation, and new ventures.

Shameen Prashantham is Associate Professor in International Business and Strategy at Nottingham University Business School China. His research interests include new venture internationalization, in particular how this is influenced by large multinational enterprises' networks, and strategy-making. He co-edited *The Routledge Companion to International Entrepreneurship*.

Routledge studies in international business and the world economy

Born Globals, Networks and the Large Multinational Enterprise

Insights from Bangalore and beyond

Shameen Prashantham

Routledge
Taylor & Francis Group

LONDON AND NEW YORK

First published 2015 by Routledge

2 Park Square, Milton Park, Abingdon, Oxon OX14 4RN
711 Third Avenue, New York, NY 10017, USA

Routledge is an imprint of the Taylor & Francis Group, an informa business

First issued in paperback 2017

British Library Cataloguing in Publication Data
A catalogue record for this book is available from the British Library

Library of Congress Cataloging in Publication Data
Prashantham, Shameen.
Born globals, networks and the large multinational enterprise: insights
from Bangalore and beyond/Shameen Prashantham.
    pages cm. – (Routledge studies in international business and the world
    economy)
    Includes bibliographical references and index.
    1. International business enterprises. 2. Entrepreneurship. I. Title.
    HD2755.5.P73 2015
    338.8'8–dc23   2014045447

ISBN: 978-1-138-78779-7 (hbk)
ISBN: 978-1-138-06258-0 (pbk)

Typeset in Times New Roman
by Wearset Ltd, Boldon, Tyne and Wear

To BJ and Meena Prashantham, my parents, who inculcated in me a fascination with the world and a love for learning from my earliest days,
and
To Diya and Aditya Prashantham, my Chinese-speaking children of British nationality and South Asian heritage – my very own "born globals."

Contents

Figures

Tables

Boxes

Foreword

Shameen Prashantham's aim in this book is shift the conversation on international new ventures by focusing on the interface between new ventures (and smaller firms in general) and large multinational enterprises (MNEs). MNEs are a salient fact of life in the global economy and entrepreneurship research needs to acknowledge this, and to map out its implications. The key connecting concept is the business network. Business network relationships are crucial to both new ventures and to MNEs. When both types are part of the same network, their relationships are perforce asymmetric. The relationship between an MNE's internal network, of subsidiaries and alliances, with its external network of customers and suppliers is fascinating and complex – and is at the heart of the analysis of global business.

Interfirm networks – such as "the global factory" (Buckley, 2011; Buckley & Ghauri, 2004) consist of constellations of independent firms. Each firm is pursuing its own strategy but this strategy is constrained by others in the network. It is also often facilitated by others in the network. Entrepreneurs who often self-proclaim independence must account for the opportunities and threats that the network provides. As this book points out, entrepreneurship is exercised within the MNE too, here characterized as "subsidiary initiative." When business networks are correctly seen, as here, as international links, then spatial and cultural influences come to the fore. It is to Prashantham's credit that he gives due weight to spatial aspects of network relationships because it is often the physical and cultural distance between decision-maker and site of the outcome that creates negative externalities for international companies.

The analysis here is nuanced and rich, paying attention to the individual entrepreneur as well as the institution. It is also dynamic in that forming, consolidating, and extending relationships are considered as part of the analyses and as essential inputs into rational policy outcomes. The use of concrete case-studies helps to anchor the analysis. The book represents an exciting challenge to researchers both in entrepreneurship and international business because it is at the interface of these two burgeoning scholarly endeavors and there is scope for real innovation – research that is policy relevant and theoretically satisfying.

Peter J. Buckley
Centre for International Business University of Leeds
Leeds University Business School
November 2014

Preface

I took my own advice, for a change.

I concluded my earlier monograph on social capital and international new ventures[1] (INVs) with the suggestion that an important future direction for international entrepreneurship (IE) research concerns the influence of new venture's relationships with large established multinational enterprises (MNEs) on their international expansion.

The present monograph seeks to respond to that call by presenting some preliminary case-study-based research, set primarily in Bangalore's software industry, but also supplemented by other exploratory insights from the UK (Cambridge and Scotland) and China (Beijing and Ningbo). In so doing, my main aim is to issue an even more emphatic call for research on INVs – which itself represented a welcome shift in the research conversation away from an exclusive focus on large MNEs – such that there is a further shift in the conversation that explicitly recognizes, rather than ignores (or wishes away), the fact that MNEs are alive and well, and that INVs often operate in a global economy dominated by powerful MNEs.

This book is intended for academics and doctoral students with an interest in research in international entrepreneurship. The rationale for this book is twofold. First, the book addresses a lacuna in the IE literature by focusing on the role of MNE networks in new venture internationalization. Second, this book addresses a broader concern that more needs to (and could) be done to enhance the level of contribution from mainstream international business (IB) research to the IE literature. Given that pioneering scholars such as Tricia McDougall and Ben Oviatt have, quite rightly, described IE as a domain at an intersection between entrepreneurship *and* IB research, it would appear only apt for IB scholarship to enrich the IE domain. This book seeks to show one way in which this may occur: by considering INVs not in isolation from, but as actors on the global stage that *interface* with, large MNEs. Whereas IE researchers have, understandably, worked hard to distinguish INVs from large MNEs, the time may have come to now consider how to progress IE research by leveraging an area of strength of IB researchers, namely, their deep understanding of the MNE.

To be clear, I am proud to be part of the IE research community and gratified by its progress as evident from recent special issues in leading entrepreneurship journals and awards for seminal papers at the leading international business journal. Furthermore, I have been in the privileged position of chairing the IE track at the 2014 Academy of International Business (AIB) conference and co-editing *The Routledge Companion to International Entrepreneurship*. There is no doubt that exciting work is being carried out in the IE domain. But coming at this domain as an IB researcher, and based on my fieldwork in settings as diverse as Bangalore, Beijing and Cambridge, I believe there is scope – and need – for IE research to be enriched by perspectives that shed light on the MNE–INV interface.

The research I present in this monograph is not voluminous; indeed what I present are rather exploratory insights (with "exploratory" being the watchword). The reasons for restricting the data to a fraction of the work I have done over the past decade are, in the main, pragmatic: I did not want to overcomplicate the narrative and, equally pertinent, some of the studies I have conducted are reported in manuscripts that are still under review at journals, thus making their inclusion inappropriate. With a fair wind, some of these will appear in the public domain not long after this monograph is in print.

My conviction about the need for a greater research focus on the INV–MNE interface has been strengthened by stimulating panel discussions that I instigated at the 2012 and 2014 AIB conferences, in which I deliberately involved scholars from outside mainstream IE research. At the first panel in 2012, Peter Buckley called for more meaningful theorizing of MNE–INV engagement within the context of emergent notions around MNE networks such as the global factory. Julian Birkinshaw referred to MNE–INV engagement as a two-way street that typically gets examined from one perspective or the other but not both, as it ideally ought to be. Ram Mudambi and George Yip noted the growing prevalence of MNE–INV collaboration in emerging economies. Charles Dhanaraj pointed to the prospect of MNEs and INVs coevolving, a thought echoed by Anoop Madhok at the follow-up panel in 2014; he suggested it was time to "bring back the multinational" into IE research. Beth Rose, in similar vein, commented that the MNE had perhaps gone missing in IE research.

It therefore seems timely to seek to make sense of the MNE–INV interface. So doing can enrich not only research on INVs but also the study of large MNEs.

I am pleased that I heeded my advice. I hope some others will be encouraged to do so too.

Shameen Prashantham

Note

1 Although I use the term "born globals" in the title (partly in acknowledgment that it is a catchy phrase!), throughout the monograph I use the term "international new ventures." I tend to view the former as a subset of the latter.

Acknowledgments

A monograph such as this would not be possible without the cooperation of research informants. I owe a profound debt of gratitude to Sanjay Shah and several of his colleagues including Kalpa Shah and Paritosh Shah at Skelta (now, Invensys-Skelta). Learning about the case of Skelta–Microsoft collaboration was an important breakthrough in my research on the MNE–INV interface. Another significant development for me was being exposed to the case of Gridsum–Microsoft collaboration in China. I thank Gridsum's Qi Guosheng and Xu Yun for their generous cooperation. More generally, I have been enlightened by studying various efforts by Microsoft to partner with new ventures, and I thank Mathew Clark, Dave Drach, Girish Joshi, Vaqar Khamisani, Mukund Mohan, Amir Pinchas, Amaresh Ramaswamy, Rajiv Sodhi, Yueda Xiong, and other informants at Microsoft.

Special thanks to Avinash Raghava, formerly of Nasscom (India's trade body for software) and now the driving force behind the ecosystem-building activities of iSpirt, a private initiative fostering innovation among software product ventures in India. I continue to learn much from him about the unfolding of what is proving to be an exciting story of internationalization and entrepreneurship.

In China, informants relating to IBM's collaboration with new ventures through the Ningbo Smart City initiative in China, especially You Ting of the Ningbo Government and Larry Qin of IBM who now heads Smarter Logistics, the entity through which IBM works with local actors, have provided me invaluable new insights into the phenomenon. I remain grateful to various informants associated with the Scottish Technology and Collaboration initiative.

My thinking about MNE–INV engagement has benefited greatly from collaborations with some truly wonderful senior scholars. I thank Stephen Young, my former doctoral supervisor and perennial mentor, for his ongoing collaboration and advice on numerous papers, which have greatly enriched my understanding of the MNE. Charles Dhanaraj has been a constant source of support and encouragement in working with me to develop my ideas, including the research presented in Chapter 6. A special word of thanks to Julian Birkinshaw who worked with me on the "dancing with gorillas" thesis and continues to allow me to pick his brain on this fascinating subject.

Other collaborators have helped me access valuable case-studies, and thereby new insights. In Bangalore, K Kumar and Suresh Bhagavatula keep me in touch with the latest developments "on the ground" and were instrumental in connecting me with Sunil Maheshwari (CEO, Mango Technologies) and his partners at Qualcomm, Rakesh Godhwani, Thia Rajagopalan, and Sean O'Leary, who have all been important informants. Girish Balachandran, my brother-in-law, generously shared his Cambridge research that led to a book chapter which has been expanded upon here.

I also thank other scholars, outside the IE community, who have supported my efforts to encourage a dialogue around the need to incorporate an understanding of MNE networks in studies on INVs through panels at AIB and SMS conferences, including Peter Buckley (who has also kindly provided a foreword to this monograph, for which I am most grateful), Rishikesha Krishnan, Anoop Madhok, Ram Mudambi, Beth Rose, and George Yip. Some of them have since become collaborators on ongoing projects relating to MNE–INV engagement. Watch this space.

I am truly grateful to my two academic homes over the period of my research on MNE–INV engagement: the Centre for Internationalization and Enterprise Research at the University of Glasgow, and subsequently the Nottingham University Business School (NUBS) China, where I am especially grateful to Dean Carl Fey for helping create a very supportive research climate.

I gratefully acknowledge funding from the UK Economic and Social Research Council (grant RES-072–27–0005), the Carnegie Trust for the Universities of Scotland, the University of Glasgow's Adam Smith Research Foundation, and NUBS China's Outstanding Researcher Support Scheme.

I thank Stella Yu, Assistant Research Fellow at NUBS China, for her excellent support of my fieldwork in China and assistance with the final formating of this manuscript.

I thank Routledge for giving me another opportunity to work with them. It was Terry Clague who originally reposed faith in me with the opportunity to do the first monograph and Jacqueline Curthoys did the same in relation to this second one. Sinead Waldron has exhibited tremendous patience and meticulous attention to detail in guiding me through the process of putting the manuscript together, as she had also done on another recent project, *The Routledge Companion to International Entrepreneurship*, that I coedited with Stephanie Fernhaber. I am grateful to them all.

In various chapters I have drawn upon some of my published work on MNE–INV engagement, and am thankful for permission to do so to Elsevier (for material in Chapters 2 and 4), Edward Elgar (Chapter 5), Springer (Chapters 6 and 7), and Ivey Publishing (Chapter 10 and Appendix). Formal acknowledgment is provided in the respective chapters.

Last but not least, my family has been a source of unstinting support. This has been true of my parents, BJ and Meena Prashantham, since my youngest days. My younger brother Naveen has been a great affirmer of my research efforts. Academic life coincided with married life for me, and I am grateful to my wonderful wife Deepali for her love, and for constantly providing me with the space to pursue my professional aspirations. I thank my in-laws, Narayana and Vimala

Balachandran, for their daughter(!), and for their own encouragement of my endeavors. Finally, I note the great blessing of having two wonderful children in Diya and Aditya, who are constant reminders of what truly matters in life. I dedicate this monograph, with great affection, to them and to my parents.

Abbreviations

3D	three dimensions
3G	third generation
ANOVA	analysis of variance
BPM	business process management
CEO	chief executive officer
DVR	digital video recorder
ERP	enterprise resource planning
FDI	foreign direct investment
GPRS	general packet radio service
GSM	global system for mobile communication
GSMA	Global System for Mobile Communication Association
H	hypothesis
HQ	headquarters
IB	international business
IBM	International Business Machines Corporation
ICT	information and communication technology
IE	international entrepreneurship
IIM	Indian Institute of Management
IMP	industrial marketing and purchasing
INV	international new venture
IP	intellectual property
IPTV	internet protocol television
ISV	independent software vendor
IT	information technology
LAN	local area network
MNE	multinational enterprise
Nasscom	National Association for Software and Services Companies
NSRECL	NS Raghavan Centre for Entrepreneurial Learning
NV	new venture
NXP	Next Experience (formerly Philips Semiconductors)
OEM	original equipment manufacturer
OLS	ordinary least square
PC	personal computer

R&D	research and development
SE	standard error
SI	systems integrator
SME	small- and medium-sized enterprise
SOC	system on chip
UI	user interface
UX	user experience
VAR	value added reseller
VC	venture capital
VoIP	voice over Internet protocol

Part I

Conceptual underpinnings

1 Networks and new venture internationalization

Introduction: the motivation for this book

The central argument of this monograph is this: international entrepreneurship (IE) research is due a shift in the conversation. Specifically, research on international new ventures (INVs) and born globals ought to take cognizance of the role of multinational enterprise (MNE) networks.

As Zahra (2005) pointed out when commenting on Oviatt and McDougall's (1994) Journal of International Business Studies (JIBS) Decade Award-winning paper, the INV notion resulted in an important shift in the research conversation of the time, away from an exclusive focus on large (elephant-like, in Zahra's colorful metaphor) MNEs to (gazelle-like) INVs, that is, new ventures that seek to derive "significant competitive advantage from the use of resources and sale of outputs in multiple countries" (Oviatt & McDougall, 1994, p. 49). There is no doubt that this was an important shift in the research conversation.

However now, over two decades on, it appears important to recognize that acknowledging the importance of INVs need not preclude acknowledging the continued existence – and dominance – of large MNEs in the global economy. This monograph seeks to argue for the prospect of INVs and MNEs engaging and thus potentially influencing new ventures' internationalization trajectory.

During the past two decades IE research on INVs and born globals has attracted much attention (Jones, Coviello, & Tang, 2011; Oviatt & McDougall, 2005; Zahra, 2005). Signals of the domain's prominence include special issues in leading entrepreneurship journals (Coviello, McDougall, & Oviatt, 2011; McDougall-Covin, Jones, & Serapio, 2014) and the prestigious Decade Award for two seminal papers on INVs and born globals (Knight & Cavusgil, 2004; Oviatt & McDougall, 1994) in the leading international business journal.

Although considerable progress has been made in highlighting and explaining the empirical reality that internationalization is not the preserve of the large MNE (Zahra, 2005), a deficiency in the extant literature is that rather little is known about how new venture internationalization is influenced by large MNEs. Some efforts have been made to identify the effects of INVs' ties with key overseas customers (Yli-Renko, Autio, & Tontti, 2002), venture capitalists (Fernhaber, McDougall-Covin, & Shepherd, 2009) and domestic companies (Yu,

Gilbert, & Oviatt, 2011), but the role of MNE networks in facilitating (or not) new venture internationalization is surprisingly under-researched. This is so despite research surfacing the prospect that new ventures do partner with MNEs. For instance, in Coviello's (2006) pioneering and insightful inductive qualitative research on INVs' network dynamics, one of her three INV cases had an enduring tie with a large MNE on which it "piggybacked" into international markets. But the specifics of this particular relationship were outside the scope of that study. Also, Prashantham and McNaughton (2006) described start-ups' efforts to build ties with large MNE subsidiaries, but stopped short of theorizing the conditions under which those relationships lead to new venture internationalization.

The prospect that MNEs may proffer a conduit for new venture internationalization has been noted in the past (Acs, Morck, Shaver, & Yeung, 1997) but not developed in a meaningful way. Perhaps part of the reason that for this lacuna is that the INV literature was rather more preoccupied initially with differentiating between the internationalization of new ventures and that of established MNEs (Zahra, 2005). Yet, while useful progress has been made in INV research concerning the role of capabilities and networks, with the exception of scholars like Gabrielsson and Kirpalani (2004, p. 555) who advocate that "the born global must utilize large channels provided by multinational corporations," the INV literature appears to "wish away" the role of the MNE. That is, little is known about the interface between INVs and MNEs. Given that the large MNE remains the most dominant actor in the global economy, it appears naïve to fail to consider the potential for MNEs to act as a conduit for INVs' international growth, and, more importantly, to examine the determinants of this occurring.

This is a theoretically relevant lacuna in the literature because the innovation strategies and business model choices of large MNEs shape the institutional environment in which new ventures operate and, in turn, pose opportunities and constraints that new ventures must navigate in order to successfully internationalize. The time now seems ripe for a more concerted effort to incorporate the role of the MNE in our understanding of the INV phenomenon. In my earlier monograph I had called for IE research to consider "the potential role of MNEs as a source of social capital" for INVs (Prashantham, 2008, p. 126). I have reiterated this call more recently by pointing to "the global entrepreneurial ecosystems that are emerging, with multinationals at the nodes not only feeding the growth of a large number of new ventures, but also being nourished and served by the very firms that they help to grow" (Prashantham & Dhanaraj, 2015) and, furthermore, by arguing that:

> Contemporary developments in firms' strategy and technological prowess have meant that the phenomenon of new venture internationalization can no longer fail to explicitly take into account the influence of large multinational enterprises (MNEs) and the interfirm ecosystems that they orchestrate.
>
> (Fernhaber & Prashantham, 2015, p. 2)

This slim monograph represents a preliminary step to address this call. It is structured in three parts:

- Part I (Chapters 1 to 3) delves into and synthesizes relevant prior relevant literatures; Chapter 2 is particularly significant in that it draws on IB literature that IE scholars generally do not take into cognizance, at least explicitly.
- Part II (Chapters 4 to 7) provide some exploratory insights drawing upon case-study research in Bangalore and survey data on Indian software ventures, supplemented by brief case-studies from Cambridge, UK, and Zhongguancun, a high-tech district in Beijing, China.
- Part III (Chapters 8 to 10) discuss implications for research, policy, and practice and contain further case-illustrations from India, China, the UK, and the US.
- Finally, for academics keen to bring research-led insights into the classroom, a teaching case on INV–MNE collaboration is included in an Appendix.

International entrepreneurship: an overview

In a sense, IE research emerged from an *en masse* recognition of accelerated internationalization in certain firms, virtually from inception, and therefore by implication, a refutation of the gradual internationalization process depicted by Uppsala research in the 1970s (Johanson & Vahlne, 1977; Johanson & Wiedersheim-Paul, 1975). Many entrepreneurship scholars were pioneers of IE research (see in particular the contributions to the 2000 IE special issue in *Academy of Management Journal*: Autio, Sapienza, & Almeida, 2000; McDougall & Oviatt, 2000; Zahra, Ireland, & Hitt, 2000), and they have lent the domain solidity in examining the role of knowledge and networks, drawing upon research at the intersection between strategic management and entrepreneurship.

Scholars whose pioneering efforts seek to foster a research agenda at the strategy/entrepreneurship interface suggest that the internationalization of smaller firms is a topic that can be fruitfully examined from a strategic entrepreneurship perspective. Hitt, Ireland, Camp, and Sexton (2001) identify internationalization – along with external networks, resources/organizational learning, and innovation – as a naturally occurring domain in strategic entrepreneurship. Smaller firms lack the resources of their large counterparts. Yet many are able to successfully leverage limited resources in an enterprising yet sensible manner. It is therefore appropriate that research on the internationalization of small and new firms be approached from both strategic and entrepreneurial perspectives.

Hitt et al. (2001, p. 480) note, "Entrepreneurship is about creation; strategic management is about how advantage is established and maintained from what is created.... Wealth creation is at the heart of both entrepreneurship *and* strategic management." Scholars have pointed out the need for an entrepreneurial mindset as they engage with risks and dangers presented by international expansion (Oviatt & McDougall, 1994). Equally, attention has been drawn to the importance of a strategic orientation (Welch & Welch, 1996) in the key choices to be made in terms of market selection, entry mode choice, and timing of entry. A strategic entrepreneurship perspective is consistent with internationalizing new ventures' need to "punch above their weight," as it were, and resourcefully use their limited means to internationalize (Zahra, 2005).

Other scholars echo the call for integrating strategic and entrepreneurial perspectives. Venkataraman and Sarasvathy (2001) colorfully argue that strategic management and entrepreneurship are incomplete without the other – much as Romeo would be incomplete without a balcony, and vice versa! Shane (2003) discusses the need for entrepreneurial strategies that synthesize opportunity recognition and strategic choice. McGrath and MacMillan (2000) call for strategists to adopt an entrepreneurial mindset. These two fields are therefore seen as offering mutually beneficial perspectives (Zahra & Dess, 2001).

The three other domains of strategic entrepreneurship identified by Hitt et al. (2001) can all be related to resourceful internationalization. There are certain *resources* that firms need to possess themselves. The influence of Penrose (1959), whose work inspired the resource-based view of the firm (e.g., Barney, 1991), is evident in the new venture internationalization literature. In particular, knowledge is seen as a vital resource (Wiklund & Shepherd, 2003). As Yli-Renko et al. (2002, p. 280) observe,

> Given the importance of knowledge as a central value-adding resource of firms, it is not surprising that the current dominant theories on the internationalization process of new and small firms treat knowledge as a central enabling and driving resource.

Reflecting the wider literature that emphasizes the role of market and technological knowledge with respect to smaller firms (Wiklund & Shepherd, 2003), the internationalization literature documents the role of market knowledge as a regulator of resources (Johanson & Vahlne, 1977) and of technological knowledge as an enabling resource (Oviatt & McDougall, 1994). An important complementary perspective to the resource/knowledge-based view is that of *organizational learning*. As Hitt et al. (2001, p. 483) assert, "Knowledge is generated through organizational learning." Both traditional (e.g., Johanson & Vahlne, 1977) and more recent (e.g., Sapienza, Autio, George, & Zahra, 2006) perspectives of internationalization highlight the importance of learning (Cyert & March, 1963). Linking this notion with that of external networks, a significant potential outcome for internationalizing firms is that "social capital facilitates learning" (Hitt et al., 2001, p. 482); in other words, "external networks can be valuable because they provide the opportunity to learn new capabilities" (Hitt et al., 2001, p. 481).

A key manifestation of knowledge and learning, including via social capital, is in terms of *innovation*. The literature is replete with exhortations for firms to succeed at innovation. The significance of innovation is evident from Hitt et al.'s (2001, p. 481) suggestion that innovation "is considered by many scholars and managers to be critical for firms to compete effectively in domestic and global markets." The role of innovation in internationalization is evident, at least implicitly, in the literature. McDougall and Oviatt's (2000) definition of international entrepreneurship identifies cross-border innovation as a component. Also, innovation can be expected to precede international expansion, given that "the capability to develop and introduce new products is a primary driver of a successful global strategy" (Hitt et al., 2001, p. 484). Technological knowledge and capabilities are strongly associated with INVs (Oviatt & McDougall, 1994). Finally, parallels have been identified between the processes of innovation and internationalization – in other words, internationalization is an innovative process (Knight & Cavusgil, 2004).

Of all the domains of strategic entrepreneurship, perhaps none is more relevant to new ventures' resourceful internationalization than *external networks*, the focus of this volume. External networks are an important means by which internationalizing firms are able to augment their limited resource base. As Hitt et al. (2001, p. 481) observe, "the greatest value of networks for entrepreneurial firms is the provision of resources and capabilities needed to compete effectively in the marketplace." Thus, in terms of the four domains of strategic entrepreneurship, this volume is primarily concerned with the relationship between external networks and internationalization.

The above interrelationships are depicted in the figure below.

Networks and new venture internationalization

Zahra (2005, p. 21) observes: "It is resourcefulness, not the mere amount or even types of resources, that matters." For INVs, resourcefulness is often manifested in the manner in which they cultivate and leverage network relationships. Indeed, a characteristic of many INVs is their "reliance on network relationships for international growth" (Coviello & Munro, 1997, p. 383); they often develop social capital and access resources via network relationships in ways that are "proactive and strategically aggressive" (Coviello, 2006, p. 716).

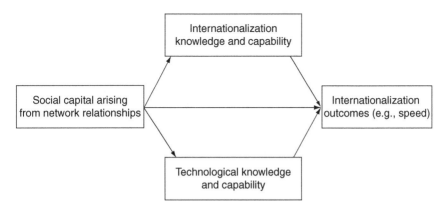

Figure 1.1 Network relationships and new venture internationalization (source: adapted from Prashantham, 2005).

Several IE scholars have drawn on social capital theory to conceptualize and study this phenomenon. Social capital helps INVs to overcome resource-poverty and augment capabilities, and is thus an important means by which INVs cope with their liabilities of newness and foreignness (Chetty & Pahlberg, 2015; Coviello, 2006; Prashantham & Dhanaraj, 2010; Yli-Renko et al., 2002). Social capital emanating from network relationships provides internationalizing small and new firms with vital network resources (Gulati, 1999). According to Putnam and Goss (2002, p. 6), "the idea at the core of the theory of social capital is extremely simple: Social networks matter." Social capital theory is complementary to knowledge-based theories and particularly relevant to new ventures that must "develop firm-specific assets while obtaining complementary external resources through their social networks" (Lee, Lee, & Pennings, 2001, p. 616). Social capital emanating from network relationships has been found to provide access to valuable information and opportunities.

In this volume, social capital is taken to mean

> the sum of the actual and potential resources embedded within, available through, and derived from the network of relationships possessed by an individual or social unit. Social capital thus comprises both the network and the assets that may be mobilized through that network.
>
> (Nahapiet & Ghoshal, 1998, p. 243)

The rationale for the choice of this definition is three-fold. First, this definition is conducive for research on firm-level social capital, including social capital derived from interfirm relationships, which is the focus of the present volume. Second, this definition is integrative of previous work, which is useful given the diversity of views on social capital; for instance, it combines both the public and private good perspectives and is neutral on social capital typologies (Adler & Kwon, 2002; Inkpen & Tsang, 2005). Third, Nahapiet and Ghoshal's (1998) definition – along with their ideas – establishes a relationship between social capital and knowledge wherein repeated and intensive social interaction facilitates the transfer of knowledge (Yli-Renko, Autio, & Sapienza, 2001; Zahra et al., 2000). This approach therefore sits harmoniously with the knowledge-based view of the firm which is dominant in the internationalization literature.

According to Portes (1998), it was Bourdieu (1986, p. 248) who provided the first systematic analysis of social capital, which he defined as "the aggregate of the actual or potential resources which are linked to possession of a durable network of more or less institutionalized relationships of mutual acquaintance or recognition." That one kind of social tie (e.g., friendship) can achieve a different purpose (e.g., work-related advice) is a long-held belief in sociology (Portes, 1998). Social relations – as distinct from market or hierarchical relations – underlie social capital. Of course, market or hierarchical relations may, over the course of time through repeated interaction, yield social relations and therefore social capital (Adler & Kwon, 2002). The social capital concept has formalized the notion that benefits can be derived from social ties and encapsulated it in a manner that has attracted considerable interest beyond the confines of sociology. For the purposes of the present discussion, the key facet of social capital is that it allows new ventures to achieve levels of internationalization and performance that they would not have been able to achieve on their own. In other words, *social capital enables resourceful internationalization.*

The role of network relationships and social capital in new venture internationalization is well recognized in the IE literature (Chetty & Pahlberg, 2015; Jones et al., 2011). Oviatt and McDougall (2005, p. 544) acknowledge that "networks help entrepreneurs identify international opportunities, establish credibility, and often lead to strategic alliances and other cooperative strategies." Also, as Zahra (2005, p. 24) notes, "Building relationships and gaining access to existing networks can help to shorten and expedite INVs' learning."

Insights from my research

My own research reiterates the importance of proactiveness in building and leveraging social capital; notably, a longitudinal qualitative study suggests that expanding network ties actively (i.e., *building social capital*) and extracting learning benefits from extant ties (i.e., *leveraging social capital*) differentiate new ventures that attain high international growth from those that fail to do so (Prashantham & Dhanaraj, 2010). This study is a direct extension of the preliminary work reported in my earlier monograph (Prashantham, 2008). My conceptual and empirical research suggests that some forms of social capital, within a firm's *portfolio* of ties, are more beneficial for certain outcomes than others. That is, networks need to be leveraged discerningly. My conceptualization of internationalization speed makes distinctions between bonding and bridging as well as strong and weak ties, each combination of which is theorized to impact specific dimensions of absorptive capacity (Prashantham & Young, 2011).

Empirically, in relation to overseas (host-market) network relationships, I found ethnic ties to have a positive effect on the level of entry mode commitment (i.e., the likelihood of using modes beyond exporting) of Indian software ventures, and this in turn was associated with the proportion of international revenues (Prashantham, 2011). Subsequent analyses reveal that ethnic ties are more beneficial for ventures based in high-reputation locations such as Bangalore, but that on balance, *non*-ethnic ties are more potent for driving international revenues than ethnic ties (Prashantham, Dhanaraj, & Kumar, 2015). Furthermore, in relation to domestic (home-market) network relationships, I found that in general ties in the home economy are less effective for driving international revenues than specific aspiration-raising industry body ties (Prashantham & Birkinshaw, 2015). Furthermore, another specific category of home-market relationships, namely, ties with foreign MNE subsidiaries, has a positive effect on internationalization capability (Prashantham & Dhanaraj, 2015). The latter is directly germane to the focus of this monograph and is therefore included as part of the exploratory findings reported in it (see Chapter 6).

Thus, as noted in my previous monograph, three facets of social capital, with respect to internationalizing new ventures, seem especially relevant. These facets, discussed briefly below, are:

- the development of social capital
- the leverage of social capital
- the management of portfolios of social capital.

Developing social capital

New ventures often have certain network relationships that can play a significant role in initial market entry (Coviello, 2006). It would seem likely that such founding relationships can have path-dependent consequences in terms of the subsequent development of the firm. Initial network relationships are often directly attributable to the entrepreneur and/or top management team (McDougall, Shane, & Oviatt, 1994). Over time, however, additional network relationships can – and indeed, must – be built. These relationships will likely influence subsequent international expansion. Oviatt and McDougall (2005) argue that initially strong ties are important to ventures but over time a set of weak ties are more likely to provide information and opportunities that facilitate accelerated internationalization. As the portfolio of network relationships expands, and especially as the ventures' confidence and capabilities grow (Prashantham & Dhanaraj, 2010), international growth accrues.

However network relationships are not easy to come by and cannot be taken for granted. Research at the strategy/entrepreneurship interface suggests that ventures can develop the capability to replenish extant network relationships (i.e., its stock of social capital) with the addition of new ties (Hitt et al., 2001). However, while ventures' network range, density, and centrality are bound to increase over time (Coviello, 2006), they must overcome key barriers and be able to achieve visibility, efficiency, and intimacy with respect to their network of relationships.

Achieving *visibility* is an important challenge for the smaller firm. It is one thing for a large established MNE to seek strategic alliances and quite another for a small, often young, firm to attempt to establish network relations. While there are specific smaller social networks within a given milieu wherein even smaller firms *can* gain visibility, this requires time and effort and often it is the entrepreneur who bears the burden of networking activity that must be undertaken if the smaller firm is to become, and remain, well known among key actors. Difficulty arises from these firms' liability of foreignness (Zaheer, 1995) – which has been viewed by some scholars as a symptom of deficient international social capital (Arenius & Autio, 2005) – and liability of smallness (and of newness, for young firms). As Zahra (2005, p. 23) suggests in relation to INVs:

> INVs usually experience three types of liability. The first relates to their newness and inexperience, which limits their access to resources and existing

networks. Newness raises questions in the minds of other stakeholders about INVs' credibility and potential viability. The second liability stems from their size, as many INVs are small. This limits the slack resources of INVs and, as a result, their ability to withstand the challenges of internationalization. The third and final liability arises from the foreignness of INVs, which means that they have to work hard to overcome barriers to entry, build links to their customers and suppliers, and gain the acceptance of potential customers.

The next aspect of developing social capital can be referred to as the achievement of *efficiency* in relationships, once they are formed. The point being made here is that social capital is more likely to result when a firm is seen to be efficient and competent in its interactions. Efficiency in carrying out its part in a transaction or engagement ensures that a firm instills confidence and trust in the other actor(s) involved. As Gulati (1995, p. 92) notes, trust is built over time through repeated interactions. Implicit in this assertion is the importance of new ventures ensuring that they "deliver", that is, do a good job of whatever it is that has been undertaken. Initial interactions and impressions can be particularly important in establishing the reliability of the firm as an efficient player.

Finally, not in all but in some cases, it becomes possible and appropriate for new ventures to build *intimacy* with the other actor(s). Intimacy implies knowledge about the other actor(s), which in turn increases the odds that any assistance provided is timely and relevant. Frequency of interactions over time leads to stronger ties (Granovetter, 1973) which can yield useful benefits (Krackhardt, 1992). Even moderate levels of intimacy in relatively weaker ties can lead to the exchange of useful information and trade leads (Chetty & Pahlberg, 2015; Prashantham & Young, 2011). An important case of network relationship where intimacy can be particularly valuable is that of the involved customer, defined as "a customer who regularly makes purchases … and with whom the relationship also involves considerable interaction and information exchange and the discussing of past, present and future needs" (Yli-Renko et al., 2002, p. 293). Such relationships can be a valuable source of technological knowledge, thereby resulting in useful innovation and internationalization outcomes (Zahra et al., 2000).

Leveraging social capital

As noted, the initial network relationships of a small internationalizing venture can often be attributed to the entrepreneur and/or top management team. The extent to which a firm is initially endowed with social capital can vary greatly. The work of Bourdieu (1986), for instance, would suggest that ventures where the top management team is drawn from the elites of society – marked by attendance at prestigious educational institutions, for example – possess greater stocks of social capital. Certainly in the context of management education, the popular press emphasizes the importance of connections that are fostered at business schools through an MBA degree, implying that alumni networks from top educational institutions constitute a valuable source of social capital.

Similarly, another determinant of the stock of social capital that a firm is endowed with is the prior professional affiliations of the founding team. Former employees and colleagues can be an important source of information and advice (Nebus, 2006). Also, as with educational institutions, former employers can signal pedigree which in turn helps to overcome barriers to social capital, such as a lack of visibility, while seeking to form network relationships (e.g., with banks). Finally, friends and family cannot be discounted as an important source of social capital. A variety of studies by entrepreneurship scholars (e.g., Davidsson & Honig, 2003) indicates that family and friendship ties can result in tangible help in the form of startup capital as well as intangible assistance (e.g., moral support). Thus, in a variety of ways, a new venture may be well endowed with social capital.

A well-endowed stock of social capital of itself, however, cannot guarantee success for the firm. Rather, social capital must often be "leveraged" in order to yield useful network resources such as information (Gulati, 1999). New ventures seem to vary in their capability to leverage social capital through, for instance, integrating knowledge within and outside its boundaries, or adeptly tapping into a relatively small set of network relationships with a view to achieving initial successes (Lorenzoni & Lipparini, 1999). Building upon these successes, such firms could expand further, adding additional ties to their portfolio of network relationships in the process.

However, it is also conceivable for smaller firms to have a sizeable number of network relationships and yet fail to utilize them effectively. This could occur for a variety of reasons: (1) the top management team may not actively recognize these relationships as a valuable resource; (2) the top managers may be bashful when it comes to asking for help; (3) the managers may make suboptimal requests of network relationships. For instance, weak ties may be better used in obtaining novel information while strong ties may be more likely to yield timely assistance (Granovetter, 1973). If, however, top managers have inappropriate expectations that all ties, whether strong or weak, will yield timely help, then they are likely to face disappointment in their interactions with less intimate associates.

It is worth making the point that the main emphasis in terms of leveraging social capital is on *active*, rather than passive, utilization of network relationships. This would be reflected in the difference between consciously attending a carefully selected set of industry conferences in order to build and maintain visibility, and failing to do so. It suggests that there is virtue in communicating within key close relationships, the nature of assistance that would be truly beneficial. What it certainly does *not* imply is that phony or opportunistic behavior in relation to building networks will yield fruit. At best, such efforts can lead to positive outcomes in the short term. In the medium to long term, such behavior will destroy social capital. Furthermore, cultural differences and nuances will likely have to be taken into account while interacting with other actors. Persistence in making a request may be appreciated in one culture and frowned upon in another. Thus efforts to leverage social capital have to be accompanied by cross-cultural sensitivity.

Finally, it is suggested that the leveraging of social capital is likely to yield useful *learning* outcomes. As noted earlier, social capital can facilitate the creation and acquisition of market and technological knowledge, thereby leading to useful innovation and internationalization outcomes. Social capital fosters trust and decreases barriers to the exchange and combination of new knowledge (Nahapiet & Ghoshal, 1998). This is likely to be increasingly the case as firms develop their visibility, efficiency, and intimacy vis-à-vis their networks of relationships.

Managing social capital portfolios

Building upon the idea that network relationships differ in their characteristics and potential benefits, it would seem that firms possess *portfolios* of different network relationships. There are various ways of identifying social capital types. Granovetter (1973) differentiated between strong and weak ties which primarily differ in terms of their degree of intimacy and frequency of interaction. Putnam and Goss (2002) distinguish bonding from bridging social capital. According to Putnam and Goss (2002, p. 11), "Bonding social capital brings together people who are like one another in important aspects (ethnicity, age, gender, social class, and so on), whereas bridging social capital refers to social networks that bring together people who are unlike one another." In other words, bonding social capital pertains to social groups that are homogenous or similar; bridging social capital pertains to heterogeneous or dissimilar groups (Putnam, 2000).

In the context of new venture internationalization, important differences exist between network relationships in the local milieu and those in international markets. In other words, geographic location of social capital (local/domestic versus foreign/overseas) is another important dimension that differentiates among social capital types in a new venture's social capital portfolio. Again, the entrepreneur or top management team is often crucial in determining the extent of local and overseas network relationships that a new venture possesses. When these individuals have studied and/or worked abroad, they may have access to network connections that yield valuable social capital (McDougall et al., 1994). Furthermore, friends and family may live abroad, constituting a valuable source of coethnic social capital. Research has shown how relationships with organizations outside the home market provide the initial information and contacts that make international growth possible (Agndal, Chetty, & Wilson, 2008; Coviello, 2006; Yli-Renko et al., 2002), and also how such relationships enable the capability development and adaptation needed for enduring success (Prashantham & Dhanaraj, 2010; Yu et al., 2011).

However, in general, new ventures are likely to have a greater number of local network relationships compared to their network relationships in international markets. The latter are therefore coveted connections and the first instinct of new ventures appears to be to look overseas to its existing network relationships (Johanson & Vahlne, 2003) and to make further efforts (e.g., via trade missions) to develop further connections. Such an intuitive preference for overseas or foreign network relationships is understandable. Indeed, foreign network relationships do yield valuable benefits in terms of international expansion. Coviello and Munro's (1997) insightful research into the evolution of new ventures' international growth patterns as a consequence of their network relationships suggests that initial relationships with large customers can be especially valuable in providing a breakthrough in initial international market entry. In some cases clients may themselves expand internationally, in the process providing new international business opportunities for the internationalizing new venture (Bell, 1997). Network relationships in international markets can yield valuable information and leads, as well as advice (e.g., on the timing of market entry) that may be difficult to obtain elsewhere. Internet technology makes communication with network relationships easier and so valuable opportunities, information, and advice can emanate from social capital in international markets.

The benefits of international networks notwithstanding, the value of *local* network relationships ought not to be overlooked. There may be a tendency to do so, however, in the context of internationalization, given firms' instincts to look beyond their own national boundaries for valuable networks (Johanson & Vahlne, 2003). Overlooking networks in the firm's own local milieu would, however, be inappropriate. The local milieu is crucial in terms of providing the inputs that go into the creation of globally mobile offerings in the first place (Fernhaber, Gilbert, & McDougall, 2008). In other words, for small knowledge-intensive ventures, the local milieu is ultimately associated with innovation, resources, and learning (Hitt et al., 2001). Where agglomeration leads to specialization, new ventures may also benefit from reputation effects and access to infrastructure. Intriguingly, local milieus also attract MNEs to set up local subsidiaries (Birkinshaw & Hood, 2000), which constitute a potential source of social capital that could lead to interesting possibilities, both locally and internationally.

The important point here is that new ventures must take a holistic perspective in recognizing their wider portfolio of network relationships, which could have potential direct and indirect benefits, both in international markets *and* in the local milieu (Zhou, Wu, & Luo, 2007). Taking a portfolio approach increases the odds that firms will have realistic expectations of network ties without becoming overly reliant on any. It could also provide an antidote to negative effects of social capital such as groupthink or overembeddedness (Yli-Renko et al., 2001). Internationalizing new ventures that curb their instinct to look for social capital exclusively in international markets are likely not to overlook valuable resources in their own backyard, as it were. However discernment is needed in the local milieu as well, given mixed results about the effects of local ties. Some studies have suggested that strong home-country relationships have a positive impact on a firm's international growth and competitiveness (Boethe, 2013), some have found that certain home-country relationships may suppress international growth (Milanov & Fernhaber, 2014), while others have found no significant effect (Yu et al., 2011).

Combining the notions of "bridging" and "local" social capital emanating from MNEs can be valuable for INVs. This is, however, a perspective on which the IE literature is surprisingly silent. Chapter 2 therefore delves into some relevant literatures on MNEs and their associated networks, and Chapter 3 draws on these understandings to offer preliminary conceptualization on the role of MNE ties in new venture internationalization.

Postscript: Uppsala research and the turn toward a network approach

As the final part of this chapter, I thought it useful (even if somewhat tangential) to highlight the evolution in Johanson and Vahlne's thinking, often referred to as the Uppsala approach (because the scholars initially worked together at that Swedish university), over the past four decades which indicates an ever-growing emphasis on the role of networks in firm internationalization. Given that their thinking from the 1990s onwards (which coincides with the advent of INV research) shares theoretical underpinnings, that is, the business network perspective with other work on MNE networks that emanated from Uppsala University as well (Andersson, Forsgren, & Holm, 2002, 2007; Forsgren, Holm, & Johanson, 2005), we might infer that the suggestion of researching the MNE–INV interface sits rather comfortably with their more recent formulations of the internationalization process. Hence in this final section I briefly trace the evolution of their thinking as articulated in a series of seminal papers, and reiterate the message – although they do not explicitly make it themselves – that an important future research direction concerns the MNE–INV interface (Gabrielsson & Kirpalani, 2004).

As noted earlier, research on the accelerated internationalization of INVs is oftentimes pitted against the more gradual internationalization process depicted by the work of Johanson and colleagues at Uppsala in the 1970s. The evolution in thinking espoused by Johanson and Vahlne over the past four decades is relevant to my present endeavor for two main reasons. The first is that their recent thinking is highly affirmative of the role of network relationships in facilitating new venture internationalization (although the accent in IE research is on social network theory rather than their preferred business network theory). The second is that, while they do not explicitly highlight the potential influence of MNE networks in new venture internationalization, their work shares theoretical common ground with other important work emanating from Uppsala on MNE networks – which provides useful conceptual background and is discussed in Chapter 2.

The early work of Johanson and colleagues in the 1970s (Johanson & Vahlne, 1977; Johanson & Wiedersheim-Paul, 1975) came to represent an understanding of internationalization as being gradual and cautious. Johanson and Wiedersheim-Paul (1975) presented longitudinal case data from four Swedish multinationals that suggested that internationalization follows a gradual establishment chain along increasing levels of psychic distance over time. This formed the empirical basis for the more theoretical treatment in Johanson and Vahlne (1977). That conceptualization posited that a firm's internationalization commitment increases with its knowledge of foreign markets, which is accumulated experientially over time. The major obstacle to such learning was seen to be psychic distance. Johanson and Vahlne (1977) arguably anticipated resource- and knowledge-based perspectives of international strategy in terms of the core of their theorizing. However, in INV research Uppsala research is primarily identified with a flawed prediction of the speed of internationalization of firms and, in conjunction with Johanson and Wiedersheim-Paul (1975), represents the "strawman" against which INV research was largely positioned, especially initially.

There has since been an evolution in their thinking. The role of networks has come to be emphasized thus leading to some resonance with INV research (Chetty & Pahlberg, 2015). This was due to another important strand of Uppsala research that has led to a voluminous literature on business networks. Referred to as the industrial marketing and purchasing (IMP) research stream, this work recognizes the network-based interconnections that influence firm behaviors. Perhaps the best-known model known to IB researchers was the Johanson and Mattsson (1988) model of network-based internationalization, which was built upon in subsequent iterations of Johanson and Vahlne's (1990, 1992, 2003) model in which networks play an important role.

The first major network-oriented revision to their thinking was perhaps the work of Johanson and Vahlne (1990). Network-related notions were added, drawing upon Johanson and Mattsson (1988), and this line of thinking was further modified in Johanson and Vahlne (1992). After the concept of the "international new venture" was formally introduced to IB audiences in Oviatt and McDougall (1994), following other critiques (e.g., Bell, 1997; Coviello & Munro, 1997; Jones, 1999) of Johanson and Vahlne (1977), a stronger statement on the role of networks, this time explicitly addressing an IE audience, was made (Johanson & Vahlne, 2003). This article again emphasized the role of networks but in addition, rather surprisingly, downplayed the role of entry modes; thus it represented a further shift in thinking that emphasized networks' influence. With regard to the emergent body of work on accelerated internationalization, Johanson and Vahlne (2003, pp. 83–84) observed that "a common feature of much of this research is that it places attention on networks and network relationships when trying to understand and explain the rapid internationalization of the firms." They went on to suggest that "there is a need for new and network-based models of internationalization" (Johanson & Vahlne, 2003, p. 84).

Subsequent restatements depict, I would argue, increasing alignment between basic notions of networks and knowledge in a strategic entrepreneurial perspective of INVs and those of Johanson and Vahlne. In Johanson and Vahlne (2006) the authors added notions pertaining to opportunity recognition (an apparent reaction to Oviatt and McDougall's (2005) redefinition of IE), but also explicitly drew upon notions of social capital (e.g., Nahapiet & Ghoshal, 1998).

Perhaps the most significant reformulation of the 1977 model appears in Johanson and Vahlne (2009). The notion of "liability of outsidership" (vis-à-vis networks) was highlighted; that is, becoming an insider within business networks is key to the internationalization process. It is this liability, rather than a more generic liability of foreignness (associated with psychic distance) emphasized in the 1977 model, that represents the true obstacle to internationalization. Another point of difference from the early work is that in the 2009 model, firms were viewed as exchange units rather than as production units, and learning about foreign markets was seen as a social process (cf. Madhok, 1995) rather than a unilateral one. Such an understanding of internationalization appears compatible with a networks-based perspective of international entrepreneurship, as noted. More significantly this approach shares theoretical underpinnings with another strand of research that came out of Uppsala, namely, the work on embedded MNE networks – and which offers valuable background conceptual fodder for the agenda of this monograph which is to call for a further shift in the IE research conversation to explicitly consider the MNE–INV interface.

In sum, I have highlighted the evolution in Johanson and Vahlne's work and sought to make the point that important ideas have emanated from their work with (indirect) links to the MNE embeddedness work. In Chapter 2, relevant IB literatures – including other Uppsala research (Andersson et al., 2002, 2007; Forsgren et al., 2005) – provide a basis for recognizing the scope for meaningful engagement at the (hitherto largely overlooked) MNE–INV interface.

2 MNE networks

A blindspot in INV research

Introduction: bringing back the multinational

While the INV literature usefully highlights the fact that international expansion is not the preserve of established MNEs, it has somehow failed to come to grips with the fact that MNEs never "went away"! However, with a few exceptions (e.g., Acs et al., 1997; Gabrielsson & Kirpalani, 2004; Prashantham & McNaughton, 2006), extant accounts of new venture internationalization arguably convey such an impression. While INV scholars have generally demonstrated a strong understanding of the strategic entrepreneurship underpinnings of INV behaviors and outcomes, the IE domain has arguably suffered from a superficial understanding of the established MNE. This chapter therefore provides a decidedly incomplete – but hopefully useful – overview of the MNE and its associated networks. There are three key areas of focus.

- First, I refer to IB research on MNE embeddedness that complements various perspectives on MNE networks (e.g., Andersson et al., 2002, 2007; Forsgren et al., 2005). It may be enlightening for IE researchers with a predominantly entrepreneurship orientation to take cognizance of the significance of Uppsala research – which is all too often caricatured (although not without basis) as a "strawman" that fails to recognize the prospect of accelerated internationalization. There is, however, far more to Uppsala research; this includes important notions of business networks and, specifically, the idea that MNE subsidiaries are dually embedded, to a greater or lesser extent, in host markets *and* the interfirm network.
- Second, I draw upon the literature, largely pioneered by Birkinshaw (2000), on MNE subsidiary initiative and entrepreneurship. Dually embedded MNE subsidiaries' entrepreneurship often takes the form of initiatives aimed at increasing the significance of the subsidiary to the parent. When the initiative is concerned with developing new knowledge by tapping into local expertise it may well involve partnering with local actors, including new ventures. This, in turn, raises the prospect of new ventures forging local links with MNE subsidiaries (Prashantham & McNaughton, 2006) which, if transformed into global links, enables their transformation into INVs.

• Third, I highlight the growing emphasis by leading scholars in the field on the interfirm networks that MNEs orchestrate. Several notions make this point such as Buckley's (2009; 2011; 2012) global factory, as do earlier normative ideas such as Doz, Santos and Williamson's (2001) metanational and Rugman and D'Cruz's (2000) flagship firm. This is a radical shift in thinking within IB research, away from the traditionally monolithic perspective of MNEs to one that actively acknowledges the importance of other actors in the interfirm network. Previous research (e.g., Ghoshal & Bartlett, 1990) noted that the network of MNE headquarters and its subsidiaries was akin to an interfirm network; the focus there, however, was predominantly on the *intra*firm network of the MNE. The more recent work referred to above, by contrast, focuses literally on MNEs' interfirm networks.

The embedded MNE

Several INV researchers with a background in entrepreneurship position their work squarely in opposition to the internationalization process research undertaken at Uppsala, which has hence appeared to have become something of a byword for obsolete thinking on (gradual) international expansion. It might be educative to gain a broader understanding of work emanating from Uppsala that advanced extant understanding of business networks that not only influenced the evolution of Johanson and Vahlne's (1990, 1992, 2003, 2009, 2011, 2014) thinking but also underpins a distinct stream of valuable research on embedded MNE networks (Andersson et al., 2002, 2007; Forsgren et al., 2005). The MNE embeddedness notion highlights the network-like properties of MNEs in relation to the links between headquarters and subsidiaries, between various subsidiaries, and between various MNE units and external actors. In this approach, distinction is made between internal and external embeddedness, and MNE subsidiaries are viewed as being embedded, to a greater or lesser extent, in both networks.

Such work builds on a business network approach that emanated from the research of the industrial marketing and purchasing (IMP) group on supplier–customer relationships, and commenced with a multicountry initiative in which Uppsala researchers played a major role. Håkansson and Snehota (1995, p. 25) note that, according to business network theory, a "relationship is not viewed as created and developed in isolation ... a relationship can also be regarded as part of a broader context." Furthermore, they observe that "the coordination of activities between two firms in a business relationship also takes place within the wider business network context.... When two firms cooperate in a focal business relationship they bring to the focal relationship their connected relationships" (Håkansson & Snehota, 1995, p. 1036). This *markets-as-networks* approach sees markets as firms "tied together directly and indirectly through networks of relationships which may extend in any direction without limit" (Blankenburg Holm, Eriksson, & Johanson, 1999, p. 468), rather than one where there are clear boundaries between the firm and the environment. Network structures are viewed as being inherently unstable, and networks and constituent relationships are expected to coevolve (Slotte-Kock & Coviello, 2010, p. 44). Turnbull, Ford, and Cunningham (1996) suggest that firms have a "relationship strategy" for generating resources and enhancing their network position. Network-related changes may be proactive or reactive, and produce positive or negative consequences (Halinen, Salmi, & Havila, 1999).

Business network theory underpins research, largely by (another) set of Uppsala researchers, on what they describe as the "embedded multinational" (Andersson et al., 2002, 2007; Forsgren et al., 2005). A key insight from this work is the notion of dual embeddedness, that is, the extent to which subsidiaries operate within internal and external business networks. Internal embeddedness refers to the relationships formed with the MNE parent company and with sister subsidiaries as internal suppliers, internal customers, or internal R&D centers. External embeddedness concerns relationships with local network partners, commonly customers and suppliers. But external relationships may include both market and non-market actors; Welch and Wilkinson (2004) highlight the possible requirement for developing relationships with government bodies (non-market actors) and for building the political embeddedness of business networks. By comparison with external embeddedness, in internal business relationships the partners are members of the same organization and hence are linked formally by administrative mechanisms and knowledge flows (Forsgren et al., 2005). Meyer, Mudambi and Narula (2011) argue that there is a tension between increasing embeddedness in the MNE network to the detriment of the subsidiary's position within the host country milieu; and, conversely, between promoting a subsidiary's loyalties to its local network at the expense of its affinity to its parent. Thus dual embeddedness may be a "double-edged sword" (Meyer et al., 2011).

From the perspective of internationalization-seeking new ventures, an important implication of the dually embedded nature of MNE subsidiaries is that they potentially represent a source of geography-spanning social capital (see Chapter 5). That is, local links forged by a new venture with an MNE subsidiary could, potentially, be leveraged to yield multiple new connections within the MNE's wider network across national boundaries. This is more likely to occur when the new venture engages with an *entrepreneurial* MNE subsidiary, as discussed next.

MNE subsidiary entrepreneurship

Dually embedded MNE subsidiaries may exhibit entrepreneurial behaviors. Birkinshaw (2000, p. 8) refers to the notion of subsidiary entrepreneurial initiative as the "proactive and deliberate pursuit of a new business opportunity by a subsidiary company," designed to develop the subsidiary's value-added scope. Subsidiary initiative can be viewed as a manifestation of corporate entrepreneurship and is "defined as a discrete, proactive undertaking that advances a new way for the corporation to use or expand its resources" (Birkinshaw & Prashantham, 2012, p. 156).

Subsidiary entrepreneurship may be oriented towards building new knowledge and competences. Indeed, Cantwell and Mudambi (2005) distinguish between competence-exploiting subsidiaries and competence-creating subsidiaries; the latter often require proactive efforts on the part of entrepreneurial subsidiary leaders (Birkinshaw, 2000). Rugman and Verbeke (2001) note that competencies generated as a result of subsidiaries' autonomous initiatives can confer subsidiary-specific advantages, that is, the idiosyncratic strengths developed by host-country managers building upon host-country specific advantages. Achieving new competencies can enhance subsidiaries' significance and bargaining power within the wider MNE and thereby the level of attention that they can attract from headquarters (Bouquet & Birkinshaw, 2008). This in turn can lead to greater knowledge flows to and from the subsidiary within the MNE network, leading to a virtuous cycle of influence building – which of course can end up being counterproductive if the subsidiary engages in rent-seeking behavior (Mudambi & Navarra, 2004).

Achieving such competences entails combining knowledge transferred from the network with newly created knowledge and subsidiary knowledge embedded in idiosyncratic host-country locations. However accessing the latter is not something MNE subsidiaries can always accomplish on their own; thus they may seek to partner with local actors. Phene and Almeida (2008) note that innovation-seeking MNE subsidiaries' absorption and utilization of knowledge are influenced by sourcing and combinative capabilities that are applied to internal *and* external knowledge sources. Unsurprisingly then, Cantwell (2013, p. 18) notes that "the source of technological creativity and the entrepreneurial initiation of new *business network formation* is increasingly to be found at the subsidiary level" (emphasis added). Indeed, a wide variety of partnerships dominate in high-technology sectors where technological development is rapid and complex with uncertain benefits (Hagedoorn & Narula, 1996). Cantwell (2013) suggests that competence-seeking initiatives may increasingly take the form of project-based activity involving external actors, as MNEs shift away from closed to open networks. He thus envisages entrepreneurial subsidiaries engaging in internal *and* external network formation. Consequently, new boundaries are emerging within the MNE because of the development of more internationally decentralized innovation networks.

From the perspective of internationalization-seeking new ventures, an entrepreneurial MNE subsidiary represents the ideal sort of MNE-related entity with which to commence the process of building an international relationship with the MNE. That is, the mere fact of an MNE subsidiary's dual embeddedness does not guarantee openness to entertaining overtures from a new venture. However, when led by entrepreneurial leaders, such a subsidiary will be much more likely to do so. Entrepreneurial subsidiaries could, potentially, represent "pipelines" (Lorenzen & Mudambi, 2013) that allow new ventures to span cross-border boundaries and internationalize via MNE networks – which is a key argument of this volume. Furthermore, not only are there engagement opportunities through (ad hoc) entrepreneurial initiatives at the level of MNE subsidiaries, there is a growing recognition in IB scholarship of systematic efforts driven by the MNE as a whole to cultivate and orchestrate interfirm networks – that could, potentially, include internationalization-seeking new ventures. I turn to the topic of MNE network orchestration next.

MNE network orchestration

Twenty-first-century research in IB and strategy has witnessed the emergence of concepts which, while varying in the detail of their substance, convey a remarkably consistent message: it is no longer appropriate to view MNEs as independent entities because their strategies and performance are increasingly manifested within interfirm networks that they seek to orchestrate (Buckley, 2012; Cantwell, 2013; Doz et al., 2001; Rugman & D'Cruz, 2000).

A prime example of this shift towards a network-centric perspective of the MNE is Peter Buckley's notion of the global factory (Buckley, 2009, 2011, 2012; Buckley & Ghauri, 2004). The global factory depicts the interfirm network that MNEs orchestrate as having three components: core functions that include branding, design, engineering, and R&D; distributed manufacturing; and local market adaptation including warehousing and distribution. It has been argued that the global factory represents "the ideal structure" through which MNEs can deal with the central tension – well known in IB research – of having to "reconcile pressures to be globally efficient with the need to be locally responsive" (Buckley, 2012, p. 79). The rationale for this network-oriented approach by MNEs is attributed to there being greater options than in the past for the cost-effective externalization and spatial distribution of economic activity. Buckley (2012, p. 77) observes:

> Action within the firm on improving business processes and agency costs may entail expansion or contraction of the firm as individual elements of each business process ... can be evaluated by comparison with the market alternative and can be externalized if it is profitable to do so (outsourcing) or can be relocated if this reduces overall costs (offshoring). These two decisions – the first on internalization/externalization control choice and the second a location decision – have led to the creation of the "global factory."

This perspective of course echoes understandings of the large corporations in the wider literature on innovation and strategy where a network-centric perspective has become increasingly salient (Dhanaraj & Parkhe, 2006; Nambisan & Sawhney, 2011). Thus a network perspective (Dyer & Singh, 1998; Lavie, 2006) complements the traditional focus on knowledge as a key driver of MNEs' competitive advantage in IB research (Buckley & Casson, 1976; Kogut & Zander, 1993). Madhok's (2006, p. 5) observation about shifts in IB research from "an emphasis on ownership to relationships" seems to hold true for research not only on international strategic alliances but also on MNEs more generally. As Buckley (2012, p. 79) observes:

The global factory is, of course, a network ... held together by control of key assets and flows of knowledge and intermediate products. Networks, like any other form of organization, have both benefits and costs (the latter are often ignored).

Other work has also highlighted the growing significance of MNE networks. One such perspective is that of Rugman and D'Cruz (1997; 2000) who introduced the idea of the flagship firm. Perhaps the clearest statement of the concept appeared in Rugman and D'Cruz (1997, p. 403): "A flagship firm is defined as a multinational enterprise which has taken on the strategic leadership of a business network consisting of four other partners: key suppliers, key customers, selected competitors and the non-business infrastructure." Successful flagship firms need to foster trust and develop collaborative relationships with their partners. Arguably, the flagship firm notion anticipated future concepts such as the global factory (Buckley & Ghauri, 2004; Buckley, 2009, 2011, 2012). It does appear a pity that the flagship firm has been somewhat overlooked by mainstream IB research. Rugman and D'Cruz (2000) usefully highlight the complexity of managerial decision-making that MNEs must contend with. Perhaps the most significant value-addition of the flagship firm notion is that of "non-business infrastructure" which draws attention to, *inter alia*, the role of non-market actors such as the state or state-related actors. Thus opportunities for new ventures to engage with MNEs that operate as flagship firms may, in certain instances, entail intermediation by non-market actors (e.g., Prashantham & McNaughton, 2006).

Also, from a primarily normative perspective, Doz et al. (2001, p. 5) exhorted MNEs to "view the world as a global canvas dotted with pockets of technology, market intelligence, and capabilities," and therefore as a source of multiple external knowledge sources. According to the authors, MNEs ought to learn from the world by looking to new innovative milieus outside classic hot spots in order to tap into (especially tacit) technological and market knowledge. Conceivably this would entail MNE units partnering with local actors including new ventures that possess such valuable tacit knowledge.

Thus from the perspective of internationalization-seeking new ventures, an opportunity presented by global MNE networks is to build complements to the orchestrating MNE's offerings and this could, potentially, open up opportunities in new ventures' home *and* host markets, often with support from the MNE's organizational infrastructure (Prashantham & Birkinshaw, 2008). Of course, it goes without saying that the new venture must possess significantly high levels of technological capability for such opportunities to arise. But this holds true of INVs in general; the scope for a new venture to internationalize is enhanced by technological distinctiveness (Knight & Cavusgil, 1996; Oviatt & McDougall, 1994). MNE networks represent possibilities for the new venture that would be difficult for it to attain by itself or through the entrepreneur's informal interpersonal ties that much of the prior INV literature focuses on. This is also in sharp contrast to earlier depictions in the IB literature of fairly low-level linkages (i.e., purely contractual arm's-length engagement) between MNEs and local small firms.

Indeed, Buckley (2006, p. 687) has been explicit about the potential link for meaningful engagement between entrepreneurial ventures and MNEs orchestrating interfirm networks: "electronic communication has opened new areas for small firms to fill in completing the networks of the MNE … as part of a symbiotic network with large firms" (Acs et al., 1997).

The MNE–INV interface: beyond siloed research on MNEs and INVs

It should be apparent from the foregoing discussion that IB scholars have come to recognize the scope for MNE subsidiaries to be competence-creating, not merely competence-exploiting (Cantwell & Mudambi, 2005). This is consistent with exhortations to learn from the world if MNEs are to build and maintain competitive advantage vis-à-vis rivals (Doz et al., 2001). There is therefore considerable scope for MNEs to engage with local firms, including highly disparate ones such as new ventures, the motivation for which stems from the MNE's strategic imperative of the pursuit of new knowledge, innovation, and capabilities. Taking Chapters 1 and 2 together, it can be seen that in both MNE and INV research, great emphasis is placed on what firms know (knowledge and capabilities) and who they know (networks and social capital). And of course, each affects the other: social capital can lead to knowledge (Nahapiet & Ghoshal, 1998) while (relational) capabilities can lead to new networks (Kale, Dyer, & Singh, 2002).

But despite these obvious commonalities in themes, the MNE and INV research streams have progressed in conspicuously parallel paths, paying little attention to each other. Notwithstanding the valuable insight that the IB literatures on MNE networks, the embedded MNE and MNE subsidiary entrepreneurship provide, it should be acknowledged that, inasmuch as the INV literature has neglected the influence of MNE networks, so too has mainstream IB literature largely ignored the interdependencies between large MNEs and smaller entrepreneurial firms in their home and host markets. Neither does the MNE embeddedness literature nor the research stream on MNE subsidiary entrepreneurship delve deeply into the alliance-forming behaviors of MNE subsidiaries in the pursuit of locally embedded knowledge pools.

Consequently, relationship-building between MNE subsidiaries and local actors generally represents a black box, thus representing an important research opportunity for mainstream IB research (Birkinshaw & Prashantham, 2012). This is a subject of considerable importance because accessing local knowledge in a given setting is not always easy for MNEs. Not only do these entities generally suffer from the liability of foreignness, they may also experience challenges in their search for new knowledge within local milieus. Even those MNE subsidiaries that have, over time, acquired the status of an insider rather than an outsider might not be readily able to search for and identify relevant specialist knowledge because their networks are rarely sufficiently broad and deep, especially when they are pursuing knowledge that is new to the firm. In such situations, allying with local actors can be beneficial – but even this is not straightforward or easy, especially when the MNE subsidiary has to step outside of the comfort zone of its extant business networks. Compounding the difficulty of engaging with strangers is the vast difference between MNE subsidiary and local actors when relevant knowledge is embodied within *new* ventures. The sheer asymmetries between MNEs, on the one hand, and new ventures, on the other, mean that the odds of MNEs and indigenous ventures forming links are not very high to begin with (Prashantham & Birkinshaw, 2008). And even when such relationships are established, the likelihood of these developing in a smooth matter does not appear very high in the light of the constraints arising from differing statuses and organizational structures leading to a generally fragile interface between the two sets of actors (Doz, 1988).

But there is growing (at least anecdotal) evidence of MNE–INV engagement. Indeed, it should be acknowledged that Acs et al. (1997) did note the prospect of new ventures internationalizing via MNE "conduits." Arguably this conceptualization represents a passive stance on the part of new ventures, in the sense that their focus is depicted as being simply on innovation with the MNE taking over the innovation's diffusion into international markets. Indeed, subsequently Acs and Terjesen (2013) referred to such ventures as "born locals." While a welcome addition to the literature, not least in terms of the recognition of the existence and influence of large established MNEs, this line of argument does not adequately reflect contemporary developments in IB research concerning the nature of MNEs, their subsidiary units, and the networks that interfirm MNEs increasingly orchestrate (as seen in this chapter). Emergent understandings of the nature of the MNE would suggest that much more *active* engagement between MNEs and INVs could, in theory at least, accrue.

Thus although it remains a reality that some of the key challenges to MNE–INV engagement stem from the MNE's greater bargaining power (see also Alvarez & Barney, 2001) and the transaction costs associated with asymmetric actors engaging with each other (Prashantham & Birkinshaw, 2008), network-centric MNEs are increasingly demonstrating a proclivity for engaging for external actors in the pursuit of supply chain linkages, complementary offerings, and external knowledge (Buckley, 2012; Cantwell, 2013; Doz et al., 2001) such that active, rather than passive, engagement between MNEs and INVs is perhaps not as far-fetched as when Acs et al.'s (1997) ideas were first published. Hence more recent attempts to describe links between MNEs and INVs use more active metaphors, such as Vapola's (2011) notion of the "battleship strategy" of MNEs whereby complementary offerings of internationalization-seeking new ventures are proactively sought and marshalled by MNEs in ways that are mutually beneficial and through commercial activities that cross national borders.

In sum, active engagement between internationalization-seeking new ventures and MNE networks has been ignored by INV researchers, and MNE scholars have generally overlooked MNE links with INVs. And yet the scope for and significance of MNE–INV engagement is not difficult to conceive of when one examines key notions in the literature on MNEs and their associated networks. The key point being made is that there is much in the IB literature to indicate the *potential* and *motivation* for MNEs to engage with new ventures; this represents an important opportunity for internationalization-seeking new ventures. The next chapter, therefore, provides preliminary conceptualization of how INVs may build and leverage social capital with large established MNEs.

3 MNE networks and new venture internationalization

MNE ties potentially represent a source of social capital that is local (initially in terms of where the initial ties are forged) and bridging, in terms of the dissimilarity between the partners (Putnam, 2000) and the access to novel information, ideas, and opportunities (Burt, 1992). While seemingly obvious, this observation is significant for IE research stems because, while the INV literature usefully highlights the fact that international expansion is not the preserve of established MNEs, it has somehow failed to come to grips with the effects of MNEs on INVs. Somehow, the role of MNE networks has been largely missing in this stream of research.

With a view to redressing this deficiency, the previous chapter sought to highlight relevant ideas concerning MNEs and their networks. Although the prospect of MNEs partnering with INVs specifically is only implicit in this work, the scope for MNE–INV engagement can be inferred, given the growing imperative for MNEs to tap into knowledge pools around the world. The notion of the embedded MNE (Forsgren et al., 2005) distinguishes between MNEs' internal and external business networks and points to scope for new ventures, among other actors, to collaborate with MNEs because the latter's internal strategic imperatives may drive external alliancing activity. The literature on MNE subsidiary entrepreneurship (Birkinshaw, 2000) suggests that such partnering efforts are more likely to be manifested in entrepreneurial subsidiaries, and new ventures may find such actors to be especially open to partnering with them. Furthermore, the work on global network orchestration (e.g., Buckley's (2012) notion of the global factory) indicates that the opportunities at the MNE–INV interface are likely to rise further as interfirm network-building by MNEs acquires serious strategic undertones (see also Cantwell, 2013; Doz et al., 2001; Rugman & D'Cruz, 2000).

Building on these understandings of MNEs, and drawing on the ideas of developing, leveraging, and managing portfolios of social capital from Chapter 1, the remainder of this chapter conceptually discusses the potential for INVs to engage with MNEs.

Developing MNE ties[1]

The need for partnering proactiveness

Several contemporary large multinational enterprises (MNEs) have developed interfirm ecosystems as a basis for engagement among business units and external firms (Dhanaraj & Parkhe, 2006; Katila, Rosenberger, & Eisenhardt, 2008). Such networks are likely to attract a heterogeneous set of actors, several of which are *asymmetric* vis-à-vis the focal MNE in terms of organizational size, structure, and power (Cao, 2006). A case in point is entrepreneurial new ventures that enter these networks. Particularly in technology-intensive sectors, such interfirm networks attract new ventures as participants. They are attractive to MNEs chiefly on account of their innovativeness. On their part, the new ventures often seek access to valuable resources (Prashantham & Birkinshaw, 2008). Little is known, however, from the perspective of new ventures, as to purposive actions that could enable them to develop and leverage social capital with MNEs.

Given that similarly sized firms are generally more likely to forge ties with each other (Cao, 2006), the sheer *asymmetry* between new ventures and MNEs in size, organizational structure, and power could be an impediment to the potential for social capital that could be developed and leveraged between these sets of firms. There are seldom clear-cut role counterparts across these dissimilar organizations (Doz, 1988). Also, new ventures tend to have a greater need for large established firms than vice versa and there is a consequent imbalance in mutual dependence (Katila et al., 2008). Interfirm asymmetry reduces the odds of the paths of these different firms crossing naturally, and increases the odds of stringent, unfavorable terms and conditions being imposed on new ventures which dissuade them from engaging (Alvarez & Barney, 2001). Subsequently, interfirm asymmetry reduces the odds of interfirm routines and absorptive capacity being developed owing to each actor's distinct templates for organizational activity (Lane & Lubatkin, 1998). Thus, asymmetric interfirm ties seem unlikely to form and – if they do form – to be effective (Cao, 2006).

And yet MNEs are potentially a source of bridging social capital to new ventures in that they can be a source of novel information, opportunities, and ideas; furthermore, they are less likely to suffer from the information redundancy of bonding social capital (Prashantham & Dhanaraj, 2015). New ventures are more likely to seek out and utilize such social capital when they are oriented towards innovation and internationalization. But of course such an orientation does not guarantee that fruitful relationships will ensue. Preliminary research suggests that the manner in which new ventures and MNEs interact, for instance, in everyday settings over a period of time has a bearing on how effectively social capital is developed amongst them (Prashantham & McNaughton, 2006).

An interesting question to consider therefore is how new ventures overcome interfirm asymmetries to develop and leverage social capital with large MNEs. Some new ventures are more adept than others at partnering with MNEs because

Table 3.1 Proactiveness of new ventures in forming alliances over time

	Forming	Consolidating	Extending
Nature of proactiveness in relationship-building	Identifying and availing of formalized network entry points into the MNE ecosystem	Using ecosystem events to cultivate informal everyday interaction with key individuals to begin joint activity	Arbitraging goodwill across boundaries to increase MNE unit/partner nodes
Underlying knowledge-base to enact this dimension of proactiveness	Understanding the management innovation(s) of the MNE vis-à-vis partnering (e.g., partner programs)	Identifying key individuals who can act as "interpreters" of the MNE's culture, systems and rituals	Comprehending the roles and priorities of units and partners in the differentiated MNE network
How it overcomes asymmetry	Provides institutionalized mechanisms to address the lack of role counterparts (Ring & Van de Ven, 1994)	Enables joint activity despite divergent traditions of organizational routines (Doz, 1988)	Helps in navigating the organizational complexity of large MNEs (Dhanaraj & Parkhe, 2006)
How this is distinct from symmetric ties	Not the same as proactive frontal initiation of ties	Not the same as proactive bonding and coordination	Not the same as linear increase in relationship scope
Consequences for interfirm ties between new ventures and the MNE	Fosters structural embeddedness (interactions) Initially likely to begin as a many → one relationship as the MNE has multiple simultaneous ties through a partner program	Fosters relational and cognitive embeddedness (trust and shared narratives/goals). Relationship evolves into more of a one → one relationship as traction develops with the MNE	Fresh cycles of structural, relational and cognitive embeddedness. Relationship later incorporates ties to multiple MNE units for a one → many relationship.

of their relational capabilities, that is, their capacity to form and nurture interfirm ties (Prashantham & Birkinshaw, 2008). More specifically, interest is in exploring the role of proactiveness over time, based on Sarkar, Echambadi, and Harrison's (2001, p. 702) premise that 'firms that are proactive in forming alliances are likely to enjoy higher performance'. Table 3.1 encapsulates conceptualization of this dimension of relational capability.

Given technological distinctiveness, a new venture's ability to successfully cultivate and leverage a relationship with a large MNE stems from its relational capabilities and entrepreneurial proclivity, which jointly indicate *proactiveness* in relationship-building. To elaborate, some new ventures are likely to be more adept than others in proactively forging relationships with MNEs.

Furthermore, consistent with Prashantham and Birkinshaw's (2008) notion of "dancing with gorillas," relationship-building and -leveraging are treated as a process over time rather than a one-shot affair. Proactiveness in forging ties with MNEs may enable new ventures to forge ties with MNEs in the first place and subsequently to span boundaries within the MNE to extend the scope of the relationship over time. However there is still scope to explore proactiveness more fully, and other relational capabilities, that enable new ventures to overcome asymmetry whilst partnering with MNEs.

Finally, it is worth highlighting the growing relevance of these issues in the Indian context where MNE subsidiaries play a prominent role in economic development (Kumar, 2009). Relationships between new ventures and large MNEs are particularly salient for both sets of actors when the former develop distinctive intellectual property (IP). Even though power asymmetries may to some extent be assuaged by a new venture's technological distinctiveness, there remain organizational asymmetries and concerns about value appropriation to contend with (Cao, 2006; Prashantham & Birkinshaw, 2008). Historically, IP creation by innovative new ventures has been well established in advanced economies. However the growing potential for new ventures in emerging economies such as India indicates both the scope for and the ambition of (Kumar, 2009; Kumar & Krishnan, 2003a) new ventures to ascend what Kumar and Krishnan (2003b) refer to as the *value curve*.

Leveraging MNE ties[2]

Strategic renewal: the dual innovation–internationalization challenge

Strategic renewal entails the acquisition and use of new knowledge through innovative behavior that leads to capability development and ultimately a modification of the firm's product-market domain (Floyd & Lane, 2000, pp. 154–155). Addressing strategic renewal explicitly in the present context is useful in that it highlights the *dual* challenge of innovative behavior (e.g., new product development) *and* subsequent change (e.g., international market entry). Achieving strategic renewal is not easy. Key to the challenge is "the tension between exploration and exploitation" (Crossan & Berdrow, 2003, p. 1087). Put simply, exploration is concerned with acquiring new knowledge whereas exploitation focuses on the utilization of extant knowledge (March, 1991). In the present context, the exploration of technological knowledge is vital to achieving pre-internationalization innovation outcomes. However, firms tend to focus on exploitation rather than exploration. As March (1991, p. 73) observes, "Compared to returns from exploitation returns from exploration are systematically less certain, more remote in time, and organizationally more distant from the locus of action and adaptation." And yet, in order to take advantage of opportunities, new ventures may also have to engage in knowledge exploration. This leads to a tension between focusing on a firm's current viability through exploitation and its future viability through exploration (Levinthal & March, 1993).

The exploration–exploitation tension of course also applies to the realm of technological innovation. Exploratory innovation relates to such activities as the development of new product offerings, as distinct from exploitative or incremental innovation where extant offerings are modified (Smith & Tushman, 2005). The merits of pursuing exploratory innovation are evident from March's (2006) observation that, in the absence of exploration, exploitation causes stagnation; new and useful directions will not be discovered. For a new venture seeking international growth, exploratory innovation is unlikely to be an end in itself. Rather, it is a means to enable international market entry, thereby achieving growth. The expectation is that the outcome or result of the exploratory innovation will allow the venture to target new customers in defined markets (Abernathy & Clark, 1985). In this case of course, the defined markets extend beyond the national borders of the firm's domestic market. Thus, new ventures may engage in exploratory innovation, motivated by the prospect of international expansion, in order to develop more suitable product offerings.

Floyd and Wooldridge (2000) propose that strategic renewal entails three underlying processes: idea generation, initiative development, and strategic renewal. Strategic renewal begins with the generation of ideas, that is, the consideration of a variety of possibilities entailing changes to the product-market domain of the firm with a view to strengthening performance. Certain ideas are then transformed into initiatives that may begin with pilot projects or are launched on a trial basis. Initiative development is especially significant in that capability learning outcomes may be greatest during this process (Floyd & Lane, 2000). Finally, strategic reintegration occurs when initiatives become part of the firm's mainstream activities, often involving organizational members beyond the more narrowly defined initiative team. In the context of a new venture, such a distinction may be more blurred in comparison to a large multi-unit organization. Nonetheless, in new ventures too it seems likely that initiatives reach a concluding phase beyond which their activities are perceived as normal rather than novel.

Strategic renewal is essentially about the creation of new knowledge in the pursuit of new products and markets (Floyd & Lane, 2000); but it is also said to be best viewed as a system of relational exchange in social networks (Floyd &

Wooldridge, 2000). Hence, the ideas that follow draw on social capital theories of knowledge from the strategic management literature. The premise here is that social capital could lead to exploratory innovation by facilitating knowledge formation. The social capital theory of knowledge formation is based upon the assumption that firms are social repositories of knowledge (Kogut & Zander, 1992). The basic logic is that social capital facilitates the creation and acquisition of knowledge by reducing barriers to the exchange and combination of resources, in particular knowledge (Nahapiet & Ghoshal, 1998).

The role of bridging social capital

Social capital facilitates knowledge formation in terms of three dimensions. First, the structural dimension of social capital allows greater proximity and interaction among actors through, for example, greater network closure (Nahapiet & Ghoshal, 1998). Second, the relational dimension increases the confidence of actors that they will not be opportunistically exploited, notably through the development of trust, facilitating thereby information exchange and joint problem-solving (Uzzi, 1997). Third, the cognition dimension enhances the efficacy of knowledge transfer through the development of shared meanings among actors (Inkpen & Tsang, 2005). This logic applies to the new venture context as well; in fact, the accentuated resource constraints in this setting make it even more likely that social capital will be crucial in knowledge accumulation (Davidsson & Honig, 2003). For new ventures, social capital's facilitation of knowledge accumulation has direct relevance to technological innovation outcomes (Yli-Renko et al., 2001).

Ties with such dissimilar firms are likely to overlap a little with the focal firm's other homogenous ties (e.g., with other new ventures) and are referred to here as bridging ties (McEvily & Zaheer, 1999). Bridging social capital is associated with dissimilar actors, and relates to a typology that distinguishes between bonding and bridging social capital (Putnam, 2000).[3] In contrast to bridging social capital, bonding social capital relates to relationships involving socially homogenous actors; for instance, Davidsson and Honig (2003) refer to family ties as a source of bonding social capital for entrepreneurs. Social capital that new ventures can leverage to acquire new knowledge that arises from network relationships with larger firms is an example of bridging social capital (Alvarez & Barney, 2001). For new ventures, bridging social capital is likely to be more difficult to form compared to bonding social capital. Indeed, bridging social capital may constitute a relatively low proportion of ventures' initial stock of social capital (Davidsson & Honig, 2003) but is potentially valuable because it could facilitate exploratory innovation in three ways.

First, the benefits from bridging ties can be considerable, particularly in terms of the novelty of the information, ideas, and opportunities that they yield (McEvily & Zaheer, 1999). Novel information arises primarily owing to the lower information redundancy with respect to bridging ties; in other words, dissimilar actors have fewer common links and therefore less overlap in information exchange (Granovetter, 1973). Non-redundancy in ties reflects weak or missing links across sets of ties, referred to as structural holes. New ideas may be generated when structural holes are spanned, resulting in unforeseen possibilities, to the mutual benefit of all parties involved (Burt, 2004). Fresh opportunities may arise when referrals for new business are made and when actors draw upon their own social networks.

Second, bridging social capital may be helpful in spurring new ventures to adopt a mindset that accommodates the need for engaging in exploitative *and* explorative innovation simultaneously (Smith & Tushman, 2005). De Carolis and Saparito (2006) argue that social capital provides stimuli, particularly new information, from the environment that influences entrepreneurial cognitive biases in a manner that reduces perceptions of risk. Bridging social capital could, by virtue of exposing the new venture to diverse perspectives, usefully suppress uncritical groupthink processes that may develop through deeply embedded (i.e., bonding) network relationships (McEvily & Zaheer, 1999). This is not to decry the virtue of bonding ties, especially within the new venture (Davidsson & Honig, 2003). However, the challenge to the existing mindset that may result from interactions with bridging ties will likely ensure that the new venture is open to and remains focused on new possibilities, including that of exploratory innovation (Burt, 2004).

Third, bridging social capital can be a source of legitimacy for new ventures (Alvarez & Barney, 2001). New ventures suffer from a liability of newness stemming from the absence of an established track record. In addition, they face a liability of foreignness while entering international markets, which is arguably compounded by their resource poverty (Sapienza et al., 2006). Bridging social capital could mitigate these liabilities if the partner involved in the bridging tie has credibility associated with longevity of operations and an international reputation (Yli-Renko et al., 2002). Also, the partner's resources and capabilities in technology and international business could compensate for the new venture's skill deficiencies (McEvily & Zaheer, 1999).

Ties with MNE subsidiaries: social capital dimensions and strategic renewal

Bridging social capital arising from local MNE subsidiaries provides an interesting case. Apart from fulfilling the criteria of bridging ties that have potential to facilitate strategic renewal, MNE subsidiaries are inherently international in that they are embedded simultaneously within an international organizational network and the local milieu (Inkpen & Tsang, 2005). Of significance, potentially, are boundary-spanning MNE subsidiary managers who can tap into individuals and resources within and beyond their own subsidiary in the MNE network. Particularly when such boundary-spanning individuals are involved, ties with local MNE subsidiaries could influence idea generation so that the ideas are better suited to the international marketplace. Initiative development involving joint activity with the MNE subsidiary is more likely to incorporate an international component. And strategic reintegration is aided by extending the activity, potentially, in a range of international markets. Three social capital dimensions of ties with local MNE subsidiaries are considered below in turn.

Structural social capital

The structural dimension of social capital refers to "who you reach and how you reach them" (Nahapiet & Ghoshal, 1998, p. 244); the focus is on access to network ties. However in the case of new ventures seeking to engage with MNE subsidiaries, gaining access to these bridging ties is not straightforward. Knowledge-intensive industries may possess a dual structure comprising indigenous firms and the local subsidiaries of MNEs which often appear to inhabit parallel small worlds. The difficulty in accessing bridging ties with local MNE subsidiaries could arise from a liability of newness which in turn constrains new ventures' network centrality within the local milieu. In sum, new ventures will likely encounter the problem of being unable to bridge structural holes between their interfirm networks and those of MNE subsidiaries (Burt, 2004).

So how can new ventures span structural holes? McEvily and Zaheer (1999, p. 1134) note the potential role of regional institutions that provide collective support services (e.g., trade bodies) to act as "networks intermediaries for interaction and information exchange among firms" that are otherwise unlinked. This could lower new ventures' search costs and mitigate their lack of legitimacy. As McEvily and Zaheer (1999, p. 1140) observe, "The search economies generated by intermediaries stem from their maintaining an extensive network of ties to different parts of a social system." These ideas are consistent with Prashantham and McNaughton's (2006) findings about the Scottish Technology and Collaboration initiative that sought to assist new ventures in building structural social capital with local MNE subsidiaries. Such initiatives relate to a regional public policy agenda to foster economic development through foreign investment (Young, Hood, & Peters, 1994). A key role of the intermediary is not only to help link two organizations but also to enable the entrepreneur of the new venture (ego) access the relevant individuals within the multinational subsidiary (alter) at the interpersonal level.

How does structural social capital affect strategic renewal? A key idea of relevance here is that structural social capital is related to network access. Greater network access can increase the volume of ideas to which the new venture is exposed. This is particularly the case in bridging ties because, as Burt (2004) argues, behavior and opinion are more homogenous within than across groups. The heterogeneity of stimuli from bridging ties is more conducive to idea generation (Floyd & Wooldridge, 2000). Novel information about market trends and competitive factors, for instance, can enhance the possibilities that a new venture becomes aware of, and hence the number of ideas generated. Structural social capital also aids initiative development by providing access to complementary capabilities which, when combined with the new venture's own, can translate ideas into initiative. And when the initiative approaches the end of its lifecycle, reintegration can be undertaken by the new venture with greater clarity as a consequence of the clear lines of communication between the new venture's entrepreneur and key managers in the partner organization. Synthesizing the above thinking, it is argued that structural social capital can facilitate strategic renewal by increasing the informational benefits of social capital, thereby enhancing internationalization-seeking the new venture's opportunity set (Gulati, 1999).

Relational social capital

The relational dimension of social capital refers to "relations people have, such as respect and friendship" (Nahapiet & Ghoshal, 1998, p. 244). Thus trust is vital, but not easy to develop between new ventures and MNE subsidiaries. Even if it were possible to develop structural social capital by leveraging a regional institution (or some other honest broker), there is no guarantee that respectful, friendly, and trusting ties will ensue. A potential hindrance in this specific context is the perceived lack of autonomy of some MNE subsidiaries which could trigger anxiety among new ventures that joint activity may be abruptly terminated if the MNE headquarters were to alter the subsidiary's mandate and priorities. Thus the very attribute of multinational subsidiaries that makes them attractive to internationalization-seeking new ventures, namely, that these are inherently international entities, can also be a source of mistrust. In sum, new ventures will likely encounter the not uncommon problem of alliance instability which may be accentuated in the case of new ventures and multinational subsidiaries (Inkpen & Tsang, 2005).

So how can new ventures manage alliance instability? Inkpen and Tsang (2005) point to the importance of interpersonal ties in fostering trust at the inter-firm level. In the present context this is likely to be especially true of interpersonal ties between the new venture's entrepreneur and the key decision-makers within the MNE subsidiary. Lewicki and Bunker (1996) suggest that interpersonal relationship and trust are not interchangeable. The development of interpersonal trust calls for individual-level competences on the part of the entrepreneur in establishing rapport and empathy, which in turn help him or her make a considered judgment of whether the other individual(s) ought to be treated with trust or suspicion (Lewicki & Bunker, 1996). Developing empathy with an individual in dissimilar circumstances is a non-trivial pursuit and is more likely to occur when the entrepreneur has shared experiences, for example, prior employment or transactions, with an MNE (Putnam, 2000). These interpersonal ties potentially translate into trust at the interfirm level and, importantly, result in buy-in on the part of key managers of the multinational subsidiary. Their commitment could help to mitigate the inherent instability arising from the potential limits on the autonomy of multinational subsidiaries.

Why is the development of relational social capital vital to the strategic renewal of internationalization-seeking new ventures? The quality of novel ideas generated could be improved through free and frank debate engendered by trust

(McEvily & Zaheer, 1999). When there is trust there is greater likelihood for discussions about novel ideas to be marked by candor that allows ideas to be thought through better and thus improved (Burt, 2004). Furthermore, trust aids the initiative development process by fostering focused activity; trust frees new ventures from the distraction of monitoring the relationship to ensure it is not being exploited in terms of value appropriation (Alvarez & Barney, 2001). Also, in relation to reintegration, a trust-filled relationship likely provides flexibility during the project's conclusion to allow adjustments that improve the "fit" between the new venture's new and old activities. Taken together, relational social capital may facilitate strategic renewal by enhancing new ventures' creativity especially in the ability to identify the application of nascent ideas; as Burt (2004) argues, the source of an idea is much less significant than the value it produces.

Cognitive social capital

The cognitive dimension of social capital refers to "resources providing shared representations, interpretation and systems" (Nahapiet & Ghoshal, 1998, p. 244). A key facet here is like-mindedness. However, arguably this is the most difficult dimension of social capital to develop in ties involving new ventures and local MNE subsidiaries. By definition, dissimilar actors lack the systemic and cultural resources that readily lead to like-mindedness (Inkpen & Tsang, 2005). As Lane and Lubatkin (1998) have argued, the odds of new knowledge being generated through interfirm activity are heightened through similarity between partner firms. The dissimilarities between new ventures and MNE subsidiaries, as noted, are considerable and include asymmetries in their resource base, long-term objectives, and organizational structure thus potentially hindering knowledge development and transfer (Prashantham & Birkinshaw, 2008). In sum, new ventures will likely encounter the problem of asymmetry in formal organizational systems (Lane & Lubatkin, 1998).

So how can new ventures compensate for this inherent asymmetry? Given the dearth of research into the cognitive dimension of social capital, Nahapiet and Ghoshal (1998) suggest turning to strategy scholars who draw upon cognitive psychology. Of particular interest is Johnson and Huff's (1998) notion of "everyday innovation/everyday strategy." They argue that innovation- and strategy-related activity in both large and small organizations is not confined to formal activities. Rather, informal activities undertaken in the everyday course of business hold considerable significance in achieving innovation outcomes and strategic change. Moreover, informal routines may be better suited than formal activity to fostering low-cost improvisation and thereby organizational learning. Apart from being well suited to their resource-poverty, this approach could help new ventures to make up for their lack of formal organizational systems by providing sufficient common ground for the partnering firms. Nimble-footed informal everyday interorganizational routines increase the odds of developing further alternative resources to organizational systems, such as heuristics and ad

Table 3.2 New venture ties with MNE subsidiaries: social capital dimensions and strategic renewal

Social capital dimension	Associated competence	Network logic	Effects on strategic renewal		
			Idea generation	Initiative development	Strategic reintegration
Structural (access) Who you reach and how you reach them (Nahapiet & Ghoshal, 1998, p. 244)	Resourceful utilization of bridging mechanisms, e.g., regional institutions to access key individuals within local MNE subsidiaries.	Helps span structural holes. For new ventures, MNE ties may be hard to access due to a lack of legitimacy and network centrality.	Greater likelihood of involving relevant individuals within MNE partner organization	Access to complementary capabilities of the MNE partner organization that can be combined with the new venture's own.	Greater clarity and concreteness in achieving closure of project for both new venture and MNE subsidiary.
			In sum, structural social capital can facilitate strategic renewal by enhancing new ventures' opportunity set.		
Relational (trust) Relations people have, such as respect and friendship (Nahapiet & Ghoshal, 1998, p. 244)	Cultivation of trustful interpersonal relationships with key MNE subsidiary managers to gain their personal commitment and buy-in.	Helps cope with inherent alliance instability. New ventures are vulnerable to MNE decisions to terminate projects.	Process of idea generation more likely to be marked by candid and constructive discussions with key MNE managers.	Commitment from key MNE managers allows focused joint activity because of lesser need to monitor the partnership by the new venture.	Greater flexibility in experimenting at the end-stage of the project to improve "fit" between new and existing activities of the new venture.
			In sum, relational social capital could facilitate strategic renewal by enhancing new ventures' creativity.		
Cognitive (like-mindedness) Resources providing shared representations, interpretation and systems* (Nahapiet & Ghoshal, 1998, p. 244)	Engagement in relatively informal everyday joint routines with MNE managers, e.g., prototype demonstrations to obtain feedback from potential international customers.	Helps transcend asymmetry in formal organizational systems. New ventures lack MNEs' developed routines; results in sub-optimal inter-organizational learning.	Refinement of product ideas through joint pilot projects and experiments with the MNE subsidiary.	Joint activity with MNE subsidiaries more likely to commence without delay and momentum built.	Greater scope for extending and sustaining cross-border interorganizational routines in conjunction with the MNE.
			In sum, cognitive social capital can facilitate strategic renewal by enhancing new ventures' bias for action.		

Note
* Dissimilar actors, e.g., new ventures and MNE subsidiaries, are typically deficient in these by definition.

hoc routines, which in turn facilitate and strengthen a meeting of minds manifested in common goals and expectations (Yli-Renko et al., 2001). This, in turn, is a key aspect of cognitive social capital.

Cognitive social capital is potentially a vital ingredient in the strategic renewal of internationalization-seeking new ventures. Informal activity, such as bouncing product ideas off or demonstrating a prototype to prospective international clients that the MNE subsidiary has access to, could help to refine the new product ideas. Such activity also enables momentum to be built rapidly once ideas are translated into initiatives because individuals from the partnering organizations have already commenced the *doing*, as opposed to merely the discussing, of joint activity. In other words, static inertia can be easier to overcome. Finally, in relation to reintegration as the initiative comes to an end, greater like-mindedness through everyday activity increases the odds of it being extended or of a new joint initiative being undertaken, thus increasing the economies of scope of the tie (Nahapiet & Ghoshal, 1998). In a sense, dynamic inertia may (usefully) set in when there is cognitive social capital. In sum, cognitive social capital can facilitate strategic renewal by enhancing new ventures' bias for action. The above theorizing is summarized in Table 3.2.

MNE ties in the INV's social capital portfolio: adding value by balancing tensions

MNE relationships hold particular interest because they can, potentially, *span* geographies. The interest in MNEs as a source of social capital lies, at least partially, in the scope it may provide new ventures to deal with various tensions and trade-offs that they must deal with. Drawing upon my earlier monograph (Prashantham, 2008), three such tensions are discussed below, each relating to the three key themes of developing social capital, leveraging social capital, and managing social capital portfolios.

Developing social capital: the overembeddedness trap

As firms develop social capital, they forge an identity for themselves within a network of relationships. It is argued that as these firms' network range, density, and centrality increase, so does their social capital (Coviello, 2006). In many ways, the consequences of being embedded within a network are positive; firms' influence, solidarity, and information benefits can increase (Adler & Kwon, 2002). However, network relationships also have a "dark side." One of the key problems is the constraining effects that network relationships may have. Firms that are overly embedded in their social networks may get caught up in a mode of groupthink, a potential problem of which is that they cease to be sufficiently critical in their thinking (Uzzi, 1997). Furthermore, overembedded firms are less inclined to behave in a manner that adversely affects the status quo and therefore prefer to engage in incremental, rather than radical, entrepreneurial behavior

(Simsek, Lubatkin, & Floyd, 2003). Radical entrepreneurial behavior, which is more likely to be associated with radical innovation outcomes (Zahra, 1996), could lead to competition and friction and may therefore be shunned by the overembedded firm.

Thus a tension that confronts innovative new ventures is a dilemma between getting deeply embedded in a social network – which can result in greater solidarity and support (Adler & Kwon, 2002; Granovetter, 1973) – and remaining only lightly embedded. Put differently, a tension pertains to how innovative new ventures can participate in their social networks without diminishing their propensity for radical entrepreneurial behavior. Admittedly, not all firms may be conscious of this dilemma or strongly focused on radical entrepreneurial behavior; indeed, some firms may be content to engage in incremental entrepreneurial behavior. However, those new ventures that are serious about developing technological innovations face a dilemma in terms of the extent of the breadth and depth of their network relationships – in other words about the extent of their embeddedness within interfirm networks (Simsek et al., 2003).

Leveraging social capital: the ambidexterity challenge

It has been argued that effective new ventures do not passively engage within their interfirm networks, but rather leverage their social capital actively. In order to leverage their social capital firms must recognize social capital to be a resource and be able to build trust with other actors (Hitt et al., 2001). However, an issue that new ventures must consider is to what end they utilize their social capital. As seen, an important benefit of social capital is the creation and acquisition of knowledge – in other words, learning outcomes (Johanson & Vahlne, 2006; Nahapiet & Ghoshal, 1998; Yli-Renko et al., 2002). The learning outcomes may, however, vary in terms of their orientation towards exploitation or exploration (March, 1991). Differing learning outcomes (exploitation vs. exploration) may result from the nature of *activities* pursued through interfirm efforts. Lavie and Rosenkopf (2006) attribute exploitation outcomes to activities concerned with new business development, and exploration to new product development efforts. Exploratory innovation (e.g., new product development) is certainly an important dimension for many knowledge-intensive ventures. Such innovation may have been required for international expansion to have been feasible in the first place. Local network relationships may be utilized in the new product development process (Yli-Renko et al., 2001). Subsequent activities may be more exploitative in terms of achieving international sales; strategic alliances with actors possessing valuable local knowledge in international markets may be helpful in this regard (Dimitratos, Johnson, Slow, & Young, 2003).

Even after internationalization commences, the imperative for technological innovation does not cease. Ever shortening product life-cycles, competitor moves, and client feedback can all put pressure on new ventures to continue generating innovations. Thus, internationalization and innovation are ongoing and often concurrent processes where learning outcomes – both exploitative and exploratory – are constantly required. The tension between exploitation and exploration is well documented in the literature. Both represent important learning outcomes and both are required. As March (2006, p. 205) asserts, "Exploitation without exploration leads to stagnation and failure to discover new, useful directions. Exploration without exploitation leads to a cascade of experiments without the development of competence in any of them or discrimination among them." It is difficult to achieve both simultaneously because these knowledge processes are contradictory (Smith & Tushman, 2005). However firms that are able to achieve ambidexterity and consequently superior performance (Lubatkin, Simsek, Ling, & Veiga, 2006). While firm-specific factors such as top managers' cognition and behavior (Lubatkin et al., 2006; Smith & Tushman, 2005) influence firms' ability to balance exploitation and exploration, clearly an additional issue comes into the picture – learning outcomes as a consequence of social capital, as seen.

Managing social capital portfolios – the attention deficiency

It has been noted that firms possess portfolios of network relationships that differ variously – for instance, in terms of intimacy (strong vs. weak ties) or social homogeneity (bonding vs. bridging social capital). It has been argued that geographic proximity (local vs. foreign network relationships) is another relevant dimension in the context of new venture internationalization. As noted, social capital in both the local milieu and in international markets can lead to innovation outcomes. However, the spatial distribution of network relationships across national borders (local vs. foreign) can be a source of tension, given the limited amount of attention (Cyert & March, 1963; Ocasio, 1997) that new ventures have to devote to the cultivation of network relationships. Despite advances in communication technology that facilitate the nurturing of relationships (see Chapters 4 and 8), choices have to be made in terms of prioritizing attention across network relationships. International travel and face-to-face communication remain important. Entrepreneurs, who bear a great burden in terms of managing social capital as seen in this volume, have finite resources of attention and travel budgets that they must judiciously utilize. From the perspective of innovation, the acquisition of technological knowledge from international markets may require large amounts of attention to be allocated to key relationships (Yli-Renko et al., 2001; Zahra et al., 2000). The challenge of managing cross-border social capital portfolios is also exacerbated by cross-cultural differences – greater attention may be required when dealing with network relationships where these differences are considerable.

The role of MNE social capital

While scholars tend to focus on internationalization or innovation when studying small and new firms, in reality the firms have to deal with both challenges simultaneously, which leads to certain tensions. Those firms that adopt a strategic entrepreneurship perspective would seek to deal with these issues using "entrepreneurial action with a strategic perspective" (Hitt et al., 2001, p. 480). With respect to each, the potential role of MNE social capital in alleviating these tensions is briefly considered, with a view to stimulating future research.

In terms of the overembeddedness trap, relationships with local MNE subsidiaries could be a useful antidote. MNE subsidiaries are known to be fleet-footed and lightly embedded (Birkinshaw & Hood, 2000) – often to the regret of local policy-makers who would prefer their closer involvement with local actors. However, this very attribute of MNE subsidiaries could be a "blessing in disguise" for new ventures; in other words, ties with MNE subsidiaries are likely to be devoid of the intense reciprocity that may characterize other local network relationships (e.g., with other local new ventures). Consequently, new ventures may be less inhibited from engaging in radical entrepreneurial behavior (Simsek et al., 2003). Indeed, it is likely that MNE partners would encourage such behavior without feeling threatened by ventures that are unlikely to pose direct competition.

In terms of the ambidexterity challenge, MNE social capital provides scope for both exploration (e.g., new product development) and exploitation (e.g., new business development) activities. Subsidiaries of MNEs like IBM and Microsoft offer partnering programs that cover both of these activities, as long as firms use their technology platforms. Initial activities tend to comprise exploratory innovation, that is, new product development; resources that new ventures could tap into include free software and free advice from the MNE's in-house competency centers. Subsequently MNEs are often willing to promote the technological offering worldwide, that is, to engage in exploitation (new business development), especially if there are derivative sales for its own technology platform (e.g., an operating system). In reality, this of course means that a new venture would compete with several other firms that sign up for the same partnership program. Moreover, not every subsidiary or sub-unit of the MNE may be equally cooperative or interested in assisting new ventures. Nonetheless, at least in principle, frameworks are in place for partnering activities that cover both exploration and exploitation. In other words, MNE social capital can be a vehicle for ambidexterity.

In terms of new ventures' attention deficiency, the MNE provides the scope for both local and international relationships by virtue of itself being a globally dispersed multi-unit network. The new venture may have to take the initiative to become well known within the local subsidiary in the first instance, and in due course gain visibility at the MNE's headquarters and/or other subsidiaries. Nonetheless, the *possibility* exists that the MNE can provide an efficient focus for new venture's attention, thereby offsetting the burden of allocating scarce attention across milieus owing to its inherent spatial dispersion.

Thus internationalizing new ventures have to cope with various tensions – which may interact and overlap with each other, as evident from the above discussion – as they develop and leverage their social capital portfolios. It is conceivable that ties developed with MNEs via their local subsidiaries could help new ventures deal effectively with these tensions. An important theoretical consideration is that these *geography-spanning* relationships could provide an efficient means for new ventures to channel their attention in *both* local *and* international markets through MNE links. Given the ever growing pressure to identify and absorb external innovation across the world (Doz et al., 2001), many technology-intensive MNEs are making exactly such an offer to innovative new ventures through partnership programs. Provided the new venture uses the MNE's technology, the offered links could potentially facilitate product development in the local market and subsequent marketing efforts in international markets. In short, MNEs can be a source of social capital that spans geographies (local vs. international milieus) and functions (exploratory innovation via upstream activities and exploitative learning via downstream activities). Attractive though the proposition may be to some new ventures, the challenge of building visibility, efficiency, and intimacy would be, if anything, even greater when engaging with giants such as IBM or Microsoft. MNEs are complex organizations where the development and leverage of social capital call for boundary-spanning activities across various sub-units (Inkpen & Tsang, 2005; Kostova & Roth, 2003).

This chapter has sought to build on the preceding two chapters to provide preliminary conceptualization of how internationalizing new ventures may build and leverage MNE relationships as part of their social capital portfolios. The next four present preliminary findings and further ideas, emanating from my work in the Bangalore software industry which is supplemented by brief cases from other contexts, such as Beijing and Cambridge.

Notes

1 Reprinted from Shameen Prashantham & K. Kumar (2011), How do new ventures in MNC ecosystems proactively overcome interfirm asymmetries? *IIMB Management Review, 23*(3), 177–188. © 2011, with permission from Elsevier.
2 Reprinted from Shameen Prashantham (2008), New venture internationalization as strategic renewal, *European Management Journal, 26*(6), 378–387. © 2008, with permission from Elsevier.
3 Putnam (2000) emphasizes social heterogeneity in defining bridging social capital whereas Burt (2004) focuses on non-redundancy. Here an integrative approach is taken, since both facets are likely to overlap empirically owing to network biases towards homophily and propinquity.

Part II

Exploratory insights

4 Rising innovation and emergent MNE–INV engagement

As noted in my previous monograph (Prashantham, 2008), my prior research on INVs in Bangalore suggests that in the first half of the 2000s there were many opportunities for new ventures in Bangalore to internationalize (albeit in the shadow of large Indian companies such as Infosys), and that overseas coethnic bonding ties – when leveraged actively – were important facilitators of Bangalore ventures' internationalization process by yielding new business opportunities.

Follow-up work explained how those INVs fared in terms of cultivating and leveraging network ties over time, and that, without learning from extant ties and building new ties to (including *non*-ethnic bridging ties), international growth might be stymied (Prashantham & Dhanaraj, 2010). From this work it becomes clear that initial ties do matter, especially when leveraged actively, but also that initial ties may "run out of steam," as it were, in terms of the direct business opportunities they yield. Therefore, initial ties have to be leveraged for indirect learning opportunities as well, and new ties have to be cultivated. Theoretically, a key message from this work pertains to the limits of bonding ties and the need for INVs to expand their portfolio of ties to include bridging ties. This might represent a challenge, requiring these firms to move beyond their comfort zone.

The present chapter argues that an upward shift in the technological innovation levels of new ventures may mean that bridging ties – including MNE ties – become more relevant (and necessary) much earlier in the life-cycle of the venture, especially as the local milieu's sophistication increases. In such a situation, internationalization-seeking new ventures are confronted by the transition from bonding to bridging ties at progressively earlier stages as they climb the value curve.

The evolving Bangalore software industry

The Bangalore software industry has been the primary empirical setting for my research. Other scholars, such as Kundu and Katz (2003), have previously identified Indian software ventures as a fascinating context in which to study INVs and born globals. Relevant to my present endeavor, one of the merits of such a setting, when examined consistently over a period of time, is the scope to observe fairly substantial change over a relatively compressed period of time. Much has changed since the early years of the twenty-first century, when my initial work in Bangalore began. In those days, software firms were primarily operating under an arbitrage logic: they built bespoke software solutions at a lower cost than their clients in advanced economies would have to pay in their home market. Although many Indian software firms continue in this vein, my more recent interview data and case-studies suggest that aspirations have risen noticeably in Bangalore in relation to the technological innovation that underpins firms' offerings. Specifically, there has been a rise in the number of software *product* ventures developing intellectual property as opposed to software services firms operating on the basis of cost arbitrage. This trend is underlined by new software product-oriented initiatives by Nasscom, India's trade body for software, and the development of a new private initiative, iSpirt, to foster innovation and entrepreneurship among software product start-ups (Nasscom, 2014; ProductNation, 2014).

From a theoretical perspective, I have witnessed a shift in the type of network relationships that Indian software ventures seek to cultivate and utilize in the pursuit of their international expansion. As noted in my earlier monograph (Prashantham, 2008) and subsequent work (Prashantham & Dhanaraj, 2010), entrepreneurs of software services ventures in Bangalore actively leveraged their interpersonal networks. Coethnic ties in international markets, notably the US, were particularly helpful in enabling initial entry into markets whereas non-ethnic ties were more useful for growth (Prashantham et al., 2015). By contrast, in the more recent cases of software product ventures that I have been studying, interorganizational ties with large foreign MNEs have been a major target in terms of relationship-building. The rationale for this altered focus has been the perceived benefit of providing complementary offerings to, and thereby gaining the support of, an established innovation ecosystem. As noted in Chapter 2, orchestrating such ecosystems is an important part of the global strategy of many contemporary MNEs (Buckley, 2012; Cantwell, 2013; Doz et al., 2001). This is especially true of the information technology industry where MNEs such as Apple, Google, and Microsoft have been aggressively developing, and competing on the basis of, their interfirm innovation ecosystems (Nambisan & Sawhney, 2011).

This shift in emphasis from coethnic ties (which my earlier monograph dealt with) to MNE ties (the focus of the present monograph) suggests that different connecting mechanisms between local milieus are activated depending on the level of innovation of internationalizing new ventures. It is useful, in this regard, to consider concepts that Lorenzen and Mudambi (2013) use in their analysis of the economic geography of MNEs: people and pipelines. People-based networks such as diasporas (coethnic networks) provide links between local milieus as do pipelines, that is, the intraorganizational connections within spatially dispersed organizations such as MNEs. It would appear that, as innovation levels rise in Bangalore, there is a growing shift in emphasis from people to pipelines.

Clearly, modern-day software ventures in Bangalore provide an interesting and appropriate setting in which to study MNE–INV engagement.

Rising innovation and MNE–INV engagement: insights from a panel

To provide a first-hand flavor for such actors I adopt a somewhat unorthodox approach of reproducing below excerpts from a roundtable panel discussion with four award-winning exemplar software ventures in Bangalore that focus on IP rather than cost arbitrage as the basis of their competitive advantage. This panel was conducted in collaboration with Professor K. Kumar, then Chairperson of the N. S. Raghavan Centre for Entrepreneurial Learning at IIM Bangalore.[1]

Sanjay Shah, CEO, Skelta

I am going to give you a quick overview of my background and then an overview of Invensys-Skelta.[2] After completing my studies here in India, I went to the US, where after my Master's, I got together with a few others to fulfill our dream of starting a software company. However, we did not have the money for that and eventually we started Accel Computers with the intent to assemble or build computers. This coincided with the recession in the early 1990s when there was a demand for inexpensive unbranded computers, and we leveraged the opportunity and did very well, though a downturn soon followed. What started off as pure retail business where we were making margins of perhaps 100–150% and getting upfront payments for goods yet to be delivered, slowly turned into becoming predominantly government and corporate business where our gross margins were less than 10%. So the going became very tough. The model was really not right because it was all about volumes and about how quickly you can turn your inventory. Eventually we sold Accel.

My partners and I then started an ERP company called Everest Software, after which I moved on to my next venture. The dot.com bust and the downturn in the early 2000s resulted in several companies seeking help to improve their business processing and that gave birth to Skelta BPM. Skelta was started in 2003 when members of the NetGalactic Internet Solutions, an IT services company, decided to venture into the product development arena. Though the move from an IT services oriented company to product development was criticized by the market leaders, Skelta proved critics wrong by becoming the leader in the embeddable business process management and workflow product space. Skelta BPM – an enterprise class business process management platform that eliminates the risk of process initiatives, enables communication amongst all process stakeholders and drives innovation by fostering business ownership, which can be formatted and deployed with a variety of software – has been extremely successful. With a steady growth of 35% year on year, Skelta adopts a unique sales model of selling licenses remotely from Bangalore to more than 600 customers around the world. Skelta is also represented by 100 plus partners worldwide – a network of VARs, SIs, and OEMs. Skelta currently has 150 employees with aggressive plans of scaling up to 200 by 2012.[3] We have a strong leadership team.

Skelta BPM over the years has also won many accolades for the innovation. Recently Invensys Skelta was chosen as the winner of the *Red Herring* Global Award, and was a finalist for the coveted Partner of the Year Award by Microsoft. Skelta BPM was recognized by Gartner, in their report titled *Cool Vendors in Business Process Management, 2009* as one of the vendors to look out for in the BPM market.

Because of the capabilities of Skelta BPM, Invensys Operations Management, a division of Invensys, acquired the company to fill in the gaps that existed in the manufacturing vertical. The strategic acquisition by Invensys Operations Management has opened up new opportunities and Skelta is all set to bring about a radical change in the manufacturing vertical.

Sunil Maheshwari, CEO, Mango Technologies

Mango Technologies started in 2006 and we were one of the early few to value the potential of emerging markets, particularly for mobile phone devices. The entry-level and low-end devices to these markets were coming largely from China or Korea. A small segment of very high-end smart phones was primarily coming from either Microsoft or Nokia.

Not much innovation was evident on the software of the low-end phones to make them user friendly. So we set out to bring flexibility, usability, and value to such phones, while reducing the engineering costs and time to market. Unlike the trend at other engineering establishments at that time, we hired graphic artists in the team on priority rather than software engineers, notwithstanding the limited resources at our disposal.

Being first -ime entrepreneurs, we had limited cash, limited space, and no experience of running an organization. We were on the lookout for funds for expansion and were fortunate to be selected by NSRECL at IIM Bangalore, for incubation. In addition to this being a learning experience, we also earned significant credibility through that association.

A product development company in India claiming a high-value mobile technology offering for the mass market arouses considerable interest. We found ourselves in the finals of the Nasscom top 100 IT innovators. We were judged the most innovative startup in 2007 by an elite panel; GSMA chose Mango as the top innovator nominee from Asia-Pacific in 2008 and *Businessworld* included Mango in the top five promising entrepreneurs in India in 2009.

With high focus on inventing methods for a rich product with a very low memory footprint, we went through multiple iterations of evaluation with semiconductor vendors like Qualcomm, NXP, Texas Instruments, and Intel, and also OEMs like Samsung, Kyocera Wireless, and others, including some Chinese companies. We had a symbiotic relationship with our customers and almost all evaluations were paid for. Our aims were very high and required high precision engineering and centered teamwork.

Qualcomm acquired our product – the application and UI framework – and that was to be shipped with millions of chipsets as the default middleware and

UI. We were one of the few Indian companies coming up with products in the consumer technology domain, which was dominated by China, Korea, Taiwan, with Europe and the US being the center of design.

Mango continued innovating on mobility solutions and expanded it to multiple mobile platforms. We also created a lot of mobile Internet services to be accessed from smart devices in the verticals of enterprise utilities, healthcare, and education. We acquired a learning management solution from another company and brought it to mobile platforms. We remodel and extend a lot of mobile Internet services so that they are accessible and convenient on mobile devices.

Devices are becoming cheaper and smart phones are now costing what mobile phones did just a couple of years back. One more interesting development is the convergence between different kinds of devices. You have devices such as the television, tablets, smart phones, and several industrial devices and these devices are able to talk to each other. To talk to each other, they need to have something on the cloud which is common for all these devices. To enable this Mango offers "complete device software ownership" which includes deploying applications on connected devices of different form factors and focusing on UI and UX orientation and "user centric" rich functionality.

As we are based out of India we understand the technology and this market better than any other market and better than anybody else, which is where our advantage lies.

Srini Rajam, CEO, Ittiam

My presentation focuses on how small ventures can effectively work with large corporations to achieve mutually beneficial results.

Ten years ago, I was working in a large corporation, but I didn't realize that I was part of a "gorilla" then. Since then, in the last ten years, we have started and grown this small company, Ittiam. The difference now is that over the course of these ten years, even the gorillas have changed.

There are several ways in which the two can collaborate. I want to highlight three ideas that have worked for Ittiam.

The first is technology performance, which is a differentiating factor; the second is the business model – because large companies have certain ways of doing things and they like certain types of partners; and the third is market selection which in itself goes a long way in bringing the right type of partners.

Let us look at a few illustrations of these three ideas.

Technology performance: We started with this as our core competency. Our strength was in signal processing – in the areas of audio, video, and communications signal processing. We decided to try and build world-class technologies in these areas with very high performance which would touch people with different products. We were pleasantly surprised by the results which far exceeded our expectations. We discovered that if you have a great performing technology, you will attract more markets than the few you had in mind when you started out; a compelling performance differentiation will attract many more applications.

We have had significant success in audio–video communication signal processing, in different types of communication systems, and consumer entertainment devices. We have come to be known as the providers of one of the widest range of technologies for embedded systems development. The end equipment for our technology includes smart phones and tablets, video conferencing, and video surveillance, Internet protocol media broadcast and in-car/flight entertainment. We cater to a lot of industrial applications. Our offerings include head-mounted display for industrial use, DVR units for surveillance recording, IPTV encode for broadcast head end – this involves one of the highest levels of problem-solving and it brought us a range of market knowledge, and wireless LAN SOC for automotive application.

We are known for our offerings through IP and system design, and chip design. In the semiconductor chip (platform) we foresee several pockets of opportunity.

The business model: Coming from India, the business model that is well understood continues to be the one based on services but it does not suit all types of companies. We discovered that there were companies that needed not just resource access but also technology access. So we kind of pioneered this model in India where we tried to realize the total value of the intellectual property through license fee and royalty which was linked to how many end products the customers would produce. We wanted to retain the IP rights and at the same time, share the risks with the customers. We wanted to retain the IP because we were an IP company, investing in R&D, making all the roadmap decisions and taking on the risks. At the same time we wanted to offer a risk-sharing model to the customers on the terms that in case their product maps did not work out as well as they planned they need not pay the price we had asked for. This appealed a lot to our customers, even to the very big companies.

We also looked at royalty, which is like pricing a cricket bat on the basis of the runs scored. You need to have really good players here, because it is the star players who drive your success. We have also assessed the "sweet spot" for this business model, by assessing the license fee and royalty shares of the total revenue, and arrived at a range of 30 to 40% revenue share of the whole company coming from royalty. That is the kind of range at which you know you are getting good returns on your old investments and at the same time your new products are also coming along. A 100% royalty model would mean that your new IPs may not be taking off in the market. We are striving for this sweet spot (see Figure 4.1).

Market selection: Just as you are trying to choose the right partner to work with, others too would be scrutinizing your intent, your priority, the focus of your R&D and management bandwidth, elements which go a long way in striking a partnership. We have been working in this field for the past 10–15 years and we could see that in the 1990s–2000, devices that were already available in the desktop were breaking up into numerous individual products, such as the gaming device or the portable music player or a navigation device or a VoIP phone. There was a divergence then and now we are seeing a reconvergence

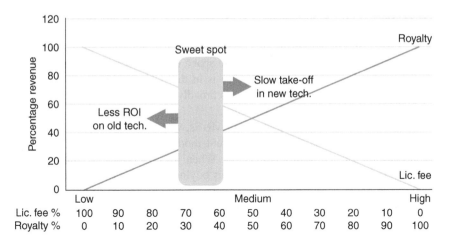

Figure 4.1 License fee and royalty share of total revenue.

except that smart phone is the new PC. Our statement of intent over the last few years has been to give the industry a host of market-proven and industry-proven signal-processing technologies and applications, within a short timeframe, which has led several noteworthy players or "gorillas" to work with us. This year, for example, we expect that about six million high-end smart phones and tablets would be carrying Ittiam's hi-definition video technology for various functions. When a small company like ours demonstrates a technology performance which perhaps a large company has just visualized, it gets their attention; the big entity feels that it has to have it and work with it immediately because suddenly their devices are being characterized very differently. We are letting our imagination fly and we aim to produce the best in class multimedia and communication for smart phones and tablets.

T. K. Srikanth, Vice President, Sasken

Sasken began as a startup in Silicon Valley in the US. We moved to India in 1990–1991 and have been fully operational for over 20 years in India and have been growing steadily. We started with design automation and since the 1990s we have been focused on the telecom space.

We have always been a technology focused company. We have taken a hybrid approach, providing both R&D services as well as IP. The mix has varied – sometimes being large on IP and small on services, and vice versa, but the DNA, the intent has been to do both. We have not consciously thought of the nature of our business as "dancing with the gorillas" but the telecom space is dominated by a few large players and we work with most of the large, established telecom companies across the value chain.

Our customer list consists of big companies, MNEs, and probably 75–80% of our revenue comes from a handful of leading MNEs. On a day-to-day basis we have to live and breathe in this ecosystem and we are constantly engaged with how to work and how to grow successfully. The challenges are huge and so are the opportunities. We are working in the space of R&D services. Some of it is direct outsourcing of services and some is in the nature of IP licensing; some could be in the nature of support services broadly tapping into the R&D chain or the R&D spend in these large companies.

While there is a lot in common to all MNEs, when we interact with them, we are very conscious that there are different modes of engagement with MNEs depending on the terms of engagement. When R&D services are directly outsourced, the MNE is our customer who is buying our services and products, so we have to be able to provide differentiated solutions/services to the MNE. We try to engage with them proactively so as to get a larger share of their wallet, of the business they outsource.

We also began to look for other approaches to engaging with the MNEs. A good example here is the juncture, in 1998–2000, when wireless technologies such as GSM, GPRS and 3G were evolving. We recognized this as a potential area of growth and we invested in developing the communication protocol stacks in these areas and our target was to license it to the big handset manufacturers – such as Motorola, Ericsson, Nokia, and Siemens (MENS).

The way to get into these companies we realized was through the semiconductor companies, those who were servicing them. That was the stage when the companies were breaking up their vertical integration. So we decided to work with the semiconductor companies, get our protocol stacks embedded with their software and get our licensing fee and royalties when they sold their products. Thus, we bundled our products/solutions with those of the MNE.

So the MNE became a channel or a reseller depending on the kind of business we did. That was how companies such as Intel became our customers. Next, we leveraged the MNE's customer reach to expand our market. While this helps you reduce your sales and marketing costs significantly, it brings with it different challenges.

A third mode of collaboration is with the MNE as your partner. This provides you with the opportunity to service the customers/suppliers of the partner MNE and reach other MNEs in the network. An MNE partner may not be in a position to provide the right kind of support to their customers – it could be customer support, field trials, or integration. If you can take over some of the work and activities of the MNE partner, such as being the integration partner for their customers, it would enable you to reach a larger set of customers – who could also be MNEs. In effect, you could be dancing with two gorillas! You could also build a brand, or build equity with an MNE, by leveraging their supply chain. For instance, your MNE partner may recommend that a supplier work directly with you and solve a specific problem before bringing a product to them. The mobile space is very complicated; you require a web of interactions and you have to constantly look for opportunities to play in one part of this space so that you can generate business in another part of the space.

However, not all MNEs outsource in the same way; the maturity of the outsourcing strategy would be different for different MNEs. Hence, companies have to understand the dynamics of the outsourcing MNE and temper their activities appropriately. (Table 4.1 outlines the differences in the outsourcing strategies of MNEs depending on the level of development or evolution of these strategies.) You have to be differently proactive while dealing with the two kinds of MNEs. With an MNE with a more mature outsourcing strategy, you both may understand what needs to be done and how, you may anticipate what the MNE wants to do, and be able to project your own plans over the next six months or one year, and, you can entrench yourself by showing your commitment, values, and ethics. However, while working with an MNE whose strategy is still evolving, you may have to help bring structure into the relationship, and be more execution oriented; you need to start thinking about the larger strategies, where the market is going, how this company will get to its market share and so on.

While the level of evolution of outsourcing of an MNE is an important parameter in determining how you work with them, the size of the MNE (or the division of the MNE you are engaged with) is another important factor. Based on my experiences, I would like to reflect on the differences between the engagement patterns of small/medium and large companies.

The size of the MNE has a bearing on how we work with these companies. (Table 4.2 outlines some salient points in the engagement patterns with small/medium and large companies.) The larger the company, the less visibility you may have on the real objectives of the project. You know what your interface group is telling you, and what they want to achieve, but whether and how that fits into the larger scheme of the large company are not very visible. If it is a small company (in the range of $100–200 million) you know exactly why they want to take a course of action, what their next step is, and where they want to

Table 4.1 Evolution level of MNE's outsourcing strategy

- **Evolved**
- Clarity of outsourcing strategy and global partner management
- Supplier as a strategic partner
- Medium-/long-term views
- Internal alignment on objectives and execution plans
- Non-threatening – to supplier and internal groups
- Integration with MNE's process and systems
- Joint investments

- **Evolving**
- Changing partnership strategy
- Tentativeness of engagements
- Internal alignment not sufficiently built
- Ongoing competition with internal groups and other suppliers
- Investment expectations without commitment on returns

Table 4.2 Engagement patterns with small/medium and large companies

- Visibility into project objectives and status
- Level of commitment/investments expected
- Access to senior management and business functions
- Speed of due diligence
- Contract process – speed and transparency
- Coordination between functions in customer organization
- Flexibility in jointly managing project scope – willingness to engage with "incomplete" solutions

go. You will probably have access to everybody in the company and get a contract completed in less than six months. Whereas, with a large company, the coordination between its functions is often a mystery and it might take years to land the contract. However, this complexity also provides opportunities. We have been in situations where we have brought additional value to the relationship by being the "bridge" in an organization helping different groups connect. For example, there have been cases where we have worked with the product development group and the product support group and have been able to proactively point out improvements. That is the kind of relationship you need to build.

Exploratory insights from Bangalore (and beyond): what can we learn?

The foregoing exposure to "voices" from leading entrepreneurial ventures in Bangalore is indicative that prospects for MNE–INV engagement are much greater when the new venture in question aims high in relation to technological innovation capabilities and output. Three of the four ventures featured in the panel (Ittiam, Mango, and Skelta) were past winners of a prestigious national innovation award instituted by the trade body for software in India, Nasscom. The other firm (Sasken) had been founded before that award was instituted but had begun life as a Silicon Valley start-up and possessed strong innovation credentials. These ventures represent the exception rather than the rule, but point to an upward trend of growing aspirations for innovation amongst a small but discernible minority of ventures in emerging economy settings such as Bangalore. Such ventures are rather different from the type of incrementally innovative Indian software ventures studied previously (Kundu & Katz, 2003; Prashantham & Dhanaraj, 2010). In this monograph I particularly focus on the case of Skelta (in Chapters 5 and 7) to surface exploratory insights into the MNE–INV interface.

The review of relevant literatures on MNE networks in Chapter 2 suggests that MNEs around the world are increasingly inclined to orchestrate intra- and interfirm networks (Buckley, 2012) to leverage their dually embedded nature (Forsgren et al., 2005) through the entrepreneurial actions of various units (Birkinshaw, 2000). A key motivation for engaging with external actors through these actions is the MNE's own agenda for furthering its innovation (Cantwell,

2013; Doz et al., 2001; Rugman & Verbeke, 2001). This, in turn, suggests scope for new ventures to further their technological capabilities through joint activity with innovation-seeking MNE subsidiaries (Prashantham & McNaughton, 2006). However given the focus of the present endeavor on the study of INVs within the *international* entrepreneurship domain, my emphasis is on how MNE ties ultimately influence new ventures' internationalization. Of course advances to a new venture's technological capabilities and output are undeniably important, and indeed a key message of this chapter is that the relevance of MNE–INV engagement is greater when technological innovations levels and aspirations rise (a phenomenon that can be seen vividly in a setting such as Bangalore). However, from the perspective of INV research, technology is a means to an end; more salient – for this research stream – is the accrual of international-ization outcomes.

Given this interest, it seems appropriate to examine the following three facets of MNE networks, from the perspective of INVs, in the remainder of this section of the book on exploratory insights from Bangalore and beyond (Chapters 5 through 7).

MNE ties as a source of geographically-dispersed social capital for INVs (Chapter 5)

As previously noted, a prominent feature of the MNE is the orchestration of network members (Buckley, 2012) that simultaneously participate in a dually embedded business networks in spatially dispersed locations around the world (Forsgren et al., 2005), some of which act in entrepreneurial ways (Birkinshaw, 2000). By definition then, MNE ties are unique compared to several other forms of network relationships that INVs typically possess, in that they contain the property of being linked with a spatially dispersed entity. This leads to the poten-tial for INVs to channel their (limited) energies to engaging with MNE partners and thereby help them address tensions associated with overembeddedness, ambidexterity, and attention deficiency, as noted in Chapter 3. The significance of spatially dispersed social capital is perhaps best appreciated in *contrast* to more spatially concentrated ties. This is therefore part of the analysis provided in Chapter 5, where Bangalore-based Skelta (briefly introduced in the panel discus-sion reported in this chapter) is contrasted with Cambridge-based Plastic Logic, in an attempt to highlight the unique spatial properties of MNE ties, which would hold true in both emerging and advanced economy contexts. As will be seen, however, this analysis has the additional merit of shedding useful light on how MNE ties are profoundly influential in an emerging economy setting.

Internationalization capability learning by INVs via MNE ties (Chapter 6)

Following on from the above discussion, a prominent feature of the MNE is that it is inherently international in its activities and therefore a repository of internationalization capability that it seeks to deploy, and replenish, in its international business operations (Johanson & Vahlne, 1977). While of course it cannot be assumed that all MNEs are highly adept at internationalization, it seems reasonable to expect that a Western MNE achieving non-trivial success in a vastly dissimilar Asian market must possess an appreciable level of internationalization capability. Especially relevant in an emerging economy context, where firms have a relatively short history of exposure to foreign markets, MNE partners may represent a far superior source of such learning outcomes relative to peer firms for local new ventures. Such learning can be usefully deployed by the new venture in its pursuit of internationalization. Thus a potentially valuable role of MNE ties for INVs – provided a sufficient level of relationship quality is attained (Nahapiet & Ghoshal, 1998) – is as a source of internationalization capability, not merely technological capability. Chapter 6 offers a test of these ideas using survey data from the Indian software industry.

Realizing internationalization outcomes by INVs via MNE ties (Chapter 7)

The MNE literature reviewed in Chapter 2 should make it clear that, ultimately, large multinationals operate out of self-interest. MNE subsidiaries in emerging economies such as China and India are likely encouraged to be entrepreneurial in order to achieve success in these lucrative high-growth markets. So, while the MNE is a source of spatially dispersed social capital (Chapter 5) and of internationalization capability learning (Chapter 6), it seems plausible that the *actual* joint activity with MNE partners that new ventures manage to engage in has a rather local focus. My research in Bangalore and elsewhere points to a "pull of gravity" (cf. Cantwell & Mudambi, 2011) exerted by entrepreneurial MNE subsidiaries on the new ventures they engage with, towards the latter's *home* market. While such joint activity can, of course, have useful payoffs, it runs counter to a new venture's internationalization goals. In Chapter 7, based on further analysis of Skelta – the canonical illustration of MNE–INV engagement in my research – I note the need for effortful actions to ensure that internationalization outcomes do accrue. A brief comparison with another successful new venture partner of Microsoft, in China, indicates that the pull of gravity may be greater is some locations (e.g., the Chinese high-technology cluster of Zhongguancun) than others (e.g., Bangalore).

Notes

1 The excerpts are reprinted from Shameen Prashantham & K. Kumar (2011), How do new ventures in MNC ecosystems proactively overcome interfirm asymmetries? *IIMB Management Review, 23*(3), 177–188. © 2011, with permission from Elsevier.
2 Skelta was renamed Invensys-Skelta following its acquisition by Invensys; in this monograph, however, the venture is referred to by its original name, Skelta. It is featured again in Chapters 5 and 7.
3 This target was achieved.

5   MNE ties

Geography-spanning social capital for INVs

Introduction: spatial embeddedness of network ties

The previously reviewed literature in Chapter 2 suggests that, potentially, MNE ties represent a means for INVs to build geography-spanning ties with entrepreneurial subsidiaries which, by virtue of their dual embeddedness in both the local milieu and their wider MNE networks, could ultimately facilitate internationalization outcomes for new ventures. The present chapter highlights this prospect by introducing the case of Skelta, a canonical illustration of MNE–INV engagement in my research, and contrasting it with a venture in Cambridge, UK, which focuses primarily on ties with much more locally embedded actors, namely, venture capital (VC) funders.[1]

Conceptually, a distinction is made between spatially dispersed and concentrated embeddedness of these distinct actors, MNEs and VC firms. Spatially dispersed embeddedness characterizes ties with major actors that are co-embedded in the local milieu and in a global network, while spatially concentrated embeddedness is associated with major actors with significant local roots that are consequently deeply embedded in the local milieu. This is an alter-centric, rather than an ego-centric, perspective of embeddedness which seems appropriate when the focal actor is a smaller young firm and the other actor (alter) is a major local player.

With respect to spatially dispersed embeddedness, the case of Skelta is introduced. As noted previously, Skelta leveraged a network relationship with Microsoft India to enhance its visibility in international markets. MNE subsidiaries represent an interesting case of local embeddedness in that they are embedded (to varying degrees) in both the intraorganizational MNE network and the local milieu (Forsgren et al., 2005). With respect to spatially concentrated embeddedness, the case-study of a spinoff venture from Cambridge University is briefly discussed. This venture formed a network relationship with Amadeus, a venture capital firm with strong roots in the local milieu – including with the venture's laboratory of origin – through which it has attracted further funding and recently commenced prototype production in Dresden, Germany. A strong innovation ecosystem comprising a technical university and sources of venture capital, as represented by the Cambridge electronics cluster, can be a vital source of network relationships for new ventures (Wright, Lockett, Clarysse, & Binks, 2006). These network relationships are more likely to demonstrate spatially concentrated embeddedness, thus presenting an interesting comparator to MNE subsidiary ties.

The emphasis in the literature has, understandably, tended to be on network relationships in international markets. Less explored is the somewhat counterintuitive notion that network relationships in the *local* milieu could influence new ventures' *international* expansion. Notable among the few studies that have taken this perspective is the work of Brown and colleagues that highlights the utility of SME (peer) networks within a regional cluster (Brown & Bell, 2001; Brown & McNaughton, 2003). Their work in the Christchurch electronics cluster suggests that SME networks can facilitate joint promotion activities and referrals. Prashantham and McNaughton (2006) have built on the idea of regional clusters yielding valuable network relationships for internationalizing new ventures. They focus on *dissimilar* companies as a source of bridging social capital (Putnam, 2000). Specifically they focus on MNE subsidiaries as a source of local social capital to internationalization-seeking new ventures through joint innovation activity (i.e., new product development) and, subsequently, international business development. Drawing upon case-study research in the Scottish software industry, they find that these potential benefits of local bridging ties are more likely to accrue when a bridging mechanism fosters the development and sustenance of these relationships.

Prashantham and McNaughton's (2006) work resonates with the broader study of networks in the strategic management field. Research by McEvily and colleagues, for example, indicates that, within clusters, smaller firms could potentially gain access to bridging ties (McEvily & Zaheer, 1999) and embedded ties (McEvily & Marcus, 2005). Bridging ties refer to relationships marked by non-redundancy, that is, the other actor is not strongly connected to the focal actor's network of relationships (Burt, 1992). Consequently there is a greater chance that these ties yield *novel* information, ideas and opportunities (McEvily & Zaheer, 1999). Embedded ties refer to relationships that, as distinct from arm's-length relationships, are characterized by fine-grained information-sharing, trust, and joint problem-solving (Uzzi, 1997). (Thus "bridging" and "embedded" are not mutually exclusive attributes of a tie.)

Drawing upon the work of Granovetter (1985) and other social network scholars, Dacin, Beal and Ventresca (1999, pp. 320–321) suggest that embeddedness refers to "the contextualization of economic activity in on-going patterns of social relations.... Embeddeness arguments take economic activity seriously but look beyond the rhetoric of intentionality and efficiency and make a strong commitment towards understanding relational aspects of organizations." Uzzi and colleagues echo this notion. Embeddedness theory "argues that the process of embedding commercial transactions in social attachments instills into future exchange expectations of trust and reciprocity that promotes unique value creation in the relationship" (Uzzi & Gillespie, 2002, p. 598); embeddedness creates "cooperative exchanges of trust and ongoing reciprocal exchanges" (Uzzi

& Lancaster, 2003, p. 391). Embedded ties are particularly useful in transferring private, as opposed to public, knowledge (Uzzi & Lancaster, 2003).

Network scholars have tended to view embeddedness not as a dichotomy (embedded vs. arms'-length ties) but as a continuum (McEvily & Marcus, 2005). The network relationships that Prashantham and McNaughton (2006) refer to between new ventures and MNE subsidiaries – which can be influential local actors – clearly share both of these characteristics: that is, bridging and embedded. Furthermore, they found that the new ventures in their Scottish sample collaborated with the local subsidiary of Sun Microsystems, a significant employer in the region and constituent of Sun's global network of subsidiaries. Thus, as Young and Tavares (2004) point out, the peculiar nature of such an actor (MNE subsidiary) lends an interesting *spatial* dimension to its embeddedness within the local milieu in that it is, simultaneously, embedded within a local milieu (Scotland) but also a global intraorganization network (Sun Microsystems). Such embeddedness is referred to as *spatially dispersed embeddedness*.

Of course, other influential actors exist in a given local milieu that could constitute a potential source of bridging embedded ties. Whereas an MNE subsidiary may be somewhat loosely embedded within the local milieu (Young & Tavares, 2004), other influential actors may be more deeply rooted (Wright et al., 2006); thus, their embeddedness within the cluster is qualitatively different. It is not difficult to conceive of, for example, more locally rooted actors in a regional cluster that possesses a strong regional innovation system. This may be particularly so within a milieu characterized by a strong tradition of university research where a number of actors could wield considerable influence – thereby constituting valuable sources of social capital to new firms; these include major indigenous companies and investors (Wright et al., 2006). Often such entities are closely associated with a university around which the cluster may have developed, and are thus deeply rooted in the local milieu. Their embeddedness, is referred to – in contrast to that of MNE subsidiaries – as *spatially concentrated embeddedness*.

How local bridging ties influence new venture internationalization will vary according to the nature of the (influential) other actor's spatial orientation vis-à-vis the local milieu, and therefore of the tie's embeddedness, spatially concentrated or dispersed, as depicted above. Consistent with the view of international entrepreneurship scholars such as Jones and Coviello (2005), the further exploration of this novel issue is best served through exploratory empirical research using an inductive case-study method, in order to get a better understanding of these differential effects.

MNE vs. VC ties: cases from Bangalore and Cambridge

In order to address the research question, an exemplar case-study is used from each of two regional clusters – the Bangalore software industry and the Cambridge electronics industry. The exemplar case-studies are drawn from wider exploratory studies. The rationale for choosing Bangalore and Cambridge is that different regional clusters may have a greater concentration of certain ties; thus, some clusters may have a strong presence of MNE subsidiaries (e.g., the Bangalore software industry) while others of VC firms (e.g., the Cambridge electronics industry).

The comparative aspect of the study is deliberate, with a view to enhancing its potential to yield valuable exploratory outcomes. Bangalore and Cambridge bear certain similarities but also differ in significant ways. Similarities include the fact that the local network is a source of international links. Also, there is considerable competition for the attention of key actors within the milieu, which means being highly innovative is a necessary condition if a new venture is to engage with a local MNE subsidiary or VC firm. A key dissimilarity is the emerging vs. advanced economy distinction which undoubtedly is reflected in Bangalore's access to MNE subsidiaries (being a significant FDI destination) and Cambridge's to VC firms (driven by a mature university-based ecosystem).

Given the exploratory nature of the research, a set of in-depth interviews (Ghauri & Grønhaug, 2002) were undertaken in Bangalore and Cambridge. The interviews covered a range of new ventures and other key local actors including MNE executives (Bangalore) and investors (Cambridge), supplemented by interviews with other industry experts including academics and trade body officials. In addition, a large amount of secondary data from company websites and industry reports were studied. The use of multiple respondents and secondary data sources was a means to achieve triangulation (Miles & Huberman, 1994).

The preliminary Bangalore and Cambridge fieldwork entailed 15 and 20 interviews, respectively. (The interview dataset on Skelta was subsequently expanded considerably; an extended narrative is provided in Chapter 7.) Interviews lasted 90 minutes on average and were tape-recorded with extensive field notes also taken. Interviewees included entrepreneurs, MNE executives, entrepreneurial support actors such as VC managers, and industry experts. An interview guide was used to ensure some uniformity in the content of the interviews to facilitate data analysis.

Data were analyzed in keeping with the approach advocated by Yin (1994). Thematic analysis of the content was undertaken first for each case-firm and then across cases. The additional expert interviews were then analyzed with a view to identifying the reiteration of or contradiction to themes identified from the interviews with the case-firms' entrepreneurs. This chapter focuses on one exemplar case-study from each of the two datasets. Both are young firms with fewer than 250 employees and thus represent small- and medium-sized enterprises.

Bangalore case-study: spatially dispersed embeddedness

Skelta was founded in Bangalore in 2002 as a software product company. Skelta's product orientation is relatively uncommon among Indian software companies, the vast majority of whom operate predominantly as services companies. Although some are skeptical about India's prospects for producing genuinely world-class software products companies, Skelta's co-founders have been adamant in their self-belief that the venture could achieve global success.

The founders include CEO Sanjay Shah, whose previous experience includes co-founding another software venture in India, iCode, which sought to offer enterprise-wide resource planning software for SMEs. Prior to this he co-founded Accel, a retailer of PCs, in Washington, DC. Shah is a graduate of the prestigious Indian Institute of Technology (Mumbai) and holds a postgraduate engineering degree from the US. Another co-founder is Paritosh Shah, who also has previous entrepreneurial experience in India and abroad and is responsible for marketing.

Skelta's flagship offering is known as Skelta BPM.NET. As evident from the name, this software application is focused on business process management (BPM) which involves the application of information technology to efficiently streamline and manage a variety of organizational processes. The second half of the product's appellation indicates that the offering is built on Microsoft's .Net platform technology, the underlying component on which software applications can be written for a Windows operating environment.

The decision to ally its product technologically with Microsoft was a significant one taken early on by the company founders. Microsoft technology was seen as attractive, given its widespread adoption by a range of companies across several countries. Technology solutions like Skelta's that are built on a Microsoft platform stand a better chance of being integrated with client companies' existing Microsoft-based applications. From Microsoft's viewpoint, such applications are of benefit too. Every time a Skelta product license is sold, so is a Microsoft operating system license.

Not surprisingly, then, a core part of Skelta's strategy has been to cultivate a deep relationship with Microsoft. Evidence of how seriously this relationship is taken is seen from the fact that the company has a separate function, alongside other conventional functions such as sales and finance, headed by a senior manager, which is referred to as the Microsoft relationship function. As CEO Sanjay Shah observes:

> Skelta shares a deep, symbiotic relationship with Microsoft and the Microsoft development community.... As a member of Microsoft's Technology Adoption Program, we have had the opportunity to work on new Microsoft technologies much in advance of their release.

It is interesting to note, however, that Skelta was able to build a cross-border, multifaceted relationship with Microsoft through efforts that began in Bangalore – its own backyard, as it were. Rajiv Sodhi, the Microsoft manager in Bangalore responsible for forging relationships with technology partners such as Skelta, notes that it was Skelta that had proactively approached Microsoft. Skelta's technology impressed Microsoft, as did the proactive approach of the top managers in seeking to gain visibility for the venture. As Sodhi comments, "We are helping Skelta. More importantly, they are helping themselves."

The Skelta–Microsoft relationship initially began at the local level through Skelta's participation in Microsoft events and other promotional activities. For example, Skelta was invited to participate in Microsoft roadshows whereby the product could be demonstrated to prospective clients in different parts of the country. Skelta's CEO was invited to speak at a seminar organized for partner organizations of Microsoft in India on how Indian software products companies could achieve local and global success. Also, when Microsoft hosted an industry-wide workshop on the topic of innovation, Skelta was showcased as an example of an innovative company.

Before long, the Indian subsidiary of Microsoft started promoting Skelta within the wider Microsoft network. To illustrate, in 2004 Skelta was invited to participate in the Microsoft Worldwide Partner Conference in Canada. The following year, Skelta was nominated by Microsoft India for an international innovation award at the Microsoft Conference in Boston, which it went on to win. In 2006, Skelta was among a set of internationally selected companies featured on Microsoft's Vista promotion website, resulting in global visibility. By this stage, Skelta had acquired about 200 clients across a range of advanced economy markets including the US, the UK, and Canada. Microsoft's Sodhi describes Skelta's strategic posture in this way:

> Skelta fostered a very strong link with Microsoft India and this link is on multiple levels ... smart people like them very quickly align themselves to Microsoft's agenda because then, you have the whole subsidiary standing behind you.... What happens as a result is that it's not a very distant point in time when you [i.e., companies like Skelta] start getting elevated to regional levels, to global levels, given the way the hierarchy works.

Thus, the Skelta experience illustrates that, given relational capabilities of pro-actively establishing a valuable relationship with a significant player such as Microsoft, Bangalore provides local firms with access to international networks via the local environment. Clearly, the local milieu in Bangalore was able to attract the presence of large players like Microsoft, and this has greatly facilitated Skelta's progress. As Skelta's relationship with Microsoft has prospered so has the company, as evident from various distinctions achieved by Skelta in 2006. It was selected for a special innovation award from the national trade body for software companies, Nasscom. It was recognized as one of Asia's fastest growing technology companies by the trade publication *Red Herring*, which had famously recognized Google's potential before many other industry observers. Perhaps most significant of all, Skelta, which had thus far been privately held, received its first round of venture capital amounting to $1.5 million from an Indian venture capital fund.

Cambridge case-study: spatially concentrated embeddedness

Plastic Logic was founded in Cambridge in 2000 as a developer of plastic electronics. Plastic Logic was spun off from Cambridge University's renowned Cavendish Laboratory, where its technology had been developed over the preceding decade or so. The company operates in the specialist area of plastic electronics, which it describes as entailing "the fabrication of electronic devices such as thin film transistors using semiconducting polymer materials." The company focuses on a new technology for manufacturing electronics and depicts its approach as one that "solves the critical issues in manufacturing high resolution transistor arrays on flexible plastic substrates." The company is working on commercializing the new technology through application in flexible active-matrix displays which are used in devices such as laptops and sophisticated mobile phones. Some experts estimate that plastic electronics will be a multibillion dollar industry by 2015.

From inception, the company has seen itself as a global company with employees, investments, and (in due course) markets coming from around the world. The company had been initially named Cambridge Polymer Logic, but the word Cambridge was subsequently dropped to signal the company's global, as opposed to parochial, mindset. ("Plastic" was preferred to "Polymer" to make the name more accessible to a lay audience.) Former CEO and current Vice Chairman Stuart Evans described Plastic Logic's orientation with respect to the international marketplace in this way:

> We are a global firm based in Cambridge. I wouldn't want anybody to think parochially about Plastic Logic. We hire people from all over the world, our investors are from all over the world, our market is all over the world, it just happens that we started in Cambridge … when we think of solving a problem, we begin looking at the world and not at Cambridge.

Notwithstanding this global orientation, it would be a fallacy to assume that the local milieu has been insignificant to Plastic Logic's birth and development; indeed, the venture's strong association with Cambridge University is striking. Apart from its origin within the university's Cavendish Laboratory, it is clear that key individuals associated with the local milieu have been influential in the company's formative stages. For instance, a co-founder is Sir Richard Friend, Cavendish Professor of Physics at the university. Another key individual has been Hermann Hauser, who earned his PhD with work at the Cavendish Laboratory and is co-founder of Amadeus Capital Partners, a venture capital firm with offices in Cambridge and London. Amadeus was a major source of seed capital for Plastic Logic. Stuart Evans, a Harvard MBA with prior stints at IBM and McKinsey, was brought on board at Amadeus's recommendation.

Its decision to ally closely with Amadeus at an early stage has had various effects on Plastic Logic. One of the most significant has been the attraction of funding beyond the seed capital stage. To illustrate, one of the investors in the next round of funding of $8 million in 2002 was the Bank of America, itself an investor in Amadeus. During this round, other investors – from Germany and Japan – were attracted as well; Amadeus's involvement with Plastic Logic from the start undoubtedly instilled confidence. Thus the seeds of many of the company's subsequent relationships were sown, as it were, in its own backyard of Cambridge, and in particular, through its links with Amadeus.

Favorable publicity was another outcome of the link with Amadeus in general, and Hauser in particular. Plastic Logic received front page coverage in the *Financial Times* during its launch, thanks to Hauser's timely positive comments to a journalist. Such assistance has complemented the considerable profile-enhancing efforts made by the company itself; indeed, Evans reckons that he "must have given 25 talks, one every couple of months all around the world, about the company and its interesting story." Evans acknowledges that the company is "helped a lot by Hermann [Hauser], who's very high profile and talks about Plastic Logic with great endearment." Another non-trivial effect of the tie with Amadeus relates to the company's accommodation in the Cambridge Science Park. When Plastic Logic sought accommodation, the general level of demand (fuelled by the Internet boom) was so high that space was not available. So when one vacancy came up, competition for it was understandably fierce. Hauser was able to use his influence to obtain that space for Plastic Logic.

But it is in attracting further funding that Amadeus's influence appears to have been the most significant. A major and, in Cambridge, unprecedented development occurred in early 2007 when Plastic Logic attracted a further infusion of $100 million to fund production of its prototype in Dresden, Germany. This is, of course, an indication that Plastic Logic has an impressive technological base and has been managed adeptly by individuals such as Evans. Although several other actors were involved, notably the American VC firms, Oak Investment Partners and Tudor Investment Corporation, it is significant that Amadeus was a participant in this round as well. As Hauser commented in the press at the time:

> Having backed Plastic Logic from day one, I am delighted that the first full commercialization of plastic electronics is now firmly in our sights. With this investment we are not only scaling up a great company – we are also creating a new electronics industry that will become a significant addition to silicon.
>
> (University of Cambridge, 2007)

Thus, the Plastic Logic experience illustrates that, given a strong platform of innovation combined with business-savvy leadership, Cambridge provides local firms with access to significant resources, directly and indirectly, through venture capitalists with deep links to Cambridge University such as Amadeus. Plastic Logic has continued to win accolades from industry commentators. The ultimate recognition of the company's potential is, of course, the recent $100 million funding, one of the largest funding rounds seen in Europe.

Analyzing the two cases in conjunction leads to the following propositions.

Opportunities

In both cases, consistent with the strategy (McEvily & Zaheer, 1999) and international entrepreneurship (Oviatt & McDougall, 2005) literatures, valuable opportunities accrued to the new ventures through bridging ties. A key consequence of these opportunities was greater credibility, and thereby legitimacy (Hitt et al., 2001). During the period of the ventures' development covered by this study, there were some noticeable differences in the manner in which opportunities accrued. For Skelta, the major influence in terms of opportunities generated through the relationship with Microsoft could be seen in international markets. Specifically, Skelta enjoyed greater international visibility through participation in international events, recognition (e.g., through awards) of its technical competence and promotion on global promotional websites. By contrast, for Plastic Logic, significant financial resources were attracted into the company and therefore, into its local milieu (notwithstanding subsequent decisions of where to locate the production function); even the company's profile within Cambridge has been significantly enhanced as a consequence. Of course, in both cases the opposite can be argued too – Skelta has gained local opportunities as well, thanks to Microsoft; and Plastic Logic has achieved international recognition through affiliation with Amadeus. But in these initial stages of both companies, the predominant influence has been in international markets for Skelta and in the local milieu for Plastic Logic. This suggests to us that there are differences in the trajectory of opportunity generation for new ventures, depending on the spatial orientation of the other actor; in the case of spatial concentration, the trajectory seems to be *magnet-like* (witness Plastic Logic's infusion of finance), whereas in the case of spatial dispersion, the trajectory is more *propeller-like* (witness Skelta's international promotion). Therefore:

Proposition 1 Spatially concentrated embeddedness in a new venture's bridging ties is associated with a "magnet-like" mechanism for the generation of opportunities; spatially dispersed embeddedness is associated with a "propeller-like" mechanism.

Knowledge

The generation of opportunities resulted in new knowledge being accessed by the ventures, which in turn influenced various economic activities pertaining to the value chain (Dacin et al., 1999; Uzzi, 1997). Irrespective of which activities were engaged in, a common benefit to both ventures was the reduction in resource-poverty as a consequence of the network relationship (Prashantham & Berry, 2004). Again, differences between the two cases can be identified. In the case of Skelta, the knowledge that it accessed was technologically more diffuse, reflecting the far greater breadth of Microsoft's knowledge-base. Such knowledge – for instance, pertaining to global software *product* sales – supplements locally available knowledge in Bangalore which is *services*-oriented. In the case of Plastic Logic, however, the knowledge that it accessed was strongly reinforcing of local specialisms. A respondent pointed out to us that a notable previous success story from the Cavendish/Amadeus "stable" had a similar interest in plastic electronics. Put differently, whereas Skelta was exposed to a wider knowledge-base, Plastic Logic was able to access a deeper knowledge-base; in both cases, these facilitated and intensified the opportunities generated for the ventures. Reflective of the particular stages in the ventures' life-cycle, in the former case the accessed knowledge was applied in downstream value chain activities (witness Skelta's international promotional efforts) and in the latter case, in upstream value chain activities (witness Plastic Logic's prototype production). In summary:

> **Proposition 2** Spatially concentrated embeddedness in a new venture's bridging ties is associated with access to a knowledge-base that reinforces local milieu specialisms; spatially dispersed embeddedness is associated with access to a knowledge-base that supplements local milieu specialisms.

Vulnerabilities

Notwithstanding the positive effects, as seen above, of local bridging ties on new ventures, the embeddedness literature points to a potential "dark side" of network relationships (Uzzi, 1997; Yli-Renko et al., 2001). Although there is no reason, per se, to suggest that it is inevitable for the two case-firms to succumb to the vulnerabilities associated with "over-embeddedness," the wider set of interviews in each of the two locations points to potential, contrasting difficulties. In the case of Skelta (or more generally, Bangalore), respondents raised concerns about the genuineness of MNE subsidiaries' commitment to the local milieu. They pointed out that, ultimately, these subsidiaries were concerned with targets in the Indian market (set for them by the MNE headquarters), and that their incentives to promote local actors in international markets were weak and transitory. Thus, ventures like Skelta may suffer from the vulnerability of *insecurity*. By contrast, in the case of Plastic Logic (or Cambridge, more generally), respondents raised concerns about the strong influence of key members – such as Amadeus's Hauser – of what they refer to as the "Cambridge mafia." While these influential individuals have contributed to many success stories, they were depicted by some interviewees as promoting a fairly standard way of doing things. Such an approach could be constraining to a new venture like Plastic Logic which could, then, be vulnerable to falling into a trap of *groupthink*. It is, of course, the very characteristics of local bridging ties that yield opportunities and access to new knowledge, as argued above, which present potential vulnerabilities. Thus, the argument concerns possible tendencies that new ventures must guard against rather than inevitable outcomes. Indeed, both ventures demonstrate characteristics that may help avoid these pitfalls – witness Skelta's dedicated Microsoft relationship function, that possibly increases the security of the relationship, and Plastic Logic's international portfolio of funders, which exposes it to a range of stimuli. Even so, caution is required about the following:

Table 5.1 Local bridging ties and new venture internationalization

	Dispersed embeddedness (MNE)	*Concentrated embeddedness (VC)*
Opportunities	"Propeller-like"	"Magnet-like"
Knowledge	Local specialisms supplemented	Local specialisms reinforced
Vulnerabilities	Insecurity	Groupthink

Proposition 3 Spatially concentrated embeddedness in a new venture's bridging ties is associated with the vulnerability of groupthink; spatially dispersed embeddedness is associated with the vulnerability of insecurity.

The table above summarizes the above arguments.

This chapter has thus far put forward the argument that local embeddedness could vary in nature and have differential effects on internationalization of new ventures in terms of differing trajectories of opportunity creation, distinct influences on value chain activities through the differing nature of knowledge-bases that are accesse,; and varying ways in which these ties potentially have a dark side – that is, constraining effects. An implication of the above is the utility of a holistic approach – both in managerial and public policy terms – whereby clusters possess both forms of network relationships that new ventures can cultivate and utilize as they seek internationalization success.

MNE networks as a substitute for voids in the entrepreneurial ecosystem

Anecdotal evidence suggests that MNE networks can be relevant for INVs in both emerging and advanced economies (Prashantham & Birkinshaw, 2008; Terjesen, O'Gorman & Acs, 2008, Vapola, 2011). My focus on the former has tended to be primarily on the grounds that the effects of social capital in general, and MNE networks in particular, are *accentuated* in such a setting. (Of course, as will be suggested in Chapter 8, further research that examines a broader range of industry and country settings is warranted.) Nevertheless, at a broad level, insights about the role of MNE ties in new venture internationalization generated from research in Bangalore are merely more magnified in such a location and ought to find broader applicability in a range of empirical contexts.

That said, it is also worth reflecting on the *differences* between emerging and advanced economies that may surface through research in Bangalore – and beyond. Thus building upon the foregoing discussion in this chapter, further observations can be made that link the role of MNE ties with the nature of the new venture's institutional environment. Indeed, research on MNE–INV engagement in an emerging economy context (such as that of Skelta's with Microsoft) raises an intriguing issue: MNE networks have a higher significance for new ventures in emerging economies to the extent that they act as a quasi-substitute for voids in the local milieu's entrepreneurial ecosystem. By way of simple illustration, a venture like Plastic Logic in Cambridge had access to abundant start-up support, including VC funds. If it were to thereafter choose to partner with MNEs it would likely be well placed to do so, having been backed by well-reputed VCs, which would act as an endorsement (Gulati & Sytch, 2007). That is, the sequence that seems most likely in the case of ventures such as Plastic Logic is that the local VC funders make decisions on whether to provide seed capital and *this* acts as a signal of quality and legitimacy to MNEs seeking innovative partners. (This was in fact what transpired in the case of Plastic Logic. My subsequent work with Microsoft's new venture partners in the UK and US also reveals a similar sequence of VC funding preceding MNE ties.)

By contrast, Skelta did not have ready access to sophisticated start-up support in Bangalore at the time of its founding. (In relative terms, of course, Bangalore's entrepreneurial ecosystem for software ventures was probably the best on offer in India but still immature relative to counterparts in advanced economies.) Thus support received from its MNE partner, Microsoft, in terms of legitimacy benefits, technology support, and general mentoring was especially valuable. In fact, *after* it had become apparent that Skelta had found favor within the Microsoft network, the venture was able to attract a modicum of venture capital in Bangalore – and this was a nontrivial accomplishment since risk capital remained relatively scarce by international standards at the time. (Rapid developments over the recent past mean the situation is much improved but in general, emerging economies lag behind their advanced economy counterparts in terms of entrepreneurial ecosystem support for radical innovation.)

Subsequent case-study research in China (referred to in Chapter 7) reveals a similar pattern and, at one level, there is a striking resemblance in the sequence of MNE and VC ties between Skelta and Gridsum, a new venture in the Zhongguancun district of Beijing (dubbed "China's Silicon Valley"), with close links to Microsoft. In China as well, notwithstanding considerable efforts by the Chinese government to strengthen the entrepreneurial ecosystem, the venture capital market is immature compared to locations such as Cambridge, UK, or Silicon Valley in the US. Much like with Skelta, it was the MNE link that came first for Gridsum. That is, its link with Microsoft *preceded* its ability to access venture capital. The Microsoft connection helped open doors to VC finding by conferring legitimacy on the new venture, thereby leading to its being taken seriously by prospective VC funders. Given the greater information asymmetry of emerging economies, VCs (especially international ones), may be more risk-averse in making funding decisions if they feel constrained in their ability to make informed decisions about first-time entrepreneurs and their ventures. In such circumstances, being associated with a well-reputed Western MNE can be an important signal that facilitates access to venture capital.

One implication of these differential patterns between advanced and emerging economy ventures is that research in a context like Bangalore, on the one hand, provides a heightened sense of MNE tie effects (making them easier to observe) and insights with broad applicability, and, on the other, in conjunction with observations from other types of settings, presents the opportunity to illuminate the moderating effects of the institutional environment on the effects of MNE networks on new venture internationalization.

Thus valuable insight can be obtained through comparative case-studies; hence the effort to incorporate a British case in Chapter 5 and a Chinese one in Chapter 7. Sandwiched by these chapters, however, is the next one (Chapter 6) where a quantitative study of Indian software ventures tests the idea that social capital associated with geographically dispersed MNEs can in fact yield internationalization capability learning and that, by contrast, peer ties yield negative benefits on this count.

Note

1 This section and the next draws upon the following material with the kind permission of Edward Elgar Publishing: S. Prashantham & G. Balachandran, 2009. Local bridging ties and new venture internationalization: Exploratory studies in Bangalore and Cambridge. In M. V. Jones, P. Dimitratos, M. Fletcher, & S. Young (Eds.), *Internationalization, Entrepreneurship and the Smaller Firm* (pp. 167–180). Cheltenham: Edward Elgar.

6   Internationalization capability learning via MNE ties

The preceding chapter highlighted the prospect of MNE ties yielding geography-spanning social capital, and suggested that this might be especially valuable in an emerging economy setting. One implication is that, potentially, new ventures can gain internationalization capability learning outcomes through MNE partners. This chapter presents a quantitative study undertaken in the Indian software industry that seeks to test this notion. Furthermore, to underline the significance of MNE ties in emerging economies as a means of compensating for weak local support, it presents a study that tests the prospect that ties with peers may be *detrimental* for internationalization capability learning.[1]

Theory and background

Relational capital and capability development

Relational capital refers to mutual trust, respect and close interactions among partners (Kale et al., 2002). It specifically highlights the affective quality of connections, that is, the relational dimension of social capital, which pertains to "relations people have, such as respect and friendship" (Nahapiet & Ghoshal, 1998, p. 244). Interorganizational knowledge transfer leading to capability development is enhanced when network relationships are characterized by relational capital because of the informational benefits of networks, that is, actors' opportunities for "receiving a valuable piece of information and knowing how to use it" (Burt, 1992, p. 13). Relational capital facilitates knowledge transfer by lowering the barriers to combining and exchanging resources, notably intellectual resources (Coleman, 1988; Dyer & Singh, 1998; Gulati, 2007; Granovetter, 1985; Nahapiet & Ghoshal, 1998). This could provide actors with access to the information and know-how underlying capabilities so they become more *aware* of capabilities and *comprehend* them better. This is especially important in the transfer of the tacit knowledge that underpins capabilities (Dhanaraj, Lyles, Steensma, & Tihanyi, 2004).

Relational capital promotes valuable information exchange, enhancing the awareness of partner capabilities, and opens potential access to knowledge underlying such capabilities (McEvily & Zaheer, 1999). Trust lubricates cooperation;

trust-based relational capital enables the free exchange of information and know-how (Kale et al., 2000, p. 221). That is, trust facilitates greater intensity, frequency, and efficiency of information exchange (Yli-Renko & Janakiraman, 2008). Trust also induces a greater willingness to take risks in exchanging information by creating a sense of security that knowledge will not be exploited beyond its intended use (Coleman, 1988; Ring & Van de Ven, 1994). This is especially valuable in contexts marked by ambiguity and uncertainty (Yli-Renko et al., 2001), as in the case of knowledge-intensive settings including software firms, which form this study's sample. Furthermore, norms of reciprocity may lead to the opening of new doors. As Dhanaraj et al. (2004, p. 430) suggest, "Learning often requires informal give-and-take." New opportunities may arise from linked firms' wider networks, sometimes serendipitously (Nahapiet & Ghoshal, 1998). Novel information, ideas, and opportunities generated in this way could strengthen the improvement of existing capabilities or the development of new ones (McEvily & Zaheer, 1999).

Relational capital also helps the focal firm to better comprehend the capability that it seeks to acquire or to grasp the underlying knowledge (McEvily & Marcus, 2005). Know-how transfer is facilitated by interaction and coactivity which provides "a forum for observation, experimentation, and demonstration" (McEvily & Marcus, 2005, p. 1034). Relational capital enables such engagement in a nonthreatening atmosphere and permits greater opportunities through which new ventures can acquire know-how (Dhanaraj et al., 2004). Furthermore, relational capital increases the odds of serendipity leading to valuable coactivity and knowledge transfer (Nahapiet & Ghoshal, 1998). Apart from facilitating learning, relational capital also reduces the prospect of opportunistic behavior by a partner (Kale et al., 2000).

Relational capital sources and internationalization capability:
MNE vs. SME partners

As appealing as the above picture is, it is incomplete if partner characteristics are not considered in the equation. In the international entrepreneurship literature, distinction among network ties on the basis of partner characteristics is relatively scant, although there is a growing literature on the effects of partner asymmetry on relationship outcomes (Katila et al., 2008; Prashantham & Birkinshaw, 2008; Vandaie & Zaheer, 2014). In the context of new ventures, ties with foreign MNE subsidiaries have the potential to aid internationalization capability development, but they also represent a set of *asymmetric* interfirm ties. It is not clear if ties with other Indian SMEs, which are likely to be far more evenly matched with, and more readily accessed by, the focal venture, provide any similar benefits. While it is well known that internationalization capability is often learned experientially, a challenge, especially for new ventures building capabilities *de novo*, is that they lack substantial prior experience. While this deficiency may be compensated for, at least to an extent, by founders' prior work experience, such knowledge tends to be narrowly focused on a specific set of international markets (Prashantham & Floyd, 2012; Reuber &

Fischer, 1997). Thus, the challenge for developing a more generalizable set of guiding principles vis-à-vis international market expansion, which represents an important downstream capability (Dhanaraj & Beamish, 2003; Knight & Cavusgil, 2004; Kumaraswamy, Mudambi, Saranga, & Tripathy, 2012), is considerable for internationalizing new ventures. While it is common that Indian software firms seek to internationalize, they vary in their success in doing so, which in turn reflects variance in their internationalization capability (Athreye, 2005; Lorenzen & Mudambi, 2013; Prashantham & Dhanaraj, 2010).

The challenge of building internationalization capability is compounded in an emerging economy where firms are latecomers to globalization and in need of catching up on various competencies (Awate, Larsen, & Mudambi, 2012). Thus, learning interactively or vicariously from firms with rich experience in internationalization offers another important learning route. The local subsidiaries of foreign MNEs constitute an obvious candidate as a source of internationalization capability learning because they are sources and recipients of knowledge flows within the MNE, with the latter often being quite substantial (Mudambi & Navarra, 2004; Yang, Mudambi, & Meyer, 2008). Given that MNE subsidiaries' very existence stems from the internationalization process of the parent, the knowledge flows they receive and the capabilities they possess, develop, and embody are likely of relevance (Schulz, 2001) to the internationalization aspirations of young Indian software firms. (However, the fact that MNE subsidiaries are likely to focus on succeeding in the Indian market and new ventures on international market success means their strategic foci differ, which in turn may limit the extent to which MNE ties actually translate into internationalization *activity*, a point that is returned to in the follow-up research question.) MNE subsidiary-derived knowledge[2] is relevant in at least three ways: it helps the focal actor to consider internationalization seriously and realistically; it reduces the perceived risk associated with international expansion by making clear-headed analysis more feasible; and it expands the focal actor's search horizon for resource mobilization by sensitizing it to relevant resources within the MNE and elsewhere.

In the context of the Indian software industry, MNE subsidiaries have been credited with being a major source of knowledge spillovers (Patibandla & Petersen, 2002; Lorenzen & Mudambi, 2013). But prior research has not considered the specific case of internationalization capability learning emanating from MNE ties for *young* Indian software firms. This perhaps reflects the fact that relationships between new ventures and MNEs face challenges in forming. Network theory posits that accessing ties with peers is generally more straightforward for actors because of the principle of homophily, that is, birds of a feather flock together (McPherson, Smith-Lovin, & Cook, 2001). Putnam (2000) uses the vocabulary of bonding and bridging ties to distinguish relationships with homogenous social actors – that is, peers – from those with heterogenous actors. But while the ease of forming bonding and bridging ties differs, Putnam (2000, p. 363) acknowledges that "bridging and bonding social capital are good for different things." More specifically, he suggests that "Bonding social capital is ... good for 'getting by,' but bridging social capital is crucial for 'getting ahead' " (Putnam, 2000, p. 23).

In the context of the Indian software new venture, a similar distinction can be made between ties with MNE subsidiaries and peers (i.e., other indigenous SMEs). That is, the former are likely to be a source of novel knowledge about internationalization capability, but at the same time represent a more difficult relationship-building task since MNE subsidiaries are so different. There is a further challenge associated with this asymmetry: even when such ties are formed, knowledge transfer is impeded by the asymmetry in the two sets of firms' knowledge-base, management practices, and organizational cultures (Lane & Lubatkin, 1998; Yang et al., 2008), which results in an accentuation of new ventures' limited power and influence (Mudambi, Schründer, & Mongar, 2004; Prashantham & Birkinshaw, 2008). This is in contrast with MNE subsidiaries' greater perceived and actual power resulting from network centrality, a strong resource base, and political clout in the host market (Brass & Burkhardt, 1993; Kumaraswamy et al., 2012). Perhaps this is why an explicit recognition of MNE ties as a source of capability development is scant in the international entrepreneurship literature within which the present study is positioned. New venture-MNE ties are therefore *unlikely* to reflect the interfirm symmetry assumed to be typical of the interorganizational learning scenario, as evidenced by this insightful description by Kumaraswamy et al. (2012, p. 377) of how the process tends to unfold:

> Repeated, frequent interactions facilitate the co-development of matching organizational structures and processes between partnering firms (Lane & Lubatkin, 1998).... Over time, a virtuous circle emerges wherein increasingly relationship-specific investments enable partners to recognize additional opportunities for collaborating and strengthening existing ties.

Given the challenges of interorganizational learning associated with asymmetric interfirm ties, the role of relational capital in overcoming barriers to knowledge transfer becomes all the more salient. That is, goodwill and trust can lead to greater awareness and comprehension of new capabilities by the new venture while lessening the odds of MNE malfeasance, thus compensating for interfirm asymmetries. Accessing relevant knowledge via relational capital with MNE ties makes the new venture *aware* of what internationalization capability entails. New doors may be opened if top managers in the focal new venture gain face-to-face time with, for instance, visiting executives from the MNE's headquarters (parent company). Interacting more widely with MNE executives who typically embody a global mindset (Gupta & Govindarajan, 2002) broadens the scope of the new venture's knowledge-base. In the Indian context, this is especially important for enhancing the quality of their international managerial practices (Kumar, Mohapatra, & Chandrasekhar, 2009). This is illustrated by the case of a new venture called Mitoken which began to engage closely with Motorola in Bangalore and thereafter in Chicago (Prashantham & Birkinshaw, 2008). Furthermore, because MNE partners as established organizations possess mature processes and systems for managing cross-border activities and relationships (Eriksson, Johanson, Majkgard, & Sharma, 1997), the focal new venture is more likely to *comprehend* internationalization capability through observation, emulation, and joint activity such as coordinated marketing efforts (Cao, 2006). Anecdotal evidence suggests that some new ventures have learned much from MNE subsidiaries. For instance, Dhruva, a Bangalore-based new venture, learned about international markets through its local association with Intel (Prashantham & Birkinshaw, 2008).

That said, while undoubtedly desirable, building relational capability with MNEs is not easy for young Indian software firms. As already noted, forming ties with dissimilar actors is inherently difficult because they tend to occupy different network locations and status levels: prominent MNE subsidiaries tend to be more centrally embedded in the local economy while new ventures are more peripheral (Cantwell & Mudambi, 2011; Mudambi et al., 2004). Their power differential means that for a young venture to gain an MNE subsidiary's attention it must be distinctive in technical competence and alliance proactiveness (Prashantham & Birkinshaw, 2008). While Hennart (2009) makes the valid observation that domestic firms also have valuable assets that get bundled with those of MNEs, here the focus is on learning outcomes that could occur without formal asset bundling. Even if this did occur, the potential and actual power in use (Brass & Burkhardt, 1993) of the MNE subsidiary greatly exceeds that of the resource-constrained new venture (Mudambi et al., 2004; Katila et al., 2008). For these reasons, some ventures "may be reluctant to seek partnerships with large international corporations" (Cumming, Sapienza, Siegel, & Wright, 2009, p. 287). Only the more savvy new ventures will be proactive in seeking relevant MNE partners and competent at "pressing the right buttons" to successfully forge links with MNE subsidiaries. Thus, it is expected there will be variance among young Indian software firms in relation to their stock of relational capital vis-à-vis MNE ties, and this is associated with the variance in their levels of internationalization capability. In sum:

Hypothesis 1 Relational capital arising from local MNE relationships is positively associated with a new venture's internationalization capability.

Note, however, that the research question is not merely concerned with the effects of MNE ties per se (which is, of itself, arguably unsurprising though non-trivial); rather, it is concerned with how these *compare* with those of peers, thus making the question novel and relevant. This is an important distinction, hitherto not made in the international entrepreneurship literature, which is important not only to underline the relevance of MNE ties in and of themselves, but also to gauge the relative impact of peer ties in an emerging economy setting. One does not know whether, when the effects of MNE ties are controlled for, such ties are also positive but less significantly so, non-significant in their effects, or –

surprisingly (and worrisomely) – significantly *negative*. Whatever the outcome, the results will have important theoretical, managerial, and policy implications.

It is suggested here that relational capital with peers can in fact be problematic, in that the effect of SME relational capital is actually likely to be negative, not merely "less positive" than MNE relational capital due to interrelated reasons. First, learning via SMEs may be suboptimal in content. This is seemingly counter-intuitive to the notion that similar firms make better "teachers" (Lane & Lubatkin, 1998). However, even though a basic tenet of sociology is that actors prefer to transact with others like themselves, Phelps, Adams and Bessant (2007, p. 14) note: "There is an important issue of whether or not it is best to construct networks from similar firms, given that this potentially ... limits the breadth of knowledge that can be exchanged by over-familiarity." Although the interorganizational learning *process* may be more straightforward between a new venture and another SME, the *content* of learning in the realm of internationalization capability may be lacking owing to limitations outlined previously. Internationalization know-how is less abundant amongst SME partners who are less likely to have mature routines in place relative to an MNE partner, especially in emerging economies like India where active outward internationalization is of relatively recent origin (Krishnan, 2010; Kumar et al., 2009; Kundu & Katz, 2003). They also are less likely than MNEs to expose the focal young actor to "contacts that are tapping fundamentally different informational domains ... therefore they are likely to discover unique opportunities and information" (McEvily & Zaheer, 1999, p. 1138).

Second, learning via SMEs may be insufficiently ambitious. Greve (2003) suggests that actors typically have implicit reference groups that form the basis of their aspirations and consequent mimetic behaviors. Selecting local SMEs as its reference group, particularly in an emerging economy, may lead to the focal young actor setting its horizons too low in the realm of internationalization. This does not contradict the earlier observation that many young Indian software firms tend to be export-oriented because this may reflect an underdeveloped domestic market rather than high levels of aspiration. There is likely variance in aspiration, and a new venture could end with a set of ties with peers whose internationalization ambitions are modest. This, in turn, could have a detrimental effect on internationalization capability outcomes because a passive orientation to learning efforts makes it unlikely that the focal young actor will undertake distinctive actions that could foster such outcomes.

Third, learning via SMEs may be distracting. Sapienza, De Clercq and Sandberg (2005) provide the insight that when new ventures engage in non-internationalization activities they "displace" learning efforts that could enhance internationalization capability because of the new venture's scarce managerial attention and resources. The cooperative behaviors noted among new ventures in some advanced economies (McNaughton & Bell, 1999) presuppose the existence of strong institutions that are not prevalent in emerging economies. Weak institutions may be compensated for by intensive relationship-building activity among indigenous peers (Xu & Meyer, 2013). Network relationships impose high costs, in time and energy, in monitoring and maintaining these relationships. Displacement of internationalization learning efforts may lead to capability learning in other domains (e.g., dealing with the local business environment), but have negative consequences for internationalization capability. Taking into account the above arguments:

Hypothesis 2 Relational capital arising from local SME relationships is negatively associated with a new venture's internationalization capability.

Methodology

Data

To test the hypotheses, a survey was conducted among young Indian software firms that had internationalized. The choice of software firms is a popular one in international entrepreneurship research because of their proclivity to internationalize and leverage network relationships (Coviello, 2006). India was an attractive setting because of the high export orientation of its software industry; 80% of all revenues accrue through international business. It has been the recipient of considerable FDI, and foreign MNEs, such as IBM and Microsoft, have a major India presence (D'Costa, 2003). The focus on a single country and industry mitigates concerns about non-measured variance associated with undesirable extraneous heterogeneity.

Data collection in an emerging economy can be a challenge. To identify a sample, a single reliable database was used, namely, the directory of the software trade body, Nasscom. It yielded a list of 351 software services firms younger than 12 years old[3] and with fewer than 250 employees[4] across Bangalore, Chennai, Hyderabad, Mumbai, and greater New Delhi. The questionnaire was pre-tested on a 50-firm sample from a different population to ascertain clarity of phraseology. It was initially emailed out, resulting in 39 responses. A follow-up effort involving the use of field researchers yielded 69 more responses. Six incomplete responses were discarded, leaving 102 usable responses. The response rate (29%) compares favorably with other similar studies (e.g., Yli-Renko et al., 2001). Respondents were the CEO or one who held a top manager position. ANOVA tests for bias showed no significant demographic differences between respondents and non-respondents, and between respondents in each wave. On average each firm was 8.6 years old, had 137 employees, and obtained 62.2% of revenues through international business.

Measures

Dependent variables

Internationalization capability was measured using a three-item Likert-type scale (Cronbach's α 0.86) based on Eriksson et al. (1997); see Appendix.

Independent variables

Relational capital arising from (1) local MNE relationships and (2) local SME relationships were separately measured using a five-item scale based on Kale et al.'s (2000) work (Cronbach's α 0.98 and 0.96, respectively); see Appendix. Consistent with some previous studies (e.g., Rindfleisch, & Moorman 2001; Yli-Renko & Janakiraman, 2008), these items yielded an aggregated perceptual measure taking into account an overall set of relationships because of practical constraints in respondents evaluating each of their numerous relationships. The informants used (CEOs and top managers) are known to be knowledgeable and accurate in their responses about such relationships (Kumar, Stern, & Anderson, 1993).

Control variables

Firm age and firm size. Following precedent, the logarithm of the number of years since founding and the logarithm of the number of full-time employees, respectively, were used to control for demographic variance (Lu & Beamish, 2001).

    Knowledge intensity. More knowledge-intensive firms often have a greater proclivity to internationalize and learn (Autio et al., 2000; Prashantham, 2005). A four-item scale adapted from Autio et al. (2000) was used (Cronbach's α 0.85); see Appendix.

    Overseas networks. Research suggests that overseas relationships facilitate internationalization (Coviello & Munro, 1997; Yli-Renko et al., 2002). Member-ship of a prominent cross-border networking organization called The Indus Entrepreneurs was used as a proxy for such relationships (dichotomous dummy variable; 1 = member and 0 = non-member).

    Activity scope. New ventures may vary in the scope of their offering which in turn influences their internationalization trajectory (Oviatt & McDougall, 2005). The number of software activities carried out was used as a proxy measure; see Appendix.

Reliability and validity

Principal factor analyses were performed on all measurement items which loaded onto the expected factors, suggesting discriminant validity. Composite reliability (Cronbach's α) scores exceeded 0.85 in all cases, indicating convergent validity. Follow-up interviews with a sub-sample (10%) provided assurance of the validity of the survey data.[5] To rule out multicolinearity concerns, variance inflation factor scores were computed and found to be less than 2 (Hair, Anderson, Tatham, & Black, 1998). Also, principal components analysis of the combined 12 items of the two relational capital constructs yielded, with orthogonal rotation, two distinct factors suggesting that the measures were not redundant. Regressions were rerun using the resulting factor scores as independent variables. To ensure the MNE and

SME relationships were comparable, respondents were asked to describe the nature of their exchange relationships as suppliers versus buyers. The difference between the extent to which MNEs and SMEs were buyers ($t=-0.268$; sig $=0.790$) or suppliers ($t=0.833$; sig $=0.407$) was non-significant. In order to address common method variance in single-respondent studies of this kind, multiple-item scales were used to measure constructs, and distributed across the survey instrument. A post hoc Harman's one-factor test did not yield a single dominant factor. Regression results remained stable when the first principle component was included as a control to account for covariance from a single survey instrument. Other post hoc robustness tests included rerunning the regression analyses with modified measures for the independent variables (e.g., other items used by Yli-Renko et al., 2001); the hypothesis results remained stable.

Findings

Quantitative results

For the formal testing of the hypotheses, data analysis was undertaken using OLS regression techniques. Correlations are depicted in Table 6.1. Table 6.2 shows regression coefficients for internationalization capability; Model 1 indicates regression results with control variables alone and Model 2 includes the independent variable(s). Apart from the demographic variables of age and size, the firm's level of technological knowledge intensity is found to be significantly associated with the level of internationalization capability.

When the independent variables are introduced, as Table 6.2 shows, increasing levels of relational capital arising from local MNE relationships lead to greater internationalization capability ($t=3.277$; $p=0.001$), in support of H1. The results for H2 are consistent with the prediction of a negative relationship ($t=-1.872$; $p=0.064$) between relational capital arising from SME relationships and internationalization capability. Overall, the findings are supportive of the hypotheses.

It is plausible that MNEs are heterogeneous in their internationalization capability and the results could vary with the internationalization capability of the MNEs. SME relational capital was measured at an aggregate level, and no data were collected on the level of internationalization of individual SME partners. However, such effects could be partially inferred by analyzing the effects of heterogeneity among the SMEs, by using firm location as a proxy of internationalization propensity. As a robustness test, the regressions were run for a sub-sample of ventures from the export-oriented locations of Bangalore and Hyderabad; the results were qualitatively similar for this sub-sample as well as that comprising the remaining firms. Future studies can build on this study's findings and could explore the effect of tie heterogeneity.

Table 6.1 Correlations

	1	2	3	4	5	6	7	8	9
1 Log age	1								
2 Log size	0.202*	1							
3 Knowledge intensity	-0.057	0.076	1						
4 Overseas networks (membership 0/1)	-0.136	0.050	-0.127	1					
5 Activity scope	0.142	0.158	0.010	-0.028	1				
6 MNE relational capital	-0.037	0.140	0.134	0.025	0.136	1			
7 SME relational capital	-0.012	0.126	0.065	0.063	0.058	0.421**	1		
8 Internationalization capability	-0.275**	0.179	0.339**	-0.018	-0.059	0.309**	-0.011	1	
9 International intensity	-0.004	0.124	-0.008	0.171	0.103	-0.019	-0.156	0.335*	1
Mean	0.893	1.931	5.722	0.12	4.99	3.261	3.485	5.036	62.20
s.d	0.252	0.442	0.961	0.325	2.062	1.858	1.701	1.320	32.59

Notes
* $p < 0.05$ (two-tailed).
** $p < 0.01$.

Table 6.2 OLS regression coefficients for internationalization capability

Variable	Model 1		Model 2	
	B	SE	B	SE
Constant	2.971***	0.980	3.080***	0.945
Log age	−1.506***	0.510	−1.447***	0.488
Log size	0.634**	0.293	0.583**	0.284
Knowledge intensity	0.416***	0.128	0.377***	0.123
Overseas networks	−0.138	0.378	−0.128	0.361
Activity scope	−0.033	0.060	−0.051	0.057
MNE relational capital			0.229***	0.070
SME relational capital			−0.140*	0.075
Adj. R^2	0.168		0.242	
Wald F	4.968***		5.478***	
Change statistics				
Δ R-squared	0.168		0.74	
Δ Wald F	4.968		0.510	
N	102		102	

Notes
* $p < 0.10$.
** $p < 0.05$.
*** $p < 0.01$.

Discussion

Contributions

The present study of 102 young Indian software firms contributes to research on international entrepreneurship by highlighting the relative ability of network relationships to assist new ventures to develop internationalization capability. H1 is a straightforward (but useful) confirmation that MNE relationships can have a positive effect on internationalization capability in new ventures by, in effect, the tapping of relevant knowledge flows to and from MNE subsidiaries (Mudambi & Navarra, 2004; Yang et al., 2008). This is useful because building high-quality interactions with an MNE is no trivial task for a new venture. This study reveals a potential payoff – namely, internationalization capability – for new ventures that overcome the challenges associated with successfully building relational capital with MNEs. The arguments and results for H2 present an unexplored *negative* effect of local SME relationships. By utilizing an emerging economy setting, the study brings out the accentuated effects of relational capital – both positive and negative – on capability development in internationalizing new ventures. In so doing it extends prior research (notably Coviello, 2006; Fernhaber et al., 2009; Prashantham & Dhanaraj, 2010; Yli-Renko et al., 2002) which helpfully highlights network relationships as a valuable source of know-how but does not investigate differential effects of relational capital sources. This study suggests that *who* SMEs know may matter more than *how much* relational capital they have per se.

At the strategy/IB interface, these insights offer a novel perspective by turning attention away from MNEs as the focal actor in interorganizational relationships to their role as partners for *other* focal actors. It provides a more holistic picture of firm internationalization compared to the typically siloed approach scholars take in studying MNEs and international new ventures separately, without reference to the other set of firms. This more holistic perspective resonates with contemporary IB perspectives, such as the global factory notion, which recognizes that MNEs orchestrate interfirm networks that may include new ventures (Buckley, 2012). Indeed, it is seen here that MNEs *can* be beneficial to indigenous new ventures. This is especially significant given the finding that if partners (such as SMEs) are *not* highly capable of yielding requisite capability learning, relational capital may end up being *counterproductive*.

This argument complements and extends research that shows that exchange relationships with customers (Yli-Renko et al., 2001) and suppliers (McEvily & Marcus, 2005) are conducive to know-how transfer to new ventures. This study suggests that for internationalization capability in new ventures, the key issue appears to be less the nature of the exchange relationship (supplier vs. customer) and more the nature of the partner as a source of capability learning. Thus from a theoretical perspective, in contrast to "relative absorptive capacity" arguments that commonality in resource base, organizational structure, and corporate culture facilitates interorganizational learning (Lane & Lubatkin, 1998), this study indicates that dissimilar actors (MNEs, in this case) can be highly effective "teachers" in certain domains (here, internationalization), and that highly similar partners (SMEs, in this case) may be ineffective. Relational capital may compensate for interorganizational asymmetry barriers to yield learning from dissimilar actors.

Limitations, future research, and implications for practice

The limitations of this work can stimulate future research. A reasonable question may arise as to whether MNE relational capital leads to internationalization capability (as argued here) or whether in fact internationally capable new ventures are adept at forging local MNE relationships. The cross-sectional nature of the data makes it difficult to rule out reverse causality. However, the historical development of the Indian software industry suggests MNE presence came first (D'Costa, 2003). Other limitations include the study's exploratory nature, reflected in its small sample size. Further research involving larger datasets and longitudinal research in multiple settings is warranted, including on *how* MNE relational capital is formed. A more fine-grained perspective can be obtained by exploring differences between leading and laggard MNE partners, and between upstream and downstream joint activities. It would also be illuminative to study how MNE manager-level knowledge spills over into local new ventures. It is also acknowledged that certain new ventures may have established ties with local SMEs because of their lack of interest in internationalization capability. Conversely, the aggregate measures of SME relational capital may mask the effects of certain dyads with individual SME partners possessing strong internationalization capability; future research could usefully tease out such effects. The stated premise remains, however, that the differential in levels of internationalization capability between a focal new venture and foreign MNE subsidiary is considerably higher than that between it and a fellow SME.

The study informs managerial practice and public policy. New ventures in advanced and (especially) emerging economies ought to leverage local MNE relationships for international capability. Equally, given local SME relationships' inefficacy in this regard, they should be mindful of the company they keep. From a public policy perspective, fostering MNE linkages in knowledge-intensive sectors could facilitate capability development in new ventures, an important outcome (Wright, Westhead, & Ucbasaran, 2007). In settings where FDI has waned or local institutions are weak, specific initiatives to broker these links by coordinating enterprise and FDI attraction policies appear advisable, given Cumming et al.'s (2009, p. 287) observation that new ventures may not always willingly partner with MNEs. Such brokering initiatives are therefore potentially useful.

Conclusion

Although network relationships have long been cast as strategic assets for new ventures seeking internationalization capability, it is important to consider when that is the case, and (perhaps even more importantly) when it is not. While it is known that relational capital facilitates capability development in linked firms, rather less is known about the *relational capital sources* associated with more and less effective knowledge transfer. This study points to the differential effects of different relational capital sources for internationalization, and supports the view that "the characteristics of partners matter" (Stuart & Sorenson, 2007, p. 218). In particular, the role of MNEs as partners to new ventures is highlighted, and is a topic warranting further investigation, including shedding further light into *how* such relationships are cultivated and leveraged for innovation and internationalization outcomes.

The last-mentioned point is picked up in the next chapter through further qualitative analysis of the Skelta case, discussed in the previous chapter.

Appendix

Table 6.3 Measurement items and validity assessment

Construct	Items 1 = completely disagree; 7 = completely agree	Factor loadings	Composite reliability (α)	Literature	Source
Internationalization capability	(1) We are knowledgeable about international business strategy, (2) We are competent at identifying international business opportunities, (3) We are competent at international marketing.	0.833 0.782 0.816	0.86	Eriksson et al., 1997	Survey
International intensity (%)	(International revenues) × 100 (total revenues)	n/a	n/a		Nasscom Survey
MNE relational capital	With respect to MNE subsidiaries in India (e.g., Microsoft India): (1) We actively utilize these relationships in our business. (2) These relationships are characterized by close interactions. (3) These relationships are characterized by mutual trust. (4) These relationships are highly reciprocal. (5) These relationships have "opened new doors" for us.	0.941 0.946 0.928 0.927 0.929	0.98	Lu and Beamish, 2001 Kale et al., 2000; Yli-Renko et al., 2001	
SME relational capital	With respect to other infotech/software SMEs in India: (1) We actively utilize these relationships in our business. (2) These relationships are characterized by close interactions. (3) These relationships are characterized by mutual trust. (4) These relationships are highly reciprocal. (5) These relationships have "opened new doors" for us.	0.894 0.936 0.895 0.896 0.894	0.96	Kale et al., 2000; Yli-Renko et al., 2001	Survey
Knowledge-intensity	(1) We have a strong reputation for technological excellence. (2) Technological innovation is a primary goal for us. (3) There is a strong knowledge component in our products/services. (4) Most of our employees have strong technical skills.	0.852 0.851 0.766 0.87	0.85	Autio et al., 2000; Yli-Renko et al., 2002	Survey
Activity scope	Overall problem definition, conceptual design, physical system design, programming, testing and reviewing, maintenance and support, and documentation.	n/a (count measure)	n/a	Generated through pre-survey interviews	Survey

Notes

1 The remainder of the chapter is taken from a recent article with kind permission from Springer Science+Business Media: Shameen Prashantham and Charles Dhanaraj, (2014) MNE ties and new venture internationalization: exploratory insights from India *Asia Pacific Journal of Management*, doi 10.1007/s10490–014–9391-y.
2 The focus here is on subsidiary-level knowledge rather than that of individual MNE subsidiary managers because only firm-level data are available. But it is acknowledged that, as insightfully pointed out by an anonymous reviewer, a more fine-grained picture can be obtained in future research by considering multilevel models that take into account manager-level knowledge within MNE partners. Furthermore, the focus here is on *foreign* MNE subsidiary ties, not ties with Indian MNEs, which field interviews suggested were relatively rare.
3 The 12-year threshold represents relative youth in an Asian context. This higher age limit compared to US-based studies is justified by the lower availability of early-stage equity funding and the typically longer maturation process for ventures (Kumar et al., 2009). The study's results remained stable at lower age cut-offs (less than ten and eight years).
4 As Keupp and Gassmann (2009, p. 601) note, the most common employee cut-offs in international entrepreneurship research are 250 and 500 employees. In this study the former was chosen because of the nascent empirical setting.
5 Ideally every questionnaire would have been completed by multiple respondents but often this is not feasible in smaller Asian firms for business and cultural reasons; hence the follow-up to confirm survey data against interviews.

7 Realizing internationalization outcomes via MNE ties

While the quantitative study in the previous chapter suggests that MNE ties yield internationalization capability learning, it seems prudent to examine *how* internationalization outcomes can be realized by new ventures given that their MNE partners – especially entrepreneurial subsidiaries – may be primarily interested in *their* own success in the new ventures' home market (as inferred from the material on MNE subsidiaries and networks in Chapter 2). To get better insight into the processes driving the model, and discuss *how* MNE ties may enable new ventures to learn – and importantly, internationalize thereby, I return to case-findings on Skelta[1] to provide a rich understanding of the phenomenon. Here, Skelta is described in somewhat greater detail than in Chapter 5.

The Skelta case: an expanded narrative

The inductive study of a young Bangalore-based firm, Skelta, which forged a relationship with Microsoft India, and succeeded in undertaking cross-border activity through this relationship entailed 27 in-depth interviews over a three-year period involving three field visits to Bangalore. The interviews typically lasted for 60–90 minutes. These were tape-recorded and transcribed, yielding, on average, 11 pages of single-spaced transcripts per interview. The interviews involved Skelta's CEO (four interviews), Microsoft managers (six interviews), other Skelta managers (eight interviews), and industry experts such as academics (nine interviews). The interview questions were structured around simple, open-ended questions to prompt descriptions of how the Skelta–Microsoft relationship had evolved, for example, "What happened when you and he met?" and "What happened afterwards?" with follow-up questions to elicit additional detail when necessary. Interview data were supplemented with more than 50 items of archival material including news clippings and PowerPoint presentations shared by Skelta. Also, it became possible to observe a worldwide partner conference in Los Angeles in which Skelta participated. These additional data points enabled triangulation with the interview data, thereby strengthening confidence in the findings.

The approach to the data analysis corresponded to what Orton (1997) describes as iterative theory-building where researchers "cycle back and forth between theory and data" (Orton, 1997, p. 419). As recommended by Yin (1994), coding of the interviews, tape-recordings and notes was followed by independent coding of a sub-set of the interview data by an MBA student under the supervision of the principal investigator. There was concurrence in 90% of the data; for the remainder, discussions were held to reconcile the differences. Mechanisms were identified to account for Skelta's ability to translate a local MNE tie into cross-border activity.

The case-firm, Skelta, sought to establish a relationship with Microsoft because its core product was built on that MNE's technology platform. One of the co-founders had prior exposure to Microsoft in the United Arab Emirates and the US. Skelta was proactive in its efforts to forge a link with Microsoft. It focused its efforts, in the first instance, on building a local relationship with the Bangalore-based India subsidiary of Microsoft. Microsoft India was quickly impressed by Skelta. Skelta stood out not only because of its technical competence but also on account of its business savvy. Microsoft's Rajiv Sodhi who worked with Skelta described his impressions in this way:

> Skelta fostered a very strong link with Microsoft India on multiple levels. They recognize that Microsoft is a big company that will have its own agenda. And so smart people like them very quickly align themselves to this [agenda] because then, you have the whole subsidiary standing behind you.

Furthermore, to Skelta's good fortune, the timing of its proactive efforts to reach out to Microsoft coincided with the latter's own efforts to engage with Indian software SMEs, the centerpiece of which was the introduction of a structured partnering program for independent software vendors (ISVs). Having established a formal link through the ISV partner program, Skelta sought to cultivate a multifaceted relationship with Microsoft, covering both technical and business aspects. The impetus to move the relationship forward was aided by the appointment of Sanjay Shah, a US returnee veteran of the software product space, as CEO. Skelta signaled its intent to treat the Microsoft link with the utmost seriousness by creating a Microsoft relationship function within its fledgling organizational structure, through which a range of activities were undertaken. At this stage Sanjay Shah, the CEO observed:

> Skelta shares a deep, symbiotic relationship with Microsoft and the Microsoft development community. A senior Manager plays a pivotal role of Microsoft evangelist within Skelta and heads the Microsoft Relationship function. Our development team works closely with Microsoft and the Microsoft community.

As the relationship with Microsoft India grew, Skelta sought to extend the relationship as a means to facilitating its own international expansion. Again, Skelta found it had to be proactive because Microsoft India was primarily concerned with the local market. At least three activities were a key part of the proactive effort to translate the local link with Microsoft into a cross-border relationship. First, Skelta invested time and resources to attend worldwide Microsoft partner events, especially in the US. Second, efforts were made to connect with Microsoft executives in the US, including personnel transferred to headquarters from Microsoft India (with whom they already had built a rapport) and several product managers who happened to be of Indian origin and were therefore relatively easy to build a rapport with. Third, Skelta leveraged its goodwill with Microsoft India to gain face-to-face meetings with global Microsoft executives when they visited India to enhance Skelta's visibility in Microsoft beyond the India operations.

Skelta's efforts to globalize its Microsoft relationship soon bore fruit. It received international profile-building opportunities including the CEO participating as a guest speaker at events such as a Microsoft Summit in Seoul, Korea. Also, Skelta was part of a select group of companies included in Microsoft's worldwide promotional website for its Vista operating system. Its technology was also recognized through a partner award at a Microsoft global partner summit and thereafter Microsoft India presented Skelta with an award recognizing it as "an ISV making global waves."

Skelta's top management team was, however, keen to formalize the international dimension of the relationship and lobbied hard for the introduction of a cross-border partner program that would enable it to gain greater Microsoft support for its go-to-market strategies in key markets such as the US. Ultimately, Microsoft did introduce an international ISV program, referred to as the Open Borders program, through which a select group of ISVs gained access to an account manager in one overseas market of its choice. With robust support from Microsoft India, and as a consequence of its own representations to Microsoft in the US, Skelta was admitted as the only Indian member of this select group. Also, as Skelta's international expansion gained momentum, the venture began building its own worldwide network of partners who acted as resellers in more than 20 countries. These included major markets like the US, the UK, Germany, France, Spain, and Portugal. These companies were typically, like Skelta, smaller firms that were deeply entrenched within the Microsoft ecosystem. They gave Skelta a cross-border "presence" despite not having overseas offices per se.

How new ventures leverage MNE ties to realize internationalization outcomes

The above qualitative study helps identify three mechanisms through which local engagement with a foreign MNE (namely, Microsoft) led to Skelta's cross-border activity. This is important because, in an important emerging economy such as India, MNE subsidiaries are primarily concerned with promoting their own agenda of achieving inroads into the Indian market (Awate et al., 2012; Kumaraswamy et al., 2012). They may hence exert a sort of physical attraction or "gravitational pull" on their partners toward the local market (India, in this case) where they constitute "a particularly attractive partner for *local* cooperation" (Cantwell & Mudambi, 2011; emphasis added). However the young venture seeking to develop internationalization capability may not be interested in engaging in joint activity in the domestic market. Thus, while on average MNE partners are effective "teachers" of internationalization capability to young Indian firms and indigenous peers are ineffective, this does not imply that MNE ties automatically translate into cross-border *activity* for internationalization-seeking young Indian firms. Somewhat counterintuitively, the very importance attached to the Indian market which attracts MNEs to it and makes possible the development of MNE ties for Indian ventures may mitigate the prospect of the focal actor's internationalization.

And so there is a potential tension: given the desire to succeed in the lucrative Indian market, foreign MNE subsidiaries are likely to adopt an India-centric attitude in terms of sales and marketing activity,[2] thus curtailing the prospect of the focal new venture achieving joint activity beyond its home-country market. The internationalization-seeking young Indian firm may well find itself having to overcome the "pull of gravity" (Cantwell & Mudambi, 2011) toward the home country if it is to leverage MNE ties to propel itself into international markets. Extending a local relationship with an MNE subsidiary (e.g., IBM India or Microsoft India[3]) into one involving cross-border activity is likely to entail the "effortful" accomplishment of managerial actions (Ozcan & Eisenhardt, 2009). The mechanisms are discussed below.

Arbitraging goodwill across MNE units

Theory suggests that within a multi-unit organization, it is relatively easy to establish connectivity across units given their shared goals and culture (Inkpen & Tsang, 2005; Nahapiet & Ghoshal, 1998). Spanning boundaries within an MNE has been suggested as an important way for new ventures to internationalize via global interfirm networks (Prashantham & Birkinshaw, 2008). Here, the new venture is able to build its own relational capital with the MNE partner by leveraging the fact that units with an MNE trust the judgment of their fellow units, as elaborated below.

Consistent with the perspective that relationships yield more benefits when actively leveraged (Prashantham & Dhanaraj, 2010; Stuart & Sorenson, 2007), Skelta engaged in an iterative process of building visibility and goodwill for itself within Microsoft. While the starting point for the engagement was the Indian subsidiary, top managers from the new venture actively participated in global events at which time they would highlight achievements with Microsoft India to gain the attention of Microsoft managers overseas. Any resultant activity would then be duly relayed to the India subsidiary, further strengthening its positive image. This virtuous cycle played out over a number of years, leading to mutually reinforcing positive impressions within the Microsystem at home *and* abroad. Skelta placed itself in a position to become more likely to be on managers' radar when opportunities for joint activity arose, not only in India but overseas as well. It also warranted Microsoft India showcasing Skelta as a world-class partner. Thus, progressively greater relational capital was built through effective boundary-spanning within the MNE partner's network (Birkin-shaw & Pedersen, 2008).

Cultivating coethnic internal champions

Theory suggests that solidarity and trust are more readily engendered among coethnics owing to their shared values (Coleman, 1988; Portes & Sensenbrenner, 1993). The altruistic conduct associated with coethnics creates the confidence that such ties can be forged and will prove beneficial, including in the case of internationalizing new ventures (Prashantham et al., 2015). Thus the top management team of the new venture was able to form identity-based individual ties within an organizational entity that is otherwise vastly different from its own, as highlighted below.

Consistent with Lorenzen and Mudambi's (2013) insightful observation about the potential interaction between diasporas and MNE ties in facilitating catch-up in emerging economies, Skelta's top managers took advantage of the burgeoning cadre of influential Microsoft executives of Indian origin. In some cases, they could leverage ties with individuals who had been transferred from the Bangalore operations to Microsoft headquarters in Redmond, WA. In other cases, these were Microsoft managers based overseas (typically in the US) within relevant product teams with whom it was relatively easy to build rapport. Consistent with Portes and Sensenbrenner's (1993) assertion that coethnics are prone to being altruistic, such individuals proved to be especially helpful in supporting Skelta's efforts to lobby Microsoft headquarters to establish – and then include it within – a partner program for overseas ventures. They were also intrigued by Skelta's efforts to create compelling intellectual property, a relative rarity in India, and were inclined to be supportive. In Putnam's (2000) terms, it proved important for the focal actor to cultivate and leverage bonding (coethnic) ties *within* a bridging (MNE) relationship.

Partnering with partners of the MNE

As previously noted, theory suggests that relational capital is built more readily among actors with a shared bond (Coleman, 1988; Putnam, 2000). By virtue of being fellow SME partners of the same large MNE partner, it is likely that the new venture was able to build rapport with such prospective partners relatively easily. Given the know-how embodied by the SME partners in foreign markets, relational capital was able to yield internationalization outcomes (Hitt, Bierman, Uhlenbruck, & Shimizu, 2006), as observed below.

Consistent with Dhanaraj and Parkhe's (2006) notion of network orchestration, that is, actions that build interdependencies among partners leading to value creation and appropriation, in addition to the mechanisms identified above which pertain to Microsoft's interfirm network, Skelta's executives directed managerial actions within the wider *inter*firm Microsoft network as well. By participating in events such as worldwide partner conferences, they were able to build bridges to other companies (often SMEs) in multiple markets that were also closely aligned to Microsoft. Thus, Skelta ultimately did benefit from SME ties, albeit ones in overseas, mostly advanced, markets rather than in the home market. Such firms were co-opted as partners of Skelta to act as the first point of contact for prospective and existing customers across the world and were listed on the company's website. In this way Skelta mimicked the MNE's "orchestrating" behaviors on a smaller scale, ensuring its engagement with Microsoft directly supported its internationalization and weakened the MNE's gravitational pull to the home market (Cantwell & Mudambi, 2011).

Synthesizing, two observations can be made. First, a diverse range of managerial actions may be required for the translation of learning outcomes from MNE partners into actual internationalization, including in contexts that are interpersonal (coethnics), intraorganizational (within the MNE), and interorganizational (with other SME partners). Second, common to all managerial actions were dual characteristics: they tapped into a shared identity – between MNE units, between coethnics, and between peer firms – *and* they were inherently *cross-border*. The latter point is crucial in explaining how a new venture can internationalize on the basis of a relationship with an MNE by escaping the pull of gravity such a partner likely exerts on it.

Comparing Bangalore and Beijing: boundary-spanners and the "pull of gravity"

To deepen insight into this notion of the "pull of gravity" it may be worth contrasting Bangalore-based Skelta with another venture in a different institutional environment where such effects may in fact be even stronger. I therefore focus on Zhongguancun, China. While Bangalore has been referred to as India's Silicon Valley, the Zhongguancun district (within Beijing) has been referred to as China's Silicon Valley. To make the comparison meaningful, I keep the alter (MNE partner) constant. Below the case is briefly described and brief analysis provided on differences between Skelta and Gridsum in terms of the boundary-spanning options they have access to and differential effects in relation to innovation (higher for Gridsum) and internationalization (higher for Skelta).

The key argument sought to be made is that the relationship between social capital arising from MNE partnerships and NV *innovation* is stronger in an institutional environment that is endowed with external boundary-spanners through, for instance, state-sponsored technology parks focusing on catch-up (e.g., China, more than India), whereas the relationship between MNE-based social capital and NV *internationalization* is stronger when there is greater access to internal boundary-spanners through, for instance, MNE decision-makers' sharing ethnic ties with entrepreneurs (e.g., India, more than China).

Gridsum (Zhongguancun-Beijing, China)

Gridsum was founded in the Zhongguancun high-tech district of Beijing in 2006, by a Tsinghua University alumnus who, as a student, had interned at the

Zhongguancun-located Microsoft research facility, which had been a recipient of strong support from the Chinese government. This exposure influenced an early decision to develop Gridsum's offerings based on Microsoft's platform technologies. By 2008, the NV had developed its own search engine optimization tools. A major turning point for Gridsum was a formal relationship that it forged with Microsoft through the MNE's worldwide initiative offering start-ups its software development tools free of charge. From Gridsum's perspective, this BizSpark relationship offered much more than free software; it was an opportunity to begin a formal process of relationship-building with Microsoft.

Gridsum made an early positive impression on the giant MNE by applying its own technology to help Microsoft China solve an online marketing challenge. Gridsum's relationship with Microsoft moved to a new level in 2009, when it became the first Chinese start-up to be invited to join Microsoft's elite partnering program, reserved for its 100 most innovative start-up partners, worldwide. In 2010, Gridsum received funding from Steamboat Ventures, an international firm, following an introduction made by Microsoft. In 2011, Gridsum began actively monitoring Microsoft's China strategy, in order to understand likely product launches that were on the horizon. When Gridsum learned of the imminent launch of Microsoft's Windows Phone in China, it dedicated substantial resources to develop a product for this platform.

Corporate managers in Microsoft's US offices began taking notice of this Chinese start-up, especially as China had been identified as a key market for the Windows Phone, and the Silicon Valley-based Microsoft office that managed BizSpark decided to focus even greater attention on China. A high-profile event in Beijing was arranged in which then Microsoft CEO Steve Ballmer showcased Gridsum's innovation. However, despite these accolades and its long-standing technology alliance with Microsoft, Gridsum does not undertake any business outside of China. By contrast, over 80% of Skelta's revenues accrues from international markets.

Table 7.1 provides a summary of Gridsum and the previously seen case of Skelta, and I next theorize differential outcomes for each actor.

How can these differences be explained? In the following paragraphs I highlight two types of boundary-spanning, one of which is more accessible in China (external) and the other in India (internal). I argue that these lead to a differential emphasis on extracting innovation and internationalization benefits, respectively, from MNE networks for new ventures.

Extracting innovation benefits from MNE ties: external boundary-spanners

Developing innovation via MNE networks is likely to involve transforming an arm's-length relationship into an embedded one (cf. McEvily & Marcus, 2005; Uzzi, 1997). Although weak ties (Burt, 1992) with dissimilar actors can be a source of valuable novel information,[4] at least two challenges present themselves to the focal NV. First, when firms are highly dissimilar, they tend to have low

Table 7.1 Comparison of Gridsum and Skelta

	Beijing-based NV (Gridsum)	Bangalore-based NV (Skelta)
Rationale for partnering	Compensating for limited support systems (e.g., underdeveloped venture funds).	Compensating for limited support systems (e.g., underdeveloped venture funds).
Manner of consolidating	Proactive enhancement of ties to include MNE HQ, leveraging on the allure of the domestic market. Own home market as locus of joint activity with the MNE HQ.	Proactive enhancement of ties to include MNE HQ, aided by coethnic Microsoft managers working for the India subsidiary, other business units in the USA, and HQ.
Nature of extending	Primarily focused on extending into new technological variants Systematic search for opportunities to build complementarities on the MNE partner's new technology platforms Limited access to coethnic decision-makers.	Primarily focused on extending into international markets. Systematic cultivation and leveraging of coethnic ties in decision-making roles within the MNE, while also developing links with other SME partners of the MNE to create its own partner network.

relative absorptive capacity; as Lane and Lubatkin (1998, p. 465) argue: "if student and teacher firms have very different organizational structures, the student will have difficulty assimilating knowledge from the teacher." Second, the actual exchange and transfer of knowledge that lead to concrete innovation outcomes require the formation of stronger, embedded ties. That is, innovation via MNE networks is more likely to accrue when weaker, arm's-length ties are transformed into ties characterized by fine-grained information exchange and trust building, which facilitate joint problem-solving and ultimately knowledge creation (McEvily & Marcus, 2005); such relationships reduce the barriers to exchanging resources sufficiently to permit the transfer and exchange of tacit, private knowledge domain (Uzzi & Lancaster, 2003; Nahapiet & Ghoshal, 1998).

However, building embedded ties between NVs and MNEs can be challenging. The principle of homophily predicts that deeper relationships are forged among "birds of a feather," and the considerable differences in power and resources between these sets of actors reduces the likelihood that their paths cross easily. Therefore, external boundary-spanners – including state-supported intermediaries – may be important for brokering, and helping to build, relationships between NVs and MNEs. Prashantham and McNaughton's (2006) description of a policy initiative to facilitate collaboration between local NVs and MNE subsidiaries suggests that nonmarket actors with state support are particularly well placed to act as "honest brokers" between these disparate entities. Hence the institutional environment's capacity to support boundary-spanning between NVs and MNEs may be a function of the extent of government intervention.

Emerging economies in Asia vary in the extent to which the state intervenes. Access to boundary-spanners – such as technology parks and policy initiatives – is likely to be greater in settings where political institutions are especially powerful, and the state plays the role of an institutional entrepreneur (Nasra & Dacin, 2010). While most Asian governments tend to be heavily involved in institutional reform, the scale of intervention is expected to be greater in larger economies with a long-standing history of central planning. In this regard, China is unparalleled in Asia (Child et al., 2007). Thus, notwithstanding India's not inconsiderable policy efforts, Chinese NVs are relatively better placed than their Indian counterparts with respect to being able to develop the links with foreign MNE subsidiaries that yield tangible innovation outcomes (e.g., the development of patents or prototypes).[5] Hence:

Proposition 1 The relationship between the extent of a NV's social capital arising from MNE ties and its level of innovation is stronger in institutional environments that are better endowed with external boundary-spanners.

Extracting internationalization benefits from MNE ties: internal boundary-spanners

For NVs, internationalization via MNE networks typically entails transforming a local relationship into a global one (Prashantham & Birkinshaw, 2008). Although internationalization outcomes can also accrue indirectly, via MNE ties that are confined to the NV's home market, if the firm gains internationalization-related learning by engaging with a foreign MNE subsidiary and then applies this newly acquired capability in international markets (Prashantham & Dhanaraj, 2015), the benefits of the capability will likely be magnified when applied to opportunities that emanate from further dealings with that MNE partner's wider global network (Acs et al., 1997; Vapola, Tossavainen, & Gabrielsson, 2008).

The transformation of a local MNE relationship into a global one entails the NV's obtaining connections with other sub-units, including headquarters, within the wider MNE network. The chances of this happening are greater when the NV is able to cultivate a champion internal to the MNE who can help navigate its complex internal intra- and interorganizational networks. Kostova and Roth (2003, pp. 304–305) define such an internal boundary-spanner as

> an individual employed at a subunit who currently has, or has previously had, direct contact(s) with a headquarters representative(s).... Through

these personal encounters, boundary-spanners form relationships with contacts at headquarters and, with time, develop a set of perceptions and attitudes toward those contacts, as well as headquarters as a whole.

Gaining access to MNE boundary-spanners is not inherently straightforward; in contrast to multitasking managers in NVs, MNE managers tend to have narrow, specialist roles and, therefore, little incentive to partner with a NV across space and time. The work of some social capital theorists suggests that an overriding consideration for MNE managers in choosing to champion a NV (effectively, beyond the call of duty) may be feelings of solidarity and altruism that result when actors share common bonds of identity (Putnam, 2000). One basis of bonding that has been found to be relevant in relation to the global ICT sector, in particular, is coethnic ties (Nanda & Khanna, 2010; Prashantham, 2011; Ramamurti, 2004; Saxenian, 2006). Such bonds are known to foster bounded solidarity and trust relatively readily (Portes & Sensenbrenner, 1993).

Institutional environments in emerging Asian economies vary, in terms of ease of access to internal MNE boundary-spanners, given that they are shaped by history, which leads to certain commonalities that transcend economic and cultural disparities (Ghemawat, 2003). Migration patterns may reflect past colonial ties that create shared (informal) institutional dimensions, such as linguistic connections and normative commonalities, making some settings particularly amenable to creating coethnic ties within MNE networks that NVs can cultivate and leverage. For instance, migration to English-speaking countries has traditionally been strong from British Commonwealth countries in Asia, yielding a potentially potent resource within many MNEs that can be tapped by Asian NVs. In this regard, Indian NVs may have an advantage over their Chinese counterparts with respect to using MNE ties for developing internationalization-related capabilities. Therefore:

Proposition 2 The relationship between the extent of a NV's social capital arising from MNE ties and its level of internationalization is stronger in institutional environments that have relatively easier access to internal (vis-à-vis the MNE) boundary-spanners.

In this chapter I have sought to proffer further insight into the role of MNE ties: the MNE's strong "gravitational pull" toward succeeding in India may mean that while valuable learning occurs for the young Indian firm, there may not be actual cross-border activity with MNEs. By examining an exemplar young Indian firm that successfully overcame this propensity for a MNE subsidiary to be preoccupied with its India mandate, the study provides useful understanding of the sufficient conditions for new ventures to leverage MNE ties to internationalize namely, arbitraging goodwill across MNE units, cultivating coethnic internal champions, and partnering with partners of the MNE.

Furthermore, I highlight the role of external boundary-spanners in facilitating innovation from NVs' MNE ties, which might be expected to be more prominent in China (e.g., via state-sponsored technology parks) than in India. While beneficial for promoting innovation outcomes there may be a counterproductive effect on internationalization, with foreign MNEs focusing their joint efforts with local partners single-mindedly on succeeding in that particular market (e.g., China). This perspective adds a dose of realism to the notion that MNE networks can facilitate accelerated internationalization, by recognizing that emerging economy firms may have differential levels of success in transforming engagement with local MNEs into global relationships. Thus Chinese NVs may be less successful than their Indian counterparts in internationalizing via MNE ties, due to lower access to internal boundary-spanners based on coethnic ties.

This insight represents a nuanced understanding of the role of MNE networks by highlighting the importance of interpersonal ties within interfirm relationships, thus adding to the distinction between MNE pipelines and personal relationships (Lorenzen & Mudambi, 2013) by highlighting potential *interactions* between these entities.

Notes

1 With kind permission from Springer Science+Business Media: Shameen Prashantham and Charles Dhanara (2014), MNE ties and new venture internationalization: exploratory insights from India. *Asia Pacific Journal of Management.* doi: 10.1007/ s10490–014–9391-y, 2014, j.
2 In terms of R&D activity, foreign MNEs tend not to engage with indigenous Indian firms (Krishnan, 2010).
3 As evident from these examples, the general thinking here relates to leading MNE subsidiaries. Cantwell and Mudambi (2011) insightfully observe that some MNE subsidiaries are laggards. This is a distinction that is conceptually and empirically beyond the scope of this study. But it is recognized that this represents a fascinating way forward for future research on the role of MNE ties in international entrepreneurship.
4 The firm-level logic here is consistent with John Stuart Mills's (1848, p. 581) observation about individuals over a century ago: "It is hardly possible to over-rate the value … of placing human beings in contact with persons dissimilar to themselves, and with modes of thought and action unlike those with which they are familiar."
5 Illustrative of China's greater interventionism on the part of the state is the proactive way in which the Chinese government has sought to develop Zhongguancun, a district of Beijing, into "China's Silicon Valley" whereas for India's counterpart, Bangalore, development was emergent (Wang et al., 2012).

Part III

Implications and directions

8   Implications for research

Introduction: shifting the research conversation (again)

As noted at the outset, the central argument of this monograph was stated to be as follows: IE research is due a shift in the conversation (having initially heralded a welcome shift in the research conversation to include INVs rather than focus exclusively on large MNEs) that factors in the role of MNE networks in the internationalization pathways of new ventures.

As stated in Chapter 1, acknowledging the importance of INVs need not preclude acknowledging the varying effects of large MNEs on the internationalization firms that participate to a greater or lesser extent in the interfirm networks that MNEs orchestrate. Hopefully, the preceding seven chapters have served to support this assertion by indicating the prospect for (some) INVs and MNEs to engage in ways that can have important effects on the former's internationalization trajectory.

Studying the MNE–INV interface therefore represents an important future research direction. Adopting an integrative perspective of (large, established) MNEs and INVs could help advance research on both types of actors. From a theoretical and phenomenological perspective, research at the MNE–INV interface is likely to lead to more complete accounts of how internationalizing activity unfolds. Notions such as the global factory (Buckley, 2009, 2011, 2012; Buckley & Ghauri, 2004), MNE dual embeddedness (Forsgren et al., 2005), and subsidiary entrepreneurship (Birkinshaw, 2000) can, individually and in concert, enrich INV research by providing a more accurate picture of the influences under which internationalizing new ventures may operate (see also Cantwell, 2013; Doz et al., 2001; Rugman & D'Cruz, 2000). IE research recognizes the effects of various types of network ties but the role of MNE networks in new venture internationalization is inexplicably under-researched.

Equally, research on interfirm network orchestration (e.g., Dhanaraj & Parkhe, 2006; Nambisan & Sawhney, 2011) can be enriched through a more pluralistic perspective that considers not merely the focal MNE but also participating partner-firms, especially those that operate under conditions of relatively low power at the peripheries of the network, as might be the case with new ventures. This more comprehensive perspective not only helps to improve upon preliminary but somewhat partial and passive accounts of MNE-intermediated new venture internationalization

(Acs et al., 1997; Acs & Terjesen, 2013) but also speaks to broader debates in the literatures beyond IE research. For instance, such work could help shed light on heterophilous networks (Shipilov, Li & Greve, 2011), open business models (Chesbrough, 2006), and the interplay between networks and capabilities (Vandaie and Zaheer, 2014).

This chapter seeks to highlight potential future research directions. But first I synthesize some of the key insights from the preceding chapters.

Synthesis: exploratory insights from Bangalore (and beyond)

The preliminary findings in the preceding four chapters are highly exploratory but, given the nascent stage of research at the MNE–INV interface, nevertheless illuminating. To summarize briefly, Chapter 4 highlights the particular relevance of MNE networks for internationalization-seeking new ventures when the latter orient themselves towards higher levels of innovation (compared to the more modest levels of innovation evident in the low-cost software services ventures studied in my earlier monograph). Thereafter Chapter 5 sought to shed light on the nature of social capital on MNE ties notably the geographic dispersion of the partner-entity.

Chapter 6 examined a useful consequence of this property of MNE social capital, namely, the prospect of INVs gaining internationalization learning outcomes. Finally, Chapter 7 presents the argument that internationalization capability learning of itself is not a guarantee that a new venture will actually internationalize, given that the MNE partner may be preoccupied with its (i.e., the venture's) home market. Thus insights were presented into how this "pull of gravity" may be overcome; in part, by the capacity of a venture to tap into *people within pipelines*, that is, internal champions who may act as boundary-spanners and facilitate the transformation of an initially local link with the MNE into a global, multifaceted relationship.

Thus while my earlier research showed that shifting from a focus on bonding to bridging ties over time is important for sustaining (international) growth (Prashantham & Dhanaraj, 2010), the present monograph suggests that when ventures have higher aspirations in terms of the nature and level of technology innovation, then considering bridging ties virtually from the outset becomes important. Bridging ties in the local milieu, specifically MNE ties, could help new ventures make the transition to internationalizing on the basis of highly innovative offerings by facilitating strategic renewal (see Chapters 3 and 4). MNE ties potentially represent spatially dispersed relationships for internationalizing new ventures and, within emerging economies, a substitute for weaknesses or voids in the entrepreneurial ecosystem. MNE ties could potentially facilitate internationalization opportunities by yielding (multifaceted) *spatially dispersed* relationships as an important pathway to international markets as opposed to *spatially concentrated* relationships, such as with VCs (Chapters 5 and 6). However, in a market of growing importance, such as China or India, the "pull of gravity" of foreign MNEs on new ventures to engage in joint activity in the latter's domestic market may mean that proactive efforts are needed in order to put those new capabilities to use in international markets (Chapter 7). Thus there is a bit of a tension: realizing the potential for internationalization may not be straightforward and while MNE ties appear to be source of internationalization capability, to realize internationalization outcomes new ventures may have to demonstrate agency as did Skelta.

Insights that are broadly generalizable include:

- the virtue of MNE ties as a source of local bridging social capital that is geographically dispersed (Chapter 5)
- the potential for important capability learning outcomes from MNE ties (Chapter 6)
- the need for relational capabilities and entrepreneurial actions to leverage MNE ties to *their* advantage, especially when internationalization outcomes are sought (Chapter 7).

Insights that highlight contextual variations include:

- the virtue of MNE ties as a means of filling voids in the local entrepreneurial ecosystem which heightens their significance in emerging economies vis-à-vis advanced economies (Chapter 5: Bangalore vs. Cambridge)
- the particularly great significance of MNE ties as a source of internationalization capability in emerging economies, given that peer ties may have a *negative* effect on internationalization capability (Chapter 6)
- differing magnitudes of the challenges (pull of gravity) associated with the MNE partner's own agenda in the new venture's home market – and differing network resources to address these challenges (Chapter 7: Bangalore vs. Beijing).

Figure 8.1 updates the model from Chapter 2 to reflect these notions.

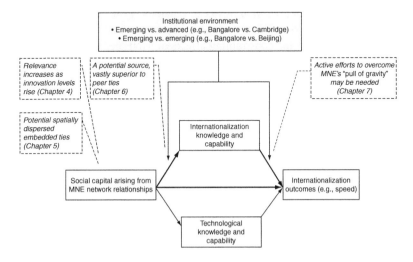

Figure 8.1 MNE network relationships and new venture internationalization.

Toward a research agenda at the MNE–INV interface

Enabling effects of MNE networks

Given the initial small-scale base of the (highly exploratory) research discussed in this monograph, an obvious way to move the research agenda forward would be to conduct large-scale studies with a broader range of industry and country contexts. The exploratory insights in this monograph points to at least three promising avenues for future research.

First, future research could test nuanced effects of MNE ties on new venture internationalization based on the premise that while social capital is generally influential, more insight is gleaned from understanding the differential effects of different types of ties. There is scope, for instance, to examine the differential effects of MNE and VC ties (as suggested in Chapter 5). Similarly, the differential effects of MNE ties and other local ties (as suggested in Chapter 6) could be tested more extensively. In both cases, hypothesis-testing studies could examine direct and mediated effects of these ties; in the latter case, of particular interest would be intermediated effects via learning outcomes in relation to technological and internationalization capabilities. A further line of enquiry in relation to nuancing the effects of MNE ties would be to distinguish between types of MNE partners, for instance making a distinction between leaders and laggards (Cantwell & Mudambi, 2011).

Second, further research could build further theory and test hypotheses concerning the relational capabilities that enable INVs to realize internationalization, as opposed to merely setting up the potential for international expansion. Of course, there may well be other important payoffs such as technological learning but from the perspective of IE research, the extent to which internationalization outcomes are achieved holds particular interest. Both the conceptual material (e.g., Chapter 3) and exploratory findings (e.g., Chapter 7) in this monograph provide some grist for theorizing further on this important issue, which I return to in the next sub-section on the constraining effects of MNE networks.

Third, future studies could usefully examine the moderating effects of the institutional environment on the role of MNE networks in new venture internationalization. The preliminary research presented in this monograph hints at at least three promising directions. One is a comparison of advanced and emerging economy contexts, in relation to both the magnitude of motivation to leverage MNE ties, which may be greater in emerging economies (as suggested in Chapter 5), and the challenges for realizing internationalization outcomes (as suggested, implicitly, in Chapter 7). Another fascinating comparison is that between emerging economies, for instance the nature of boundary-spanning engaged in by new ventures partnering with MNEs in China versus India (as suggested in Chapter 7). Finally, while the cases discussed in this monograph come from highly reputed locations such as Bangalore, Beijing (Zhongguancun), and Cambridge, an important question concerns the plight of new ventures seeking to engage with MNE partners in other, less well-endowed settings. Thus another point of comparison in future research might be that between MNE–INV engagement in clusters versus non-clusters.

Constraining effects of MNE networks

Of course, network relationships often have a dark side. As Buckley (2012) points out, this is not always recognized as explicitly as it should be. (Indeed, the empirical study in Chapter 6 surfaces the constraining effects of a different set of relationships for INVs, namely, peer ties.) In the context of INVs engaging with MNEs there is considerable risk. A number of research avenues can be identified that might shed further light on the constraining effects of MNE networks on INVs.

First, research could usefully consider the extent to which INVs are able to pursue their own agendas as opposed to having them disrupted by those of the MNE. The preceding chapter has already hinted at one of the constraining effects that MNE networks may have on new ventures: although in theory they provide pathways to international markets they might, in reality (and somewhat counter-intuitively), direct the new venture's attention to its own home market rather than international markets. Drawing upon the Skelta case, some insight was gleaned into how new ventures might proactively overcome such pressures. More research is warranted into how new ventures can effectively span boundaries within the MNE network.

Second, research could examine how INVs engage with MNEs while ensuring no harm comes to them by way of, for instance, being cheated out of property rights or due rewards. There is also a sense that new ventures are susceptible to malfeasance on the part of the large MNE; the various metaphors describing engagement between new ventures and established firms, such as "dancing with gorillas" (Prashantham & Birkinshaw, 2008), "swimming with sharks" (Katila et al., 2008), and "surviving bear hugs" (Vandaie & Zaheer, 2014), hint at this. Therefore the ideas about alliance proactiveness articulated in Chapter 3 should be tempered with sensitivity to the need for being proactive cautiously. Again, this could be an area where future research might fruitfully shed light on how new ventures balance the imperatives for proactiveness and caution. Thus, while engaging with MNEs can help new ventures address paradoxical tensions around ambidexterity, attention deficiency, and overembeddedness (Chapter 3), the very act of engaging with MNEs may result in its own tensions, such as that between the need for proactiveness on the one hand and caution on the other.

Third (and related), research might unearth network actions that enable new ventures to build relationships with MNEs that are equitable. Indeed, part of the relational capability needed by new ventures to successfully navigate MNE networks is the capacity to avoid pitfalls in dealing with the more powerful MNEs. This is not to say that new ventures have no bargaining power; many of them do, due to the quality of their innovation and MNE's perceived (inter) dependence vis-à-vis it. However, it would also appear to be the case that, on average, new ventures need MNEs more than the other way round, and that large MNEs are better placed to capture value from joint economic activity (Alvarez & Barney, 2001).

Coevolutionary dynamics

Future research of a longitudinal nature could usefully approach the phenomenon of MNE–INV engagement as a "two-way street." That is, strategic imperatives within MNEs could shape the way in which they construct and manage interfirm ecosystems thereby influencing INV pathways to international markets. But equally, as INVs evolve and develop they may in turn shape the nature and scope of MNEs' knowledge-seeking actions in host markets, including the extent to which they partner with locally-based INVs. A coevolutionary perspective would help explain how growing MNE engagement within a local setting interacts with the indigenous entrepreneurial ecosystem to facilitate greater innovation and internationalization on the part of new ventures, and could potentially shed valuable light on how local contexts and global business coevolve.

Research on coevolutionary dynamics between MNEs and INVs, while challenging to accomplish, may well have wider implications, beyond IE research, for the work on clusters, for instance, especially given that in some cases technological capacity increases, as has been the case in locations such as Bangalore and Zhongguancun, whereas in other cases the innovative capacity may decline. Enright (2000) has distinguished between clusters where economic development is independent of, dependent on, or interdependent with MNEs' contribution to the local milieu. By explicitly incorporating the prospect of MNEs partnering with local INVs, fresh insight could be obtained into how clusters (co)evolve over time and expand or contract their innovation output.

More generally, from the perspective of interorganizational relationships, such coevolutionary dynamics could also be interesting given the potential fragility of the MNE–INV interface due to the the instability of alliances and the challenge of building mutual understanding and trust between dissimilar actors (Doz, 1988). The vulnerability of new ventures may be accentuated when engaging with MNEs (a point already made above in relation to the constraining effects of MNE networks), due to differences in the partners' decision-making processes, the prospect that corporate priorities may change, and the potential for key MNE managers leaving.[1] It would be fascinating to unearth how differential partnering strategies may be associated with different coevolutionary patterns.

Finally, it is also worth noting that such coevolution could also be intriguing in emerging economies where MNEs are poised to increasingly seek out nonconventional innovation that allows them to benefit from opportunities at the "bottom of the pyramid," comprising millions of people of the lowest means (Prahalad, 2004; Govindarajan & Ramamurti, 2011). The bottom of the pyramid represents a largely untapped market for those innovative MNEs that can adopt a novel mindset and formulate relevant offerings at appropriate price points but in so doing, MNEs will almost certainly have to engage with local actors, including knowledge-intensive new ventures that possess valuable (and difficult-to-obtain) local knowledge. It is conceivable that these new ventures could achieve unprecedented innovative outcomes in concert with MNEs at the bottom of the pyramid. Given the widespread dispersion of bottom of the pyramid markets across the world, the opportunity is inherently international, as seen from the case of Bangalore-based Mango Technologies (Chapter 4; see also the illustration in Chapter 10).

Revitalizing research on global strategy and strategic entrepreneurship

Beyond the specific focus on IE research, enquiries into the MNE–INV interface could potentially enrich research in the wider fields of global strategy and strategic entrepreneurship in which research on smaller new ventures and larger established firms is voluminous but typically independent of each other. In those studies that do not differentiate between such firms (e.g., when an entire population within an industry is studied), the interface between MNEs (or large established firms, more generally) and new ventures is typically overlooked. More recently, however, with the rise of interfirm ecosystems orchestrated by large powerful actors in which new ventures participate, some research points to the prospect of overcoming challenges associated with extreme demographic asymmetry and status heterophily (e.g., Diestre & Rajagopalan, 2012; Hallen, Katila, & Rosenberger, 2014; Katila et al., 2008; Prashantham & Birkinshaw, 2008; Vandaie & Zaheer, 2014).

Such work, while useful, has only begun to scratch the surface. Although new venture-established firm engagement is a growing empirical reality, academic treatment is at a nascent stage and some of this work is primarily normative. Considerable scope exists therefore to build on the initial steps taken by scholars to develop and test meaningful theory around a rapidly growing phenomenon that is relevant to strategy, international business, and entrepreneurship scholars, and in particularly those at the strategy/international business and strategy/entrepreneurship interfaces – that is, global strategy and strategic entrepreneurship, respectively.

Research on the engagement between new ventures and established firms may take various perspectives: that of the larger established firm; that of the smaller new venture; or that of the interface (i.e., structures and mechanisms facilitating collaboration). Irrespective, a range of issues may be addressed that link to extant research themes that hold interest for global strategy and strategic entrepreneurship scholars. The following is a non-exhaustive, somewhat overlapping set of issues that future research might address:

1   Interfirm asymmetries. A fundamental issue to consider is: How do power asymmetries and dependencies affect the decision to collaborate and the management of the collaboration? In addition to variance theory testing, processual perspectives can be useful, given that in some cases relationship-building

between a new venture and an established firm represents a process over time rather than a one-shot affair (Prashantham & Birkinshaw, 2008).

2   Alliance interface management. What organizational designs of the interface are more effective than others in facilitating trust and overcoming asymmetry-induced barriers between new ventures and established firms? Given that much of the platform research takes the perspective of the eco-system orchestrator, it is worthwhile to also understand the agentic actions of low-power actors seeking to participate and thrive in these interfirm ecosystems.

3   Relational capabilities. What relational capabilities enable some new ventures to extract more value than others from their established firm partners and the accompanying ecosystem? For instance, given that "firms that are proactive in forming alliances are likely to enjoy higher performance" (Sarkar et al., 2001, p. 702), what is the role of alliance proactiveness in facilitating engagement between new ventures and established firms?

4   Competition–cooperation tensions. The dynamics of technologies and associated platforms/ecosystems may result in today's competitors becoming tomorrow's collaborators, and vice versa. This may result in a paradox (Smith & Lewis, 2011), and a paradox theory lens may be fruitfully applied to examine (potentially differential) mechanisms adopted by large and smaller players to navigate the competition–collaboration tension over time.

5   Capability learning. Research suggests that new ventures can enhance their capability set by deploying them through large partners (Vandaie & Zaheer, 2014) and that large partners seek to learn new capabilities from new ventures (Diestre & Rajagopalan, 2012). More work is warranted to examine the content, nature, speed, and efficacy of learning outcomes.

Focusing on the MNE–INV interface lends a rare perspective to the wider global strategy literature: that of a peripheral actor participating in MNE activity. As noted, scholars have identified the emergence of interfirm MNE networks, conceptualizing these variously as global factories (Buckley, 2009), flagship firms (Rugman & D'Cruz, 2000), and orchestrators of innovation (Dhanaraj & Parkhe, 2006), among others. In all of these accounts, the focal actor is the central MNE, rather than the much weaker NV that seeks to enter and thrive in the MNE's interfirm ecosystem. The literature on MNE networks and innovation can be enriched by (explicitly) recognizing positive externalities of the presence of foreign MNEs in emerging economies, and how these might differ due to institutional differences across various host markets, while explicitly incorporating the agentic actions of NVs in proactively extracting value from their MNE ties.

Research on the MNE–INV interface could also add to the burgeoning literature on strategy in emerging economies (e.g., Xu & Meyer, 2013; Wright, Filatotchev, Hoskisson, & Peng, 2005), which recognizes that both MNEs and NVs face opportunities and challenges, but tends not to consider how these disparate actors interact. Research could potentially contribute to the emerging-economy MNE literature, where the focus has primarily been on large success stories such as Tata in India and Lenovo in China, which have deep pockets and engage in acquisition-led international growth (Luo & Tung, 2007). By studying firms that are at a much more nascent stage of their life-cycle, future research might investigate an alternative pathway to international markets – developing complements to MNE ecosystem networks – as opposed to the high-cost "springboarding" into international markets represented by cross-border acquisitions.

Note

1 I thank Yves Doz for these insights in a personal conversation.

9 Implications for policy

From a public policy perspective an important issue concerns *how* MNEs and new ventures (NVs), which are highly disparate actors, are brought together to begin with. This is an intriguing issue because network theory in sociology highlights the principle of homophily – that is, birds of a feather flock together (McPherson et al., 2001), suggesting that the formation of meaningful relationships between MNEs and new ventures represents the exception rather than the rule. The sheer asymmetries between these disparate sets of actors in terms of size, status, and power result in their experiencing differing institutional logics, constraints, and opportunities (Prashantham & Birkinshaw, 2008). As a result, these actors' paths do not cross readily, resulting in a problem of missing markets which, in turn, means some form of intervention may be required to facilitate MNE–NV collaboration.

Useful insight can be obtained from my work in settings beyond Bangalore, chiefly the UK and China. I draw upon that research in this chapter. I conceptualize systematic facilitative activity as institutional work, that is, "the purposive action of individuals and organizations aimed at creating, maintaining and disrupting institutions" (Lawrence & Suddaby, 2006, p. 215). Drawing on my prior work in Scotland, three facets of institutional work appear relevant to facilitating MNE–NV collaboration: architecting, brokering, and coaching (Prashantham & McNaughton, 2006). To broaden the usefulness of these ideas, an illustration from China is provided as well.

Background

Interfirm asymmetry as an impediment to collaboration

The principle of homophily (McPherson et al., 2001) suggests that MNEs and NVs are unlikely allies; that is, MNE–NV ties are less likely to be forged compared to MNE–MNE or NV–NV ties. And yet, in the twenty-first century, there is potential attraction for MNEs and NVs to work together towards knowledge transfer and joint innovation which stems from the prospect of pooling complementary assets (Doz et al., 2001; Etemad, Wright, & Dana, 2001). MNEs are typically associated with exploiting high resource levels and knowledge in international markets, while

NVs are known for their propensity to entrepreneurially explore new knowledge within specialist niches (Buckley, 2006; Prashantham & Birkinshaw, 2008). Furthermore, absorptive capacity scholars have suggested that achieving knowledge transfer in highly asymmetric dyads, owing to their different organizational structures and cultures, is problematic (Lane & Lubatkin, 1998).

It would thus seem that MNEs and NVs are somewhat unlikely allies even though, on paper, they have good prospects for collaborating, and there is indication that they do (Doz et al., 2001; Birkinshaw & Monteiro, 2007). This suggests a need for – but also a challenge associated with – facilitating collaboration between MNEs and NVs due to the marked dissimilarity between these two sets of firms. The sheer asymmetry between MNEs and NVs in size, organisational structure, and power could be an impediment to relationship-building between these sets of firms (Cao, 2006). Such interfirm asymmetry reduces the odds that MNEs and NVs, who lack cognitive empathy, will cross paths naturally (Prashantham & Birkinshaw, 2008). They likely have contrasting goals, decision-making processes, and planning horizons (Katila et al., 2008). Put differently, they tend to operate in different institutional fields, operating with differing institutional logics.

From a practical viewpoint, there are seldom clear-cut role counterparts across these dissimilar organizations, making it difficult for NV entrepreneurs to establish contact with, and gain the attention of, MNE managers (Doz, 1988). In addition, NVs tend to have a greater need for large established MNEs than the other way round, which increases the odds of stringent, unfavorable terms and conditions being imposed on NVs by MNEs (Alvarez & Barney, 2001). Thus the dominant impression that is conveyed is that MNE–NVs ties are unlikely to form and – if they do form – to be effective (Cao, 2006). Meaningful and knowledge-intensive MNE–NV engagement might be impeded by dissimilarity between the actors since social interaction is less likely. O'Mahony and Bechky's (2008, p. 424) observations about collaboration are germane to the discussion of MNE–NV relationships:

> Collaborations can be difficult when the interests, goals, and practices of participants differ.... Even when mutual gains from collaboration can be identified, managing the boundaries of collaborations is essential if parties are to preserve their disparate interests.

How then does MNE–NV collaboration occur? The literature suggests three possibilities. First, ad hoc proactive efforts on the part of one or both of the partners could lead to MNE–NV dyads. To illustrate, one of Coviello's (2006) case-studies refers to a new venture that piggy-backed on an MNE to internationalize. Second, the MNE may introduce management innovations to facilitate MNE–NV partnerships. As an example, Birkinshaw and Monteiro (2007) describe a British MNE's use of scouting as a means of forging links with Silicon Valley start-ups. Third, policy-makers may intervene through policy efforts in order to overcome the substantial institutional barriers dividing MNEs and NVs.

A documented case of the last-mentioned route in the IB literature is Prashantham and McNaughton's (2006) description of an effort within a regional cluster in the UK to facilitate innovation links between MNE subsidiaries and indigenous software ventures. They suggest that "public policy intervention is often required to compensate for NVs' own underinvestment in social capital. Moreover, in the case of asymmetric interfirm ties – such as between NVs and MNE subsidiaries – there are significant barriers to be overcome" (p. 452). This is consistent with the broader view of policy-making in the realm of internationalization. Reflecting on policy measures to aid new venture internationalization, McNaughton and Pellegrino (2015, 239–240) observe:

> [There] is debate over the extent to which governments should have a role in promoting or supporting the internationalization of firms. One view is that governments should take a hands-off approach, limiting their role to ensuring a competitive and level playing field. However, from a practical perspective, governments at various levels in almost all developed economies take an active role, and intervene with a range of programs that address various perceived market failures.

Formal policy intervention by nonmarket actors constitutes the primary focus of the present conceptualization, although there are potential parallels between the ideas here and the institutional work of market actors (e.g., MNEs orchestrating global interfirm networks) as well, which future research could add to. The facilitative efforts by a neutral policy-making entity have the potential to achieve what neither set of actors can do on their own, and in particular are more likely to actively take into account the interests of the less powerful actors, namely, the NVs. Thus these nonpartisan facilitative efforts hold particular relevance for facilitating relationship-building between actors that are unlikely allies.

Prashantham and McNaughton (2006, p. 451) argue that "without high levels of visibility, efficiency and intimacy in local networks, NVs struggle to engage with larger actors, including MNE subsidiaries." NVs suffer from a lack of visibility; there is relatively low name-recognition of such firms, which puts them at a disadvantage in the competition for MNEs' scarce attention and resources (Cao, 2006). NVs tend also to possess less transactional efficiency which could somewhat loosen the vice-like control often exerted by MNEs in interfirm networks (Alvarez & Barney, 2001). Furthermore, NVs typically enjoy little intimacy, that is, feelings of mutual trust and a deeper understanding by the MNE partner of the focal NV's goals (Doz, 1988).

Institutional work to facilitate asymmetric interfirm collaboration

The emergent institutional work perspective examines how actors agentically create, maintain, and disrupt institutions through "intelligent, situated institutional actions" (Lawrence & Suddaby, 2006, p. 219). While institutional theory has typically focused on how institutions affect actors, institutional work is concerned with the agency enabling actors to affect institutions manifested in their practices (Lawrence, Suddaby, & Leca, 2011). Reflective of the "turn to work" in institutional theory (Phillips & Lawrence, 2012, p. 223), an institutional work perspective places agentic actions at the heart of institutional change, highlighting the goal-oriented capability and reflexivity of actors and capturing the interrelationship between structure and agency (Battilana, Leca, & Boxenbaum, 2009). An institutional work perspective is potentially useful in explicating how MNE–NV collaboration is facilitated because it helps focus analytic attention on *what* constitutes institutional work, *who* does institutional work, and *how* institutional work is carried out (Lawrence, Leca, & Zilber, 2013).

Agency in an institutional setting represents a paradox: how can actors modify the very institutions that constrain them? After all, institutions are associated with continuity; as Scott (2001, p. 187) observes, "in highly institutionalized systems, endogenous change seems almost to contradict the meaning of institution." Institutional theorists have long viewed institutional change as being associated with exogenous shock, and thus agency may channel disruptive extraneous change towards institutional change (Tolbert & Zucker, 1983). But more recently it has been recognized that institutional change may occur without exogenous shocks, through the interplay of practices within and across boundaries (Zietsma & Lawrence, 2010). The agency manifested in these efforts is not always heroic or entrepreneurial varying from small-scale iterative agency through ambitious projective agency (Battilana & D'Aunno, 2009). Thus institutional work subsumes but is broader than the heroism associated with dynamic leaders' institutional entrepreneurship.

One focus of institutional work concerns boundaries – that is, the distinctions among sets of actors. MNEs and NVs have historically tended to be part of different communities of organizations, – fields, in institutional theory parlance (Scott, 2001). Facilitating MNE–NV collaboration requires institutional work across these different communities. Hence, while institutional work at the intersection of boundaries and practices may take the form of boundary closure, connecting, and breaching, our interest here is in boundary connecting. In particular, actors who are able to span boundaries between disparate sets of actors are more likely to be able to carry out the institutional work required to "establish a shared context" (Carlile, 2002, p. 451). Such change is often triggered by knowledgeable yet semi-detached actors, rather than the central actors themselves, because they are able to identify a new way of doing things and care enough to do something about it. In relation to MNE–NV collaboration, as indicated, policy-makers are well placed to play such an outsider role.

In a setting as bifurcated as the MNE–NV divide, institutional work can be tricky to accomplish, given the differing logics and imperatives on either side of the divide (Zeitsma & McKnight, 2009). It therefore seems highly likely that institutional work in this setting requires the creative embrace of contradiction and "the ability to use the tension between contradictory elements as a source of innovation" (Hargrave & Van de Ven, 2009, p. 120). Put differently, accomplishing institutional work calls for the creative management of paradox (Lewis,

2000). This is consistent with the multiplicity of actors that are involved directly or indirectly in these endeavors and the interdependencies that are involved in interfirm collaboration which make it harder to achieve legitimacy across the different constituencies (Gulati & Sytch, 2007). Thus, paying attention to how paradox is navigated could contribute towards improvement in extant "understanding of the effort that institutional work demands" (Lawrence et al., 2013, p. 1029).

Boundary organizations – defined as "the intermediary organizations that align the divergent interests of [collaborators] ... by remaining accountable to both" (O'Mahony & Bechky, 2008, p. 426) – can help to bridge disparate actors while allowing them to maintain their distinct identity "by providing a mechanism that reinforces convergent interests while allowing divergent ones to persist" (p. 426). In the context of MNE–NV collaboration, this means the purposeful creation of boundary organizations, something regional policy-makers are well placed to undertake (McEvily & Zaheer, 1999).

The institutional work of facilitating MNE–NV collaboration

In Prashantham and McNaughton's (2006, p. 454) account of a facilitative policy effort in the UK, the objective was to bring together MNE subsidiaries with one or more NVs to build social capital and work on joint product development by overcoming barriers to MNE–NV collaboration. The attraction for the MNE was gaining access to nimble technology specialists, while the benefits for the NV included enhanced reputation through association and access to complementary commercialization and internationalization capabilities. At least two such alliances received "fast track" status and appeared to be on the path to success.

Prashantham and McNaughton (2006, p. 454) describe how the process worked:

> The intervention entails three key activities – "architecting," brokering and coaching. Architecting is the first stage and typically begins when an initial approach is made by a company (be it an NV or MNE) with a new product idea. The "architects" (two full-time staff members) identify the complementary skills needed from other actors and specific potential candidates from its database of organizations. Brokering is the next step and is undertaken by the architects (although previously this was outsourced to a networking organization). Brokering involves introducing potential collaborators and facilitating a process of determining a mutually satisfactory work arrangement (e.g., pertaining to intellectual property), often with the help of external legal experts. Coaching is included in the mix of activities based on the notion that technological compatibility is no guarantee for inter-personal harmony.

I use this framework of architecting, brokering and coaching in examining how MNE–NV engagement can be facilitated.

Architecting

While the MNE's general *ability*, in theory, to add value to NV partners and vice versa is not in doubt, whether they actually can do so readily in terms of there being a suitable fit with their own agendas and mandate (especially in the case of MNE subsidiaries operating within different local milieus) is not a given. As Latour (1987, p. 109) observes, collaborations are most likely to occur when partners "tailor the object in such a way that it caters [to] people's explicit interests." Ensuring the feasibility of MNE–NV collaboration requires the creation of alignment between the MNE's strategy and scope for collaboration with NVs, and vice versa. This is what the UK initiative sought to do, particularly to gain opportunities on behalf of the NVs. Rather than seeking to persuade the MNEs to act as "good citizens" per se, the initiative focused on the ongoing innovation agendas of those actors (and the corresponding policy activities to attract and service MNEs) and married these with a different agenda namely, that of strengthening technological and internationalization capabilities in indigenous NVs (which was the focus of separate policy endeavors). Thus the initiative bridged agendas and otherwise disparate policy concerns in a manner that was synergistic. This is echoed by McNaughton and Pellegrino (2015, p. 240):

> In general, explicit interventions that promote outward internationalization are most relevant to born globals. However, foreign investment can have valuable spin-off effects for endogenous firms, which may become indirect exporters by supplying local subsidiaries of multinational firms (Prashantham and McNaughton, 2006), or be pulled into international markets through relationships with a subsidiary and its international network.

Brokering

A challenge for MNEs and NVs is often that they lack the *opportunity* to readily find, and work with, each other. MNEs suffer from a liability of outsidership in host markets which makes it challenging to identify suitable NV partners. NVs suffer from a liability of smallness (and often newness in the case of young firms), making it difficult to free up the time and resources required to forge links with the appropriate individual managers in relevant MNEs. Therefore the UK intervention described by Prashantham and McNaughton (2006) involved the creation of a distinct project-based entity that was perceived as legitimate in that it was a neutral third party with support from the local government and software trade body but otherwise no vested interests vis-à-vis any individual firm, large or small. This entity was thus readily identifiable and MNEs and NVs could freely approach it to explore collaboration opportunities – even (or rather especially) if it did not have a specific prospective partner in mind.

Coaching

A somewhat counterintuitive notion is that the very aspects of an MNE, such as the prestige associated with it, which make them attractive partners for NVs could be a source of anxiety as well by triggering concerns about potential misappropriation of the rents generated by the more powerful partner (Alvarez & Barney, 2001; Katila et al., 2008). Such concerns are likely to be alleviated, thereby enhancing their *motivation* to collaborate with MNEs, when they see the demonstrable success of other peers who have benefited from such relationships. This is the sense in which the two "fast track" alliances noted by Prashantham and McNaughton (2006) become significant. Strenuous efforts made by the policy initiative enabled these alliances to become successful. For instance, informants from the alliances are reported to comment on the proactiveness with which the managers in the interfacing entity helped set up meetings between the MNE subsidiary and NVs on those alliances. Thus, not only is the successful outcome of initial MNE–NV collaboration valuable of itself, it also holds potentially valuable symbolic value and signaling effects that lead to institutionalized, as opposed to ad hoc or one-off, MNE–NV collaboration.

An illustration from an emerging economy setting

To shed more light on this phenomenon, a further illustration of the facilitation of MNE–NV collaboration is provided, namely, the Smart City initiative in the Chinese port city of Ningbo, in Zhejiang Province[1] in which parallels to the three facets of institutional work (architecting, brokering, and coaching) can be seen. The Ningbo Smart City Initiative sought to improve the services offered to the city's citizens in areas such as healthcare, transport, and education, through the use of information technology and intelligent devices, *and* to attract the attention of the very biggest technology MNEs to engage with Ningbo. These MNEs would, however, need to collaborate with local actors which were often innovative local NVs.

In order to make it possible for a wider set of NVs to make themselves known to MNEs like IBM that had become key players in the Ningbo Smart City initiative, the local government set up a separate entity which would manage the relationships. Local government officials were especially proactive in identifying prospective NV partners that would be able to work efficiently and effectively with the selected MNEs (e.g., IBM in the case of Smart City logistics) in order to showcase the prospect that MNE–NV collaborations could be successfully achieved. This led one local government official to actively advocate to IBM that they take a close look at the technology of Delian Technologies, a hitherto unknown Ningbo-based start-up that had come up with a cloud technology-based locking device. IBM agreed with the suggestion, leading to a successful pilot test of a solution for frozen food logistics.

Comparing this illustration from China with Prashantham and McNaughton's (2006) UK case provides insight into how actors operate under differing institutional settings (Baker, Gedajlovic, & Lubatkin, 2005; Kiss, Danis, & Cavusgil, 2012). In relation to architecting, the UK initiative focused on engaging with extant MNE subsidiaries whereas in the China initiative the strategy was to attract MNE entry. In relation to brokering, in the UK example the brokering interface was project-based (temporary) whereas in the Chinese case there was a more permanent interface, perhaps because relationship-building is viewed as a long-term activity. In relation to coaching, in the UK case intermediary managers had to modulate the pace and rhythm of MNE–NV interactions to prevent any party from overly pressurizing the other, whereas in the China case there was rather more spurring on of both sides, including the MNE.

It would therefore appear that policy-makers in emerging and advanced economies can fruitfully employ the architecting–brokering–coaching framework (Prashantham & McNaughton, 2006), but will of course wish to adapt it suitably to their local context.

Note

1 The illustration is based on 20 interviews I undertook in Ningbo, China, with 14 informants including local government officials and managers from three MNEs, six SMEs and an intermediary company created at the behest of the local government. About half of the interviews were conducted in English and the rest in Chinese through a native-speaking research assistant. Extensive field notes were taken by both of us which were then compared for inconsistencies. My notes were then content-analyzed to yield a description of the institutional work described in this section.

10 Implications for practice

Research over the past couple of decades makes it clear that internationalization is no longer the exclusive domain of large international corporations. Several small and young companies also do internationalize, often in creative and proactive ways. Entering international markets typically entails building and leveraging network relationships, because new ventures rarely have the wherewithal to internationalize exclusively on the basis of their own resources. Thus, of all the special capabilities of new ventures to globalize, arguably the most important is that of building and leveraging network relationships. This applies to both interpersonal relationships of the entrepreneur and interorganizational relationships of the venture as a whole. Interpersonal relationships with, for instance, mentors and former classmates, are likely to be particularly helpful in generating international business opportunities at the early stages of the new venture's internationalization. As the process unfolds, interorganizational relationships with customers, suppliers, and strategic partners tend to influence the pace and trajectory of the venture's internationalization. Internationalization activity in new ventures is often opportunistic and serendipitous. This is integral to the nature of entrepreneurial activity. New ventures can, and should, flexibly take advantage of unexpected opportunity. That said, new ventures are more likely to be effective at internationalizing entrepreneurially when they are also *strategic*. In particular, it pays to be strategic in relation to cultivating, nurturing and leveraging network relationships.

Being strategic entails three key partnering capabilities:

- **leveraging relationships proactively:** Relationships are widely recognized as being key to new ventures' growth and success both in general and specifically in relation to internationalization. However a passive approach to relationships will result in suboptimal network benefits. All things being equal, firms that are proactive in cultivating *and* leveraging their network relationships are more likely to succeed on the global stage. Furthermore, they not only leverage their networks proactively, but they also broaden their original network portfolios;
- **leveraging relationships reflectively:** It is important for entrepreneurs to recognize that, while generating revenues through network relationships is

important, a more sustainable benefit is gaining learning outcomes – learning new knowledge and capabilities through network relationships. This calls for deliberately devoting attention to knowledge transfer and acquisition, which can require even greater effort whilst dealing with dissimilar partners. Picking good "teachers" is important. Having the intent and patience to gain non-monetary benefits such as knowledge – which can in turn be monetized by applying it to enhance international business revenue – is crucial and may go against the natural tendency of new ventures to focus exclusively on business revenue outcomes via networks;

- **leveraging relationships discerningly:** Entrepreneurs must recognize that different types of networks are good for different things. This is important because certain relationships are easier to access than others, but their benefits may be limited to early stages of the internationalization process. For longer-term success, new ventures will have to go beyond their comfort zone to build new types of relationships. Typically, forging relationships with other *similar* entities is easier to do, but it is necessary to build a portfolio that includes links with dissimilar actors too. That is, it is important to build a holistic portfolio of network relationships over time. To do so, new ventures will need, over time, to go beyond easy-to-access network relationships, at both the interpersonal level and the interorganizational level.

All three of the partnering capabilities indicated earlier are well illustrated in the case of a new venture in Ningbo, China, called Centurion AD. The venture is the brainchild of Dwayne Mason who had previously worked in Shanghai following several years with Sony in the US. Mason founded Centurion AD in association with a former Chinese colleague, Leon Zhang, with the goal of targeting Western markets with offshored graphic art and animation production. This is an interesting example of the opportunities that Chinese ventures *can* take, despite linguistic constraints, since language is not a critical component (as in, say, software development). Of course language skills are required for smooth communication between client and service-provider. But in terms of the core output – for instance, rendering Mickey Mouse in three-dimensional animation – globally transferable skills in digital animation, rather than in conversational English, are primarily required.

To facilitate its internationalization, Centurion leveraged network relationships strategically, as follows:

- **proactively:** For instance, Mason went back to one of his previous employers in the US, and managed to persuade them to give Centurion AD some business. This enabled the fledgling start-up to rapidly get a name on its client roster;
- **discerningly:** Centurion tapped different types of networks in different ways. Thus certain local strong ties in China were leveraged for much-needed capital investment to help it get started whereas overseas weak ties in North America were leveraged to gain new international business;

• **reflectively:** Centurion sought to attain new learning outcomes about, for instance, new international markets that it might tap. A case in point is the manner in which Leon Zhang leveraged former employer relationships through which he spent time gaining information and advice about the Scandinavian market. These relationships proved to be a valuable source of learning about subtle differences between European and US clients. This knowledge eventually led to new business in Europe and widening of the company's international market portfolio, thereby ensuring it was not overly dependent on the US market.

When seeking to pursue higher levels of technological innovation, one of the key discernments that internationalization-seeking new ventures need to make is between the relative benefits of easy-to-access versus difficult-to-access network relationships. Typically, relationships with other actors of a similar status to oneself are easier to access. But such relationships can be somewhat limited in their capacity to sustain internationalization of new ventures over time, because in such networks everyone tends to know everyone else, which means having multiple relationships does not, beyond a point, necessarily generate *novel* information about business opportunities.

Therefore, some other *less* easy-to-access networks must also be considered if the new venture's internationalization is to be sustained over time. At the inter-organizational level, while relationships with other local smaller firms are generally easy to forge, and might be a useful source of moral support and advice regarding common pitfalls encountered while attempting to internationalize, cultivating and leveraging other more difficult-to-access relationships may be more effective for new ventures with high innovation aspirations.

Specifically, my research suggests that relationships with large multinational enterprises could represent a pathway to international markets, in particular for highly innovative new ventures. Partnering with multinationals, although not easy, can yield mutual benefits. In the remainder of the chapter I outline ways in which new ventures may partner effectively with multinationals.[1]

The hidden story behind dancing with gorillas

Announcing his company's strategic alliance with Microsoft in 2010, Nokia's CEO, Stephen Elop, observed: "The battle of devices has now become a war of ecosystems." Indeed, large MNEs like Microsoft, Nokia, and several others have come to build large ecosystems comprising thousands of participants that engage in various activities and points on the value chain. But unlike the relationship between Microsoft and Nokia, which brings together two formidable, large MNEs, many of these ecosystem participants are small (and often young) firms that are drastically different from the large MNE at the center of the ecosystem. For such participants, an MNE ecosystem provides a great opportunity, though it also presents a great challenge. Leveraging the opportunity while overcoming the challenge calls for adeptness at what Julian Birkinshaw, professor at the

London Business School, and I have referred to as "Dancing with gorillas."[2] Given the sheer asymmetries between start-ups and MNEs, we have argued that business as usual is unlikely to bear fruit. Instead, start-ups must form, consolidate, and extend MNE relationships through less orthodox partnering strategies. This chapter describes those strategies and suggests how smaller firms can overcome some of the obstacles inherent in partnering with multinationals.

There are three partnering strategies that start-ups can employ to work with large multinationals.

- **Forming MNE relationships:** Most MNEs wishing to engage with a partner of similar size will take a direct frontal approach to that relationship, perhaps through a dedicated alliance department or through key individuals who have direct counterparts in the prospective partner company. For a smaller firm seeking to partner with an MNE, however, the lack of access and attention coupled with the asymmetry in resources means that a direct frontal approach is likely to fail. Instead, a start-up would be better off using an indirect means of access. That is, it may be necessary to form a bridge between the two disparate organizations. Using local allies to forge MNE relationships can help gain commitment from the larger partner. So, for example, some public policy initiatives provide even greater "hand-holding" for smaller firms. For example, a British start-up, HMD Clinical, leveraged a regional initiative called Scottish Technology and Collaboration to build links with relevant decision-makers at a locally based US multinational subsidiary.
- **Consolidating MNE relationships:** Having formed a relationship with an MNE, a start-up must establish its credentials by being clear about, and focusing on, the greatest value that it can add to the relationship. It can then leverage the MNE's complementary capabilities. For instance, if the start-up's main contribution pertains to specialized technology, then it can draw upon the MNE's marketing capabilities to achieve greater international visibility. However, given the inherent instability in such relationships, the start-up should also consider tactics such as "modularizing" knowledge transfer from the MNE partner. With discrete knowledge transfers, it is possible to achieve at least partial success even if the project gets shelved or derailed at some point down the road. For example, in the case of HMD Clinical, a fruitful association with the US multinational developed but then ended earlier than planned, owing to the latter's changing priorities. Even so, valuable outcomes had already been achieved – including the successful building of a product prototype – which meant the start-up's efforts had not been wasted.
- **Extending MNE relationships:** Given the asymmetry of resources and differences in long-term objectives, a start-up's MNE relationships are bound to unfold in an unpredictable pattern. Start-ups most successful at collaborating effectively with MNEs over a long period of time are often those that build links with individuals who span organizational boundaries and who

Table 10.1 Dancing with gorillas: the "hidden story"

	Forming (initiating the relationship)	Consolidating (deepening the relationship)	Extending (multiplying the relationship)
The "hidden story"	There often is a "once upon a time," i.e., pre-founding experiences with MNEs can have profound effects on the connections forged.	There may be a "twist in the tale," i.e., midcourse corrections including dropping an MNE relationship may occur.	There isn't always a "happy ever after," i.e., aligning closely with an MNE may over time lead to overlapping offerings and goals.
What it entails	Fathoming the "beast", thereby avoiding wasteful relationship-forming efforts with an MNE by targeting the right individuals in the right units at the right time.	Ensuring a strategic fit and thus increasing the odds that the relationship with the MNE brings the best out of the start-up and vice versa.	Recognizing the potential for conflict, thus balancing cooperation and competition to the extent possible (although it should be recognized that this is not always tenable).
What it takes	Awareness; alertness – need to avoid reaching out blindly without a deep understanding of the beast.	Focus; goal-orientation – and desisting from staying in a relationship that distracts from achieving key aims.	Shrewdness – and making no naïve assumption that things will remain fine forever.

can, therefore, tap into resources and knowledge elsewhere in the MNE network. Apart from extending the relationship in geographic terms, start-ups should also seek to broaden the value chain activities they undertake jointly with MNEs to derive, where feasible, both upstream and downstream benefits, thus achieving economies of scope – getting more bang for their buck – from the relationship. To illustrate, HMD Clinical's association with the US multinational became more effective when an individual with a global technology role got involved. He was able to draw on the technical expertise of his colleagues elsewhere in Europe and even North America when needed.

Building on these ideas, as I have continued to dig deeper through my research spanning India, China, the UK, and the US, I have discovered that more often than not, there is something of a "hidden story" behind the successes of young firms that have been able to dance with gorillas. In particular, I observed three facets of the "hidden story" that are discussed below, and which can provide useful insight into the nature of the challenges associated with dancing with gorillas, and possible ways to overcome them.

There often is a "once upon a time"

When a start-up is able to forge a meaningful relationship with an MNE it quite often turns out that one or more of the top management team has already had a close association with that MNE or one like it. This prior association provides valuable insight into the structure and scale of the MNE, what makes its different constituents tick, who the key decision-makers are likely to be, and what the organization's rhythms are. When there is a deep understanding of these factors the start-up is more likely to be able to target the appropriate individuals in the relevant business units of the MNE, pitch the proposition of collaboration persuasively, and time the approach to maximize the odds of receiving a positive response. All this is, of course, easier said than done, and because of the sheer complexity and dynamism of the business environment, the inside of an MNE can be something of a moving picture.

Nevertheless, the main point here is that start-up leaders who know the lay of the land in the MNE are better placed than those who are not so aware when it comes to establishing a relationship. A British start-up, HMD Clinical, made confident strides in establishing a link with Sun Microsystems because of the founding team's prior experience in another large MNE. This experience helped them understand just how they, as a start-up, could add value to a seemingly self-sufficient MNE by introducing their own novel technology with a fleet-footedness that the MNE could simply never match.

Consider also the case of SpadeWorx Software Services, a start-up in Pune, India, which was able to rapidly develop a strong relationship with Microsoft. Compared to most of its peers, this company seemed unusually adept in knowing whom to approach and how to generate traction for its proposals. Upon further investigation, it emerged that one of the co-founders, Mandar Bhagwat, had previously worked for Hewlett Packard, on a team that worked exclusively with Microsoft in Redmond, WA. In the process, Bhagwat had become intimately aware of the way in which Microsoft worked internally and with alliance partners. This knowledge, and the contacts that Bhagwat had from his earlier job, proved invaluable when the start-up sought to engage with Microsoft. Where the founding team itself lacks such first-hand experience it may do well to hire managers who have it.

There may be "a twist in the tale"

A fascinating example of a start-up that partnered with an MNE is that of Bangalore-based Mango Technologies. It partnered with the American firm, Qualcomm. However, Qualcomm wasn't the very first MNE it reached out to. In fact, it was more of a case of "third time lucky." The first MNE that the start-up approached evinced interest in working with it. However, it became clear to Mango's founders that the joint activity that the MNE favored pursuing, although feasible and attractive in the short term for revenue generation, did not really tap into the start-up's core expertise.

Thereafter, Mango dropped that association and pursued a second MNE relationship. The joint activity embarked upon this time was suitably oriented towards Mango's technical expertise but, after about three months, the start-up realized that going down that route would divert it from reaching its ultimate goals. Once again, it dropped its MNE relationship – and this time, raised a few eyebrows because the opportunity had been a good one. However, determined to stick to their plans, the start-up's founders continued exploring other possibilities, which resulted in a partnership with Qualcomm that proved to be mutually beneficial (see Box 10.1).

Box 10.1 Mango Technologies: building an embedded MNE relationship

For an example of how a start-up can effectively engage with an MNE, consider the relationship that Bangalore-based Mango Technologies forged with Qualcomm. Mango was formed in 2006 as a start-up with a focus on building a software product with a niche focus on mobile telephony for base-of-the-pyramid market segments. Within a year, partly to raise its visibility and credibility, Mango sought to enter the incubator of a prestigious local business school, IIM Bangalore. Following a rigorous selection process, the start-up was successful in its efforts.

From inception, Mango's CEO, Sunil Maheshwari, viewed partnering with an MNE as the way forward for the company to scale up and take its technology to market. Having explored multiple options to do so (in parallel), Mango succeeded in showcasing its technology to a visiting Qualcomm manager at a partner networking event. The technology got the manager's immediate attention because it became rapidly evident to him that Mango's technology was directly relevant to his own agenda at Qualcomm. This encounter set off a string of incremental steps that reached a lucrative culmination in a sale of IP by Mango to Qualcomm, which was hailed by the Indian business media as a unique "multimillion dollar deal."[3]

The remarkable journey from a rather casual encounter to a high-profile IP sale can be a described as a progressive process of relationship "embedding." That is, over time, the relationship came to be characterized by deep trust, fine-grained information exchange, and joint problem-solving, which in turn facilitated considerable learning outcomes for the start-up. The incremental steps included the following: A process was initiated to enable Mango to demonstrate its technology more elaborately on Qualcomm's own technology platform. When this was satisfactorily achieved, following due diligence, the next step was to prepare an R&D agreement allowing Qualcomm to demonstrate but not commercialize Mango products. It also enabled Qualcomm to first evaluate Mango's products internally before exposing them to their worldwide customers. Later, a commercial agreement was signed, allowing Qualcomm to ship Mango's software along with its own chipsets. Finally, it became evident to Qualcomm that it could utilize Mango's technology most effectively by acquiring it, leading ultimately to an IP sale.

Aside from the obvious fit between the two rather dissimilar organizations, two factors appear to have been key to the successful progression of the relationship. First, Mango single-mindedly devoted itself to being flexible and delivering effectively on the technology front. Second, Qualcomm deftly negotiated internal bureaucracy to provide support for Mango's technology development efforts. This was particularly down to the efforts of key individuals, both at Qualcomm's headquarters in San Diego and at its operations in India, which emerged as "internal champions" for Mango. These efforts included, in the first instance, non-interference so that Mango was able to operate with the agility of a start-up. Thereafter they provided equipment and manpower to aid both technology and business development. They also brokered relationships with other ecosystem members, including a design company in China. And they guided Mango in some of the commercial aspects of formalizing the relationship, which was a new experience for the start-up.

Clearly, building an embedded relationship between a start-up and an MNE is not for the faint-hearted: it certainly takes some doing on the part of both parties, but when successfully accomplished, the payoff in terms of revenue and learning outcomes can be considerable.

(I acknowledge the research collaboration of Professors K. Kumar and Suresh Bhagavatula at the Indian Institute of Management, Bangalore, in studying Mango's relationship with Qualcomm.)

The main point here, therefore, is that what initially appears to be an attractive MNE relationship may turn out to be less than ideal. In some cases, a start-up may stick with what it has and sacrifice some of its original intentions in the process. Strategy scholars refer to such an approach as emergent strategy, and of itself this can be a legitimate way of progressing. In other cases (such as Mango), the start-up may stick to its guns and drop certain relationships until it has arrived at a suitable one. This is a more deliberate strategy. Whether strategy is deliberate or emergent, however, it is a distinct possibility that there are changes to the storyline. This calls for flexibility and agility on the part of the start-up.

There isn't always a "happy ever after"

In some cases, despite having developed a close relationship with an MNE, a start-up may discover that the momentum has suffered, tensions have crept in, and the prospect of discontinuing the association is a real one. While this could occur for a variety of reasons, paradoxically it may result from close alignment between a start-up and an MNE over time. Although a high degree of alignment, in terms of technology and business strategy, is a prerequisite for a close relationship with an MNE, it is conceivable that, as time progresses and the offerings of each party evolve, there may be overlapping features and functionality that lead to friction. That is, what were initially complementary offerings could turn into competitive ones.

The point here is that smooth sailing in a relationship with an MNE is not guaranteed to be a permanent state of affairs and that start-ups must be cognizant of the possibility that the more it aligns with an MNE over time, the more it could come into conflict with it.

That said, start-ups and other small firms could take heart from the fact that MNEs appear to be taking them more and more seriously, not least because – as evident from the observation noted at the outset – they recognize that they are engaged in a war of ecosystems. As a consequence, some MNEs have come up with innovations in their management of partnering with start-ups that, in turn, have been skillfully leveraged. In achieving this, it is especially vital that the start-up be proactive in cultivating the relationship on the basis of reciprocity. This is seen, for example, in the case of Linxter's thriving relationship with Microsoft (see Box 10.2). While such proactive behavior does not rule out the possibility of conflict down the road, it certainly provides scope for thoughtful entrepreneurs to navigate the rapids of MNE engagement for a considerable length of time.

Box 10.2 Linxter: proactively leveraging an MNE partnering initiative

MNEs have themselves begun to recognize the benefits of partnering with smaller firms, including start-ups. In some cases, innovative arrangements have been put in place, typically in the form a partnering program. Such initiatives provide a well-defined point of entry into the MNE's ecosystem and structure to the interactions between the young firm and MNE.

BizSpark One, a partnering program run out of Microsoft's Silicon Valley campus, is a striking example of the growing sophistication on the part of some large MNEs to actively engage with innovative start-ups. While many MNEs have partnering programs that cover a broad range of participants (including Microsoft's own "regular" BizSpark program with over 35,000 members worldwide), the BizSpark One program is highly selective. With a worldwide capacity of 100 members, the goal of the program is to identify (through a rigorous selection procedure) and invite onto the program the most innovative start-ups that are likely to make a significant impact, and whose technology is aligned with Microsoft's. In effect, Microsoft is seeking to foster the development of firms that may turn into significant partners in the future and also become examples from which the thousands of other start-ups partnering with Microsoft can learn.

The program provides start-up members with the opportunity to forge a relationship with Microsoft on a one-to-one basis (as opposed to the one-to-many approach typical of most partnering programs) because start-ups get access to a named account manager, who frequently doubles as a mentor and also connects the start-ups to outside mentors with explicit experience in areas of needs. The program is time bound, normally with a 12-month duration, and operates in a range of geographies covering both advanced and emerging economies. Formed in late 2009, the program was intentionally launched without fanfare. Instead, the goal was to "prove" itself and demonstrate its overarching goal of helping start-ups to succeed. The program's most high-profile networking event to date was the OneSummit in Silicon Valley in October 2010, which brought together BizSpark One start-ups and other network partners and venture capitalists.

Florida-based Linxter, which specializes in cloud-based messaging technology, illustrates how a young firm, by being proactive, could enable take advantage of the opportunity presented by an innovative partnering initiative such as Microsoft's BizSpark One program. The proactiveness of this start-up is evidenced in different phases of the relationship: forming, consolidating and extending.

In forming its one-to-one relationship with Microsoft via BizSpark One, Linxter's CEO Jason Milgram was building upon the visibility he had proactively built within the local software community through speaking engagements at technology conferences. In many of his talks Milgram discussed Microsoft's cloud-related technologies. This meant that when a Florida-based Microsoft manager was looking for prospective invitees to BizSpark One, Milgram was already on his radar.

In consolidating this relationship, Milgram continued to be proactive because he believed that the onus was on *him* to make the most of it. He did so in multiple ways. He leveraged the Microsoft connection by using quotes from key managers in periodical press releases. He also reciprocated on publicity opportunities through, for instance, inviting Microsoft managers to discuss their partnering initiatives for start-ups on a Linxter-run podcast series. And he initiated dialogues with other Microsoft teams as well as other start-ups, engaging with Microsoft to explore collaborative opportunities. Thus a strategy that Milgram effectively used was that of proactively creating multiple touch points within the Microsoft ecosystem.

As for extending the relationship, following Linxter's "graduation" from the BizSparkOne program, Milgram was once again firmly on the radar of relevant Microsoft managers. Linxter has since been absorbed into another Microsoft initiative that focuses on highly innovative firms that work on its cloud technology platform, as well as being inducted into a technology adoption program in the same space. Milgram was also invited to be a panelist at a session of the next Microsoft MVP Global Summit.

Reflecting on Linxter's BizSpark One experience, Milgram observes: "A program like this does not provide you a menu of items, but it gives you direct access to individuals who in turn can help you make valuable connections that help create further interactions. It's completely up to you what you make of it."

Given the considerable challenges involved, it is conceivable that some start-ups will wonder whether collaborative MNE relationships are really worth the trouble. Indeed for some smaller firms, specifically those that are content to focus on relatively less knowledge-intensive offerings and pick the low-lying fruit, engaging with MNEs may not be truly beneficial. However, for those that do have cutting-edge technologies to offer, spurning the prospect of engaging with MNEs is likely to result in missed opportunities. And there may really be little option for innovative start-ups with global ambitions but to learn to dance with the gorillas.

Notes

1 With kind permission of Ivey Publishing: Shameen Prashantham (2011, July/August), The hidden story behind dancing with gorillas: strategies for partnering with a multinational. *Ivey Business Journal*. Richard Ivey School of Business Foundation prohibits any form of reproduction, storage, or transmission of this material without its written permission. This material is not covered under authorization from any reputation rights organisation. To order copies or request permission to reproduce materials, contact Ivey Publishing, Ivey Business School, Western University, London, Ontario,Canada, N6G 0N1; T.519.661.3208, e.cases@ivey.ca, www.iveycases.com. Copyright © 2011mRichard Ivey School of Business Foundation.

2 Our ideas were initially published in an article in *California Management Review*. As we acknowledge in it, the phrase "dancing with gorillas" was inspired by a comment made by the late C. K. Prahalad at a conference. In this chapter I provide further ideas emanating from my subsequent research on the topic.

3 See, for example, http://articles.economictimes.indiatimes.com/2010–02–06/news/2839 7299_1_software-products-qualcomm-mango-technologies.

Appendix
Teaching case

Skelta and the Microsoft partner ecosystem

Shameen Prashantham wrote this case solely to provide material for class discussion. The author does not intend to illustrate either effective or ineffective handling of a managerial situation. The author may have disguised certain names and other identifying information to protect confidentiality.

On January 12, 2010, Sanjay Shah, CEO of Skelta, a software product company in Bangalore, India, received an email that drove every other thought out of his mind. The email, from Jim Davis,[1] Skelta's Microsoft relationship manager in Boston, said that Davis was leaving the company. This news was both unexpected and unwelcome. Skelta had been working closely with Microsoft from its early years as a start-up, and Davis's announcement set Shah thinking about the complex, long-standing relationship between the two companies. Shah knew he had no time to lose. He needed to make some important strategic decisions about how to manage Skelta's relationship with Microsoft going forward.

Skelta's origins

Shah joined Skelta as its CEO in 2004. Skelta was then a two-year-old software product start-up, having shed, in 2002, its previous avatar as a software services company called NetGalactic. In its new form, Skelta was committed to being a product-centric software company, which was a bold step in an Indian IT industry dominated by software services.

Shah was brought on board to run the new company because of his credibility and rich experience in the software product sector. Shah had co-founded iCode (later Everest Software Inc.), a US-based software product company, and had then served as managing director of iCode's India operations.

NetGalactic, the forerunner to Skelta, had been founded by Paritosh Shah, Kalpa Shah,[2] and Arvind Agarwal. Kalpa Shah, who had formerly been with AOL in the United States, had returned to India and started a Bangalore-based web services company that focused on developing websites. Paritosh Shah had set up a web services business in Dubai. Arvind Agarwal, a technology specialist who had developed enterprise resource planning (ERP) software products for the Indian market, joined the duo in the new enterprise.

The creation of Skelta as a product-centric company represented a major shift in the team's aspirations and focus. With Shah on board, Skelta's top management team represented diverse strengths: Sanjay Shah and Arvind Agarwal, the chief technology officer, had a strong affinity for software products; Kalpa Shah, vice president, marketing, had vast expertise in Internet marketing; and Paritosh Shah, vice president, strategic partnerships, had extensive experience of engaging with large partners such as Microsoft through prior business ventures in Dubai and the United States (see Figure A.1).

When Shah took the helm in 2004, he had been under no illusion as to the size of the challenge before Skelta. The company was embedded within the Indian IT industry, which had acquired a fine reputation for software services, but *not* for software products. In essence, Skelta had chosen the challenge of swimming against the tide.

The challenge of being an Indian software product company

India produced relatively fewer successful software product companies than countries such as Israel and the United States. Software product companies developed and executed qualitatively different strategies compared with software services companies. Software product companies needed to first identify a "problem" or "pain point" for their clearly defined market segments. Then, they needed to invest considerable time, money, and effort upfront to create an "off-the-shelf" software product. Large Western companies, such as Microsoft, were characterized as software product companies, even though many of their services involved installing, augmenting, and customizing a software product. Typically, software product companies required high levels of innovation and substantial sales and marketing efforts to be able to reach out to and convert prospective customers.

One of the major differences between a software product company and a software services company was that a software services company offered a foreign client the option of testing the company's capabilities by starting with a low-cost trial project before committing to a larger-scale project. In the case of a software

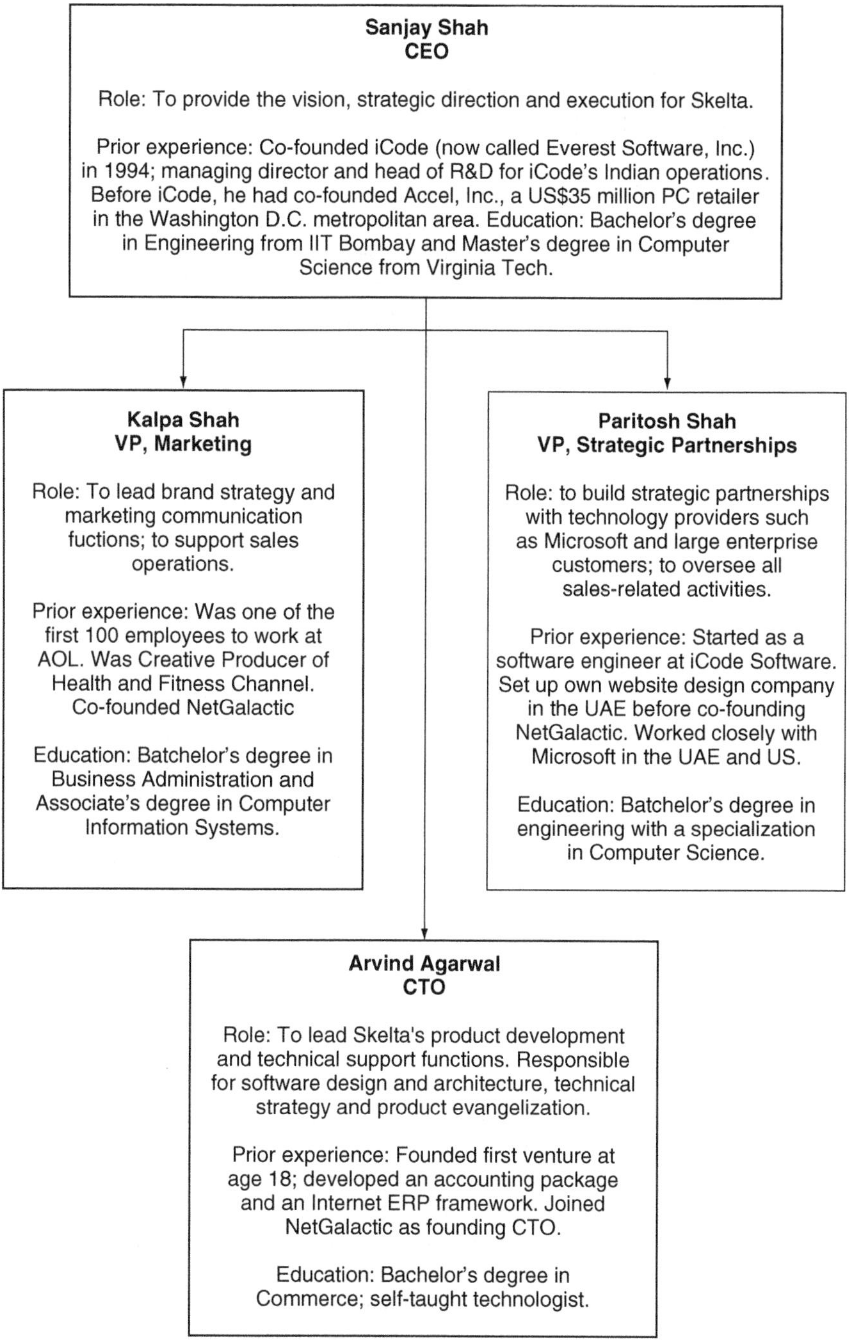

Sanjay Shah
CEO

Role: To provide the vision, strategic direction and execution for Skelta.

Prior experience: Co-founded iCode (now called Everest Software, Inc.) in 1994; managing director and head of R&D for iCode's Indian operations. Before iCode, he had co-founded Accel, Inc., a US$35 million PC retailer in the Washington D.C. metropolitan area. Education: Bachelor's degree in Engineering from IIT Bombay and Master's degree in Computer Science from Virginia Tech.

Kalpa Shah
VP, Marketing

Role: To lead brand strategy and marketing communication fuctions; to support sales operations.

Prior experience: Was one of the first 100 employees to work at AOL. Was Creative Producer of Health and Fitness Channel. Co-founded NetGalactic

Education: Batchelor's degree in Business Administration and Associate's degree in Computer Information Systems.

Paritosh Shah
VP, Strategic Partnerships

Role: to build strategic partnerships with technology providers such as Microsoft and large enterprise customers; to oversee all sales-related activities.

Prior experience: Started as a software engineer at iCode Software. Set up own website design company in the UAE before co-founding NetGalactic. Worked closely with Microsoft in the UAE and US.

Education: Batchelor's degree in engineering with a specialization in Computer Science.

Arvind Agarwal
CTO

Role: To lead Skelta's product development and technical support functions. Responsible for software design and architecture, technical strategy and product evangelization.

Prior experience: Founded first venture at age 18; developed an accounting package and an Internet ERP framework. Joined NetGalactic as founding CTO.

Education: Bachelor's degree in Commerce; self-taught technologist.

Figure A.1 Sanjay Shah's top management team at Skelta, 2004 (source: created by the case writer, based on the company's website).

product firm, however, a greater level of commitment and risk was involved upfront for both the firm developing the product offering and the customer who needed to make a purchase decision at a non-trivial price point.

Skelta's software product fell in the domain of business process management (BPM), a global and high-growth segment (see Table A.1). Skelta's objective was to help organizations improve their business processes, and, in particular, to help them cope with frequent process changes. According to Shah, reaching this goal required the ability to "define, manage, control and document how business activities were executed, including the interaction of people and/or systems."[3] Skelta's major challenge in its quest for global success was that India was not known for its software product development, despite its well-established reputation for high-quality software services (see Figure A.2 and Table A.2).

Skelta's relationship with Microsoft

Forming the relationship (2002–2004)

Recognizing that it would be an uphill task to establish itself as a serious software *product* company, Skelta made a strategic decision to forge an alliance with the globally reputed company, Microsoft. When Shah joined Skelta in 2004, the relationship was already two years old.

From its inception, Skelta had sought to establish a relationship with Microsoft for two important reasons. First, Skelta had made a strategic decision to build its software product offerings on a Microsoft technology called the .NET platform because of its widespread use among the enterprise customers, who formed Skelta's target market. Second, co-founder Paritosh Shah's previous experience with Microsoft in the Middle East and the United States had made him confident about forming relationships at the Bangalore-based India subsidiary of the global giant.

Microsoft's response to Skelta's overtures proved to be positive from two perspectives:

1   first, at the interpersonal level, Skelta's top managers quickly impressed key individuals at Microsoft India. Microsoft's managers believed that Skelta stood out not only because of its technical competence but also on account of its business savvy in terms of its corporate strategy in general and its relationship with Microsoft India in particular;
2   second, at the interorganizational level, Microsoft was, at that time, considering how it might engage more effectively with independent software vendors (ISVs), many of whom were smaller businesses, such as Skelta. Skelta's timing in approaching Microsoft was ideal as it coincided with Microsoft's launch of a structured partnering program for ISVs.

Skelta had been in the right place at the right time and had attracted a high level of attention from Microsoft managers involved in this endeavor. Skelta had the distinction of becoming one of the first members of Microsoft's new partner program for ISVs.

Skelta gained several immediate benefits on joining the ISV partner program, including cost-effective access both to Microsoft software and tools and to a range of training events that helped build Skelta's technical expertise. Several of Skelta's software developers underwent training toward Microsoft certifications. Skelta supported them by offering paid leave, reimbursement of fees, access to courseware, and incentives (i.e., salary raises) for successful employees. Developers also become active participants in Microsoft online developer communities and forums, which helped them to resolve issues that routinely arose during software development.

Further, Skelta was one of the few companies selected to participate in a Microsoft quality-certification program for ISVs, a joint initiative with Nasscom, India's apex trade body for IT companies. Toward the end of 2003, having successfully met various technical prerequisites, Skelta was officially certified as ".NET connected" by Microsoft. Skelta went on to attain gold-certified partner status, signalling that it possessed the technical capabilities and quality control required of a high-quality Microsoft partner.

Consolidating the relationship (2004–2009)

Shah's appointment as the new CEO and the subsequent 2004 launch of Skelta's first major software product offering, SharePoint Workflow Accelerator, gave Skelta the impetus to strengthen its visibility and legitimacy in the marketplace, both in India and overseas, in its effort to achieve growth.

As part of its strategy to gain a competitive edge, Shah wanted Skelta's top management team, which had established the initial links with Microsoft, to make energetic efforts to consolidate the relationship. He believed there was scope for more activities and additional links with other Microsoft business units and, thus, sought to cultivate a multifaceted relationship that encompassed both a technical and a business dimension. Paritosh Shah and Kalpa Shah focused on consolidating the Microsoft relationship on the business side, while Agarwal dealt with the technical aspects of the relationship.

Skelta engaged in a variety of activities that increased the number of its "touch points" within Microsoft, beginning with the latter's India subsidiary. Skelta extended its membership in the ISV program, which by this time had evolved and become more structured. Shah observed:

> Several small start-ups rely on Microsoft partner programs for tools, technical resources, and allied support to take their innovations to market. Participants are provided the complete software stack from Microsoft and an advisory service on product architecture and design reviews. Microsoft was able to provide expert guidance from industry stalwarts to help us validate our ideas. Opportunity maps provided an important strategic guide to help achieve better cognisance of the market and customers. They also gave us

new insight to power our competitive edge in capturing current and future opportunities.

Such interactions meant that Skelta could work actively with Microsoft India on new solutions. One initiative that resulted from their close collaboration was a software solution designed to meet regulatory requirements in India. In terms of triggering growth, a major benefit of this relationship for Skelta was the possibility of bundling its offering with Microsoft products.

Skelta was also able to gain a ringside view of Microsoft's business and technology processes. Many of these processes – joint marketing, for example – offered associated literature in the form of brochures or manuals that Skelta found useful as its own operating routines began to mature. In adopting best practices for software development, Skelta was able to draw upon Microsoft's expertise.

As the relationship with Microsoft India grew, Shah turned his sights to extending the relationship as a means of facilitating Skelta's international expansion. Skelta was deliberate in its efforts to move beyond an India focus and cultivate a global relationship with Microsoft.

Shah leveraged Skelta's goodwill with Microsoft India to arrange face-to-face meetings with global Microsoft executives when they visited Bangalore. Microsoft India was highly supportive because it felt that Skelta had proved to be a valuable and loyal partner. Such meetings gave Skelta significant exposure to thought leaders within Microsoft and enhanced Skelta's visibility in Microsoft beyond its India operations. Shah knew that Microsoft managers in India were pleased to have, in Skelta, a good example for internal and external audiences of its efforts to partner with Indian companies. As Rajiv Sodhi, a Microsoft manager, who had been instrumental in fostering the relationship with Skelta under the auspices of the ISV program, stated:

> Skelta fostered a very strong link with Microsoft India on multiple levels. They quickly recognized that Microsoft is a big company and will have its own agenda. And so smart people like them very quickly align themselves to this [agenda] because then, they have the whole subsidiary standing behind them. What happens as a result is that it's not a very distant point in time when they start getting elevated to global levels.

Skelta was proactive in its efforts to build links with Microsoft in other geographies. Apart from engaging in conference calls every two weeks with Microsoft, Skelta invested time and resources to attend Microsoft partner events worldwide, particularly those in the United States. Skelta's top managers attended events such as TechEd, which primarily attracted software developers working on Microsoft technology, and the World Partner Conference, the annual meeting of thousands of Microsoft partners (see Table A.3 for other examples).

Through these activities, Skelta cultivated new links with Microsoft managers, many of whom were in the United States. Several of the US Microsoft product managers were of Indian origin, which made it relatively easier to build rapport. Skelta also made efforts to connect with US-based Microsoft executives who had previously worked in Microsoft India and were already familiar with the company. All of these new ties added to Skelta's credibility as a Microsoft partner. Shah concurred with the observation his colleague Paritosh Shah made to a mutual acquaintance:

> Over time we understood how to get people excited within the Microsoft eco-system. We understood what the kicker was for various groups within Micro-soft, and whom to work with in what format. We were able to leverage points in Microsoft India to get to the United States and vice versa. We had to evangelize, evangelize, evangelize in order to increase mindshare.

As a participant at Microsoft's international events, Skelta seized the opportunity to showcase its products and obtain valuable feedback from a discerning audience. Skelta also regularly put itself forward for awards, with considerable success. Skelta won a Best of TechEd award in recognition of the innovativeness of its technology and was awarded a People's Choice Award from MSD2D, a Microsoft developer forum.

Such achievements gave the start-up greater visibility within the software industry at home in India. Microsoft India honoured Skelta with a special award as an "ISV making waves." Skelta was named a *Red Herring* 100 Asia company, indicating that it had the potential to shape the future of the technology industry. The company's reputation further grew when it won the Nasscom Innovation Award, one of the highest honors that an Indian software firm could aspire to. Shah recalled, "Skelta made both businesses and technology vendors sit up and take notice. Our client list boasted of industry heavyweights such as Motorola, AAA, Siemens, i-flex Solutions and Deloitte."

As Skelta's relationship with Microsoft solidified and as its own reputation grew, it found itself receiving multiple opportunities to showcase itself through initiatives in India and abroad. For example, Shah was invited to be the keynote speaker at Microsoft Community Day, in Bangalore. He was also called upon to speak at a Microsoft software ecosystem event in Seoul, South Korea, where he took the podium immediately after a talk by Microsoft CEO Steve Ballmer. Shah was also interviewed in a promotional video created by the Office Business Applications unit of Microsoft, significantly increasing Skelta's online visibility.

Skelta was invited to become part of a global structured program called the Technology Adoption Program (TAP), through which Agarwal and his team gained access to cutting-edge Microsoft technologies ahead of their release. As an example, Skelta launched its Vista-ready product versions within days of the release of Microsoft's Vista operating system. Skelta was also included in Microsoft's worldwide promotional website for its Vista operating system – the only Indian company to be featured so prominently. Skelta had, by this time, built a good understanding of the right "buttons" to press to gain its partner's attention. Paritosh Shah explained, "By understanding how they [Microsoft] are opportunistic, we could become opportunistic."

As a further affirmation of Skelta's technological prowess, a report[4] by the analyst firm Gartner labelled the company "a cool vendor," much to Shah's delight and gratification. According to the report, "Skelta Software occupies a niche of the BPM market. End-user organizations that have invested heavily in Microsoft technologies can leverage Skelta's integration to add process capabilities to these."

Extending the relationship (2009 onward)

Having established a strong bond with Microsoft both in India and overseas, Shah wanted to structure the relationship in a way that would further facilitate Skelta's international expansion. He took two broad steps toward this end: building Skelta's own global network of partners and accessing a Microsoft cross-border partner program.

Building its own global network of partners

As Skelta's international expansion activities gained momentum, it began building its own worldwide network of partners who acted as resellers in more 20 countries (see Figure A.3). This network included major markets such as the United States, United Kingdom, Germany, France, Spain, and Portugal. These companies represented the first point-of-contact for prospective Skelta customers in their respective markets. They were typically, like Skelta, smaller firms that were deeply entrenched within the Microsoft ecosystem.

Participating in events such as the Microsoft's Worldwide Partner Conference had made it possible for Skelta's top managers to identify and build links with these firms. They shared Skelta's Microsoft orientation on both the technological and business fronts, making it easier to build mutual rapport and trust. This network of resellers was instrumental in the execution of Skelta's internationalization strategy.

International business eventually represented 80% of Skelta's revenues (40% from the Americas, 30% from Europe and the Middle East, and 10% from the Asia Pacific, excluding India) and helped to sustain the organization's growth (see Table A.4).

Accessing a Microsoft cross-border partner program

Shah and other top managers lobbied hard with Microsoft executives in India and the United States to institute a cross-border partnering program (see Exhibit 7 for an overview of Microsoft's engagement with start-ups via partner programs). Skelta's goal was to gain greater Microsoft support for its go-to-market strategies in key markets such as the United States.

Microsoft eventually created a partnering initiative called the Open Borders program, which allowed a select group of ISVs to gain access to a Microsoft relationship manager in an overseas market of their choice. Thanks to robust support from Microsoft India and its own persistent representations to Microsoft headquarters in the United States, Skelta became the first and only Indian member of this exclusive band of partner companies. As a result, Skelta was assigned a dedicated relationship manager – Davis – based at Microsoft in Boston. Shah and his team saw this development as a major new opportunity to further extend and leverage its relationship with Microsoft.

Shah shifted Skelta's newly established sales office from Atlanta to Boston in an effort to keep his key US-based people close to the Microsoft relationship manager. Before long, Skelta's top managers in Bangalore had also built an excellent rapport with Davis through regular visits and frequent email exchanges.

Shah and his team found Davis to be an enterprising and supportive partner who readily helped Skelta pursue several new leads on prospective customers. Skelta's chief operating officer, Johncey George, noted, "It's been easier to get into large international organizations using Microsoft as a reference point. This relationship has helped to open doors."

Although Skelta's top managers were familiar with the US market, Davis was able to provide a nuanced perspective on market segments and on the need to take different approaches for different target audiences. After nearly a year of interacting closely with Davis, Shah and the top management team had come to value his wisdom and judgment in tackling the US market.

Challenges ahead

With Davis's exit from the company, Shah realized that he had important decisions to make about how Skelta ought to manage the Microsoft relationship going forward. He reflected that Skelta would inevitably need to determine how to proceed in its relationship with Microsoft beyond the duration of the latest partner program. It was just a matter of time. Davis's departure had merely hastened the need to address the issue head on.

Shah recalled that his colleagues had recently begun expressing their concerns about the complexity of evaluating the benefits of the relationship: 15 to 20% of sales were attributable to the Microsoft relationship, whereas other benefits were difficult to quantify. Skelta's vice president for sales, Ramesh Srinivasan observed, "You can't always pinpoint the benefits. It's like a marketing thing … the benefits don't always happen on day one."

Shah had to consider whether to aggressively strengthen Skelta's presence in the United States in an effort to work more closely with Microsoft there. Or, alternatively, did Skelta actually need to consider *reducing* the intensity of its Microsoft relationship? After all, it was a highly demanding partnership in terms of energy and time, and, on some occasions, Skelta's strenuous efforts to gain new business in conjunction with Microsoft had not been fruitful.

Shah was conscious of the danger of becoming too dependent on Microsoft. In that case, should Skelta broaden its portfolio of network relationships –

perhaps by forming new relationship with other companies? As Kalpa Shah pointed out, "In such a relationship there is the potential threat of becoming overly dependent on the large partner. It is something we should avoid."

Another point of frustration for Skelta was a lack of continuity in relationships owing to personnel changes that occurred from time to time at Microsoft. It often seemed that just when Skelta had built rapport with an individual at Microsoft, he or she was transferred to another role or left the company altogether. Skelta would then need to start building a new relationship, which was a time- and energy-consuming process. Indeed, this very problem had just arisen again.

Shah turned his attention back to his laptop and began composing an email to his top management team. He wanted to gather his senior executives together for a brainstorming session on the way forward for Skelta's relationship with Microsoft.

Table A.1 Geographic markets for BPM software solutions

	2008	*2009*	*2010*	*Growth %* *(2009)*	*Growth %* *(2010)*
Asia Pacific	132.9	155.8	180.7	17.2	16.0
Eastern Europe	32.4	37.1	44.8	14.6	20.6
Japan	150.4	163.1	167.5	8.5	2.7
Latin America	59.2	75.8	92.2	27.9	21.8
Middle East & Africa	33.6	40.3	50.0	20.0	24.0
North America	822.9	959.2	1,024.1	16.6	6.8
Western Europe	507.6	552.3	606.6	8.8	9.8
TOTAL	1,738.9	1,983.6	2,166.0	14.1	9.2

Source: Gartner, Market trends: how to profit from BPO services, 2012, www.gartner.com/id=2036515, accessed November 28, 2012.

Box A.1   The Indian software industry: a brief account

The development of India's globally oriented software industry was one of the country's most celebrated accomplishments following economic liberalization in 1991. India was catalyzed by the entry of MNCs such as Texas Instruments (especially to Bangalore, referred to as "the Silicon Valley of India"). In the 1990s, it became evident that India's abundant supply of English-speaking software engineers provided a great opportunity for India to become an attractive base from which to fix the software woes of the world. The modus operandi initially entailed numerous overseas assignments for Indian software engineers who were based in the foreign client's offices, engaging in software development activities. This approach was (often pejoratively) referred to as "body-shopping." Over time, much of the software development work was "off-shored," that is, undertaken by software engineers based in India, rather than at the client's overseas base. This approach, pioneered by companies such as Infosys, further helped to keep costs

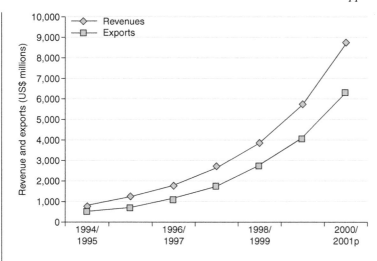

Figure A.2 Export-led growth of the Indian software industry in the 1990s.

Table A.2 Dominance of software services exports in the 2000s

(US$ million)	2005/2006	2006/2007	2007/2008	2008/2009
IT services	19,605 (83.1%)	26,260 (84.2%)	34,030 (84.2%)	39,752 (84.5%)
Products*	4,000 (16.9%)	4,942 (15.8%)	6,400 (15.8%)	7,287 (15.5%)
Total	23,605 (100%)	31,202 (100%)	40,430 (100%)	47,039 (100%)

Source: Nasscom (2009). *Strategic review 2009: The IT industry in India*, New Delhi: Nasscom.

Note
* Includes engineering services.

down. Aided by the Y2K problem[5] of the late 1990s, Indian software firms had ample opportunity to demonstrate their capacity to "do software" (see Table A.1). Many software companies subsequently grew by continuously improving the sophistication of their services. However, their focus remained predominantly on services.

Table A.3 Skelta's participation in Microsoft events and initiatives, 2008–2009

When	What	Where
March 2008	Renew partner program membership	Online
March 2008	Microsoft Sharepoint Conference	Seattle, WA
June 2008	Microsoft TechEd Conference	Orlando, FL
July 2008	Microsoft Worldwide Conference	Houston, TX
September 2008	Microsoft India Day event	Bangalore, India
September 2008	Microsoft ISV Partner Conference	Seattle, WA
April – May 2009	ISV Lead Generation Direct Marketing	Bangalore, India
May 2009	ISV Partner web meetings	Online

Source: Case writer's interviews with Skelta.

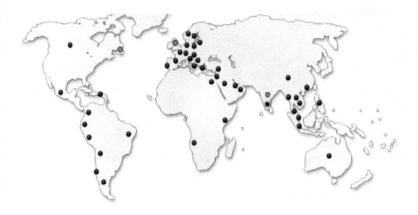

Figure A.3 World map indicating presence of Skelta's resellers (source: Skelta).

Table A.4 Skelta's organizational growth, 2006–2010

Year	Number of employees	Annual growth in revenues (%)
2006	40	80
2007	60	100
2008	90	120
2009	100	120
2010	130	80

Source: Skelta

Box A.2 A note on Microsoft's engagement with start-ups

When Skelta began to make overtures to Microsoft, the latter, like most large IT multinationals at the time, did not have a formal partner program for start-ups. Things have changed considerably since then, most notably through the launch of the BizSpark partner program targeted at start-ups.[6] According to the Microsoft website, "Since it was established in 2008, more than 50,000 companies in over 100 countries have joined BizSpark." The following are some of the key features of the program as outlined at www.microsoft.com/bizspark.

To qualify for BizSpark, a venture must be developing software, privately held, less than three years old, and making less than US$1 million in annual revenue. There is no fee to enroll. Microsoft describes this program as providing software, support and visibility for software start-ups.

In terms of software, Microsoft BizSpark membership includes a MSDN subscription for Microsoft software and tools, including Windows Azure and a wide range of products for development, testing, and production.

In terms of support, BizSpark helps start-ups by supporting the network of organizations – start-up incubators, investors, advisors, government agencies – that are equally involved and invested in software-fuelled innovation and entrepreneurship. Training resources are also available.

Start-ups have the opportunity to achieve global visibility to an audience of potential investors, clients, and partners by profiling their company and posting offers and events in the BizSpark online networking hub, BizSpark Connect. Start-ups may also be highlighted as a featured company and be promoted as BizSpark "Start-up of the Day" on Microsoft.com/BizSpark and BizSpark's social media sites.

Microsoft also has related programs, such as BizSpark *One*, which was launched in 2009. In contrast to the "breadth-oriented" BizSpark program, in this "depth-oriented" program, a select group of start-ups are offered the opportunity, on a strictly "invitation-only" basis, to engage with Microsoft one-on-one for 12 months. The program is described as follows:

> The Microsoft® BizSpark® One program identifies a small number of high-potential start-ups in the Microsoft BizSpark program comprised of more than 50,000 companies from over 100 countries around the world. Microsoft works closely through a one-to-one relationship with these companies, providing customized engagement plans to accelerate their growth including access to technical, marketing and business development resources.
>
> (www.microsoft.com/bizspark/One/)

In the context of the Skelta case, it should be noted that by the time these programs were launched, Skelta was well beyond the three-year threshold and could not have joined these programs. In any case, the issues that they face at the end of the case could well be those facing a start-up completing a 12-month tenure on the BizSpark One program, that is: How do we manage the relationship from here?

Source: The case-writer's field interviews and Microsoft, "Microsoft BizSpark," available at www.microsoft.com/bizspark, accessed November 28, 2012; Microsoft, "Microsoft BizSpark One: The Best of BizSpark," available at www.microsoft.com/bizspark/One/, accessed November 28, 2012.

Notes

1 This name has been disguised.
2 Sanjay and Kalpa Shah are married to each other; Paritosh Shah is not a relation.
3 The source of this and all quotes, unless otherwise stated, is the case-writer's field interviews.
4 Marc Kerremans et al. (2009), *Cool vendors in business process management*, available at www.gartner.com/id=911812, accessed November 28, 2012.
5 The problem resulted from the conventional use of two digits to represent a four-digit year in digital data during the twentieth century.
6 The case-writer's field interviews indicate that Microsoft was especially keen to persuade ISVs to use their technology rather than open-source options such as Linux.

References

Abernathy, J. W., & Clark, B. (1985). Mapping the winds of creative destruction. *Research Policy, 14*, 3–22.

Acs, Z. J., Morck, R., Shaver, J. M., & Yeung, B. (1997). Internationalization of small and medium sized enterprises. *Small Business Economics, 9*, 7–20.

Acs, Z., & Terjesen, S. (2013). Born local: Toward a theory of new venture's choice of internationalization. *Small Business Economics, 41*(3), 521–535.

Adler, P. S., & Kwon, S.-W. (2002). Social capital: Prospects for a new concept. *Academy of Management Review, 27*(1), 17–40.

Agndal, H., Chetty, S., & Wilson H. (2008). Social capital dynamics and foreign market entry. *International Business Review, 17*, 663–675.

Alvarez, S. A., & Barney, J. B. (2001). How entrepreneurial firms can benefit from alliances with large partners. *Academy of Management Executive, 15*(1), 139–148.

Andersson, U., Forsgren, M., & Holm, U. (2002). The strategic impact of external networks: Subsidiary performance and competence development in the multinational corporation. *Strategic Management Journal, 23*(11), 979–996.

Andersson, U., Forsgren, M., & Holm, U. (2007). Balancing subsidiary influence in the federative MNC: A business network view. *Journal of International Business Studies, 38*, 802–818.

Arenius, P., & Autio, E. (2005, July). *Social capital and new firm internationalization.* Paper presented at the Academy of International Business, Quebec City.

Athreye, S. S. (2005). The Indian software industry and its evolving service capability. *Industrial and Corporate Change, 14*(3), 393–418.

Autio, E., Sapienza, H. J., & Almeida, J. G. (2000). Effects of age at entry, knowledge intensity, and imitability on international growth. *Academy of Management Journal, 43*, 909–924.

Awate, S., Larsen, M. M., & Mudambi, R. (2012). EMNE catch-up strategies in the wind turbine industry: Is there a trade-off between output and innovation capabilities? *Global Strategy Journal, 2*, 205–223.

Baker, T., Gedajlovic, E., & Lubatkin, M. (2005). A framework for comparing entrepreneurship processes across nations. *Journal of International Business Studies, 36*(5), 492–504.

Barney, J. (1991). Firm resources and sustained competitive advantage. *Journal of Management, 17*, 99–120.

Battilana, J., & D'Aunno, T. (2009). Institutional work and the paradox of embedded agency. In T. Lawrence, R. Suddaby, & B. Leca (Eds.), *Institutional work: Actors and agency in institutional studies of organization* (pp. 31–58). Cambridge: Cambridge University Press.

Battilana, J., Leca, B., & Boxenbaum, E. (2009). How actors change institutions: Towards a theory of institutional entrepreneurship. *Academy of Management Annals, 3*(1), 65–107.

Bell, J. (1997). A comparative study of export problems of small computer software exporters in Finland, Ireland and Norway. *International Business Review, 6*, 1–20

Birkinshaw, J. (2000). *Entrepreneurship and the global firm*. London: Sage.

Birkinshaw, J., & Hood, N. (2000). Characteristics of foreign subsidiaries in industry clusters. *Journal of International Business Studies, 31*, 141–154.

Birkinshaw, J., & Monteiro, F. (2007). *External knowledge sourcing: Uncovering the technology scouting process* (AIM Working Paper Series no. 060).

Birkinshaw, J., & Pedersen, T. (2008). Strategy and management in MNE subsidiaries. In A. M. Rugman (Ed.), *Oxford handbook of international business* (pp. 367–388). New York: Oxford University Press.

Birkinshaw, J., & Prashantham, S. (2012). Initiative in multinational subsidiaries. In A. Verbeke & H. Merchant (Eds.), *Handbook of research on international strategic management* (pp. 155–168). Northampton, MA: Edward Elgar.

Blankenburg Holm, D., Eriksson, K., & Johanson, J. (1999). Creating value through mutual commitment to business network relationships. *Strategic Management Journal, 20*, 467–486.

Boethe, D. (2013). Collaborate at home to win abroad: How does access to local networks influence export behavior? *Journal of Small Business Management, 51*(2), 167–182.

Bouquet, C., & Birkinshaw, J. (2008). Managing power in the multinational corporation. *Journal of Management, 34*(3), 477–50.

Bourdieu, P. (1986). The forms of capital. In J. E. Richardson (Ed.), *Handbook of theory of research for the sociology of education* (pp. 241–258). New York: Greenwood.

Brass, D. J., & Burkhardt, M. E. (1993). Potential power and power use: An investigation of structure and behaviour. *Academy of Management Journal, 36*(3), 441–470.

Brown, P., & Bell, J. D. (2001). Industrial clusters and small firm internationalisation. in J. H. Taggart, M. Berry, & M. McDermott (Eds.), *Multinationals in a new era: International strategy and management* (pp. 10–26). New York: Palgrave.

Brown, P., & McNaughton, R. B. (2003). Cluster development programmes: Panacea or placebo for promoting SME growth and internationalisation? In H. Etemad and R. W. Wright (Eds.), *Globalization and entrepreneurship: Policy and strategy perspective* (pp. 106–124). Cheltenham: Edward Elgar.

Buckley, P. J. (2006). International expansion: Foreign direct investment by small- and medium-sized enterprises. In M. Casson, B. Yeung, A. Basu, & N. Wadeson (Eds.), *Oxford handbook of entrepreneurship* (pp. 671–692). New York: Oxford University Press.

Buckley, P. J. (2009). The impact of the global factory on economic development. *Journal of World Business, 44*(2), 131–143.

Buckley, P. J. (2011). International integration and coordination in the global factory. *Management International Review, 51*(2), 269–283.

Buckley, P. J. (2012). The multinational enterprise as a global factory. In A. Verbeke & H. Merchant (Eds.), *Handbook of research on international strategic management* (pp. 77–92). New York: Oxford University Press.

Buckley, P. J., & Casson, M. C. (1976). *The future of the multinational enterprise*. London: Holmes & Meier.

Buckley, P. J., & Ghauri, P. (2004). Globalisation, economic geography and the strategy of multinational enterprises. *Journal of International Business Studies, 35*, 81–98.

Burt, R. S. (1992). *Structural holes*, Cambridge, MA: Harvard University Press.

Burt, R. S. (2004). Structural holes and good ideas. *American Journal of Sociology, 110*(2), 349–399.

Cantwell, J. A. (2013). Blurred boundaries between firms, and new boundaries within (large multinational) firms: The impact of decentralized networks for innovation. *Seoul Journal of Economics, 26*(1), 1–32.

Cantwell, J. A., & Mudambi, R. (2005). MNE competence-creating subsidiary mandates. *Strategic Management Journal, 26,* 1109–1128.

Cantwell, J. A., & Mudambi, R. (2011). Physical attraction and the geography of knowledge sourcing in multinational enterprises. *Global Strategy Journal, 1*(3–4), 206–232.

Cao Q. (2006). *Navigating through extreme asymmetry: Partnerships between entrepreneurial ventures and established firms* (unpublished doctoral dissertation). University of Maryland.

Carlile, P. R. (2002). A pragmatic view of knowledge and boundaries: Boundary objects in new product development. *Organization Science, 13*(4), 442–455.

Chesbrough, H. (2006). *Open business models: How to thrive in the new innovation landscape*. Boston: Harvard Business School Press.

Chetty, S., & Pahlberg, C. (2015). An internationalizing entrepreneurial firm's network is their networth. In S. A. Fernhaber, & S. Prashantham (Eds.), *Routledge companion to international entrepreneurship* (pp. 117–131). London: Routledge.

Child, J., Lu, Y., & Tsai, T. (2007). Institutional entrepreneurship in building an environmental protection system for the People's Republic of China. *Organization Studies, 28*(7), 1013–1034.

Coleman, J. S. (1988). Social capital in the creation of human capital. *American Journal of Sociology, 94,* S95–S121.

Coviello, N. E. (2006). The network dynamics of international new ventures. *Journal of International Business Studies, 37*(5), 713–731.

Coviello, N. E., McDougall, P. P., & Oviatt, B. M. (2011). The emergence, advance and future of international entrepreneurship research: An introduction to the special forum. *Journal of Business Venturing, 26*(6), 625–631.

Coviello, N. E., & Munro, H. (1997). Network relationships and the internationalization process of small software firms. *International Business Review, 6,* 361–386.

Crossan, M. M., & Berdrow, I. (2003). Organizational learning and strategic renewal. *Strategic Management Journal, 24,* 1087–1105.

Cumming, D., Sapienza, H. J., Siegel, D. S., & Wright, M. (2009). International entrepreneurship: Managerial and policy implications. *Strategic Entrepreneurship Journal, 3,* 283–296.

Cyert, R. M., & March, J. G. (1963). *A behavioral theory of the firm*. New York: Prentice Hall.

Dacin, M. T., Beal, B. D., & Ventresca, M. J. (1999). The embeddedness of organizations: Dialogue and directions. *Journal of Management, 25*(3), 317–356.

Davidsson, P., & Honig, B. (2003). The role of social and human capital among nascent entrepreneurs. *Journal of Business Venturing, 18*(3), 301–331.

D'Costa, A. P. (2003). Uneven and combined development: Understanding India's software exports. *World Development, 31,* 211–226.

De Carolis, D. M., & Saparito, P. (2006). Social capital, cognition, and entrepreneurial opportunities: A theoretical framework. *Entrepreneurship Theory and Practice, 30*(1), 41–56.

Dhanaraj, C., & Beamish, P. W. (2003). A resource based approach to the study of export performance. *Journal of Small Business Management, 41*, 242–261.

Dhanaraj, C., Lyles, M. A., Steensma, H. K., & Tihanyi, L. (2004). Managing tacit and explicit knowledge transfer in IJVs: The role of relational embeddedness and the impact on performance. *Journal of International Business Studies, 35*, 428–442.

Dhanaraj, C., & Parkhe, A. (2006). Orchestrating innovation networks. *Academy of Management Review, 31*(3), 659–669.

Diestre, L., & Rajagopalan, N. (2012). Are all "sharks" dangerous? New biotechnology ventures and partner selection in R&D alliances. *Strategic Management Journal, 33*(10), 1115–1134.

Dimitratos, P., Johnson, J. E., Slow, J., & Young, S. (2003). Micromultinationals: New types of firms for the global competitive landscape. *European Management Journal, 21*, 164–174.

Doz, Y. L. (1988). Technology partnerships between larger and smaller firms: Some critical issues. *International Studies of Management and Organization, 17*(4), 31–57.

Doz, Y. L., Santos, J., & Williamson, P. (2001). *From global to metanational: How companies win in the knowledge economy.* Boston: Harvard Business School Press.

Dyer, J. H., & Singh, H. (1998) The relational view: Cooperative strategy and sources of interorganizational competitive advantage. *Academy of Management Review, 23*, 660–679.

Enright, M. J. (2000). Regional clusters and multinational enterprises: Independence, dependence, or interdependence? *International Studies of Management and Organization, 30*, 114–138.

Eriksson, K., Johanson, J., Majkgard, A., & Sharma, D. D. (1997). Experiential knowledge and cost in the internationalization process. *Journal of International Business Studies, 28*, 337–360.

Etemad, H., Wright, R. W., & Dana, L. P. (2001). Symbiotic international business networks: Collaboration between small and large firms. *Thunderbird International Business Review, 43*, 481–491.

Fernhaber, S. A., Gilbert, B. A., & McDougall, P. P., (2008). International entrepreneurship and geographic location: An empirical examination of new venture internationalization. *Journal of International Business Studies, 39*, 267–290.

Fernhaber, S. A., McDougall-Covin, P. P., & Shepherd, D. A. (2009). International entrepreneurship: Leveraging internal and external knowledge sources. *Strategic Entrepreneurship Journal, 3*, 297–320.

Fernhaber, S. A., & Prashantham, S. (2015). *Routledge companion to international entrepreneurship.* London: Routledge.

Floyd, S. W., & Lane, P. J. (2000). Strategizing throughout the organization: Management role conflict in strategic renewal. *Academy of Management Review, 25*, 154–177.

Floyd, S. W., & Wooldridge, B. (2000). *Building strategy from the middle: Reconceptualizing strategy process.* London: Sage.

Forsgren, M., Holm, U., & Johanson, J. (2005). *Managing the embedded multinational: A business network view.* Northampton, MA: Edward Elgar.

Gabrielsson, G., & Kirpalani, V. H. M. (2004). Born globals: How to reach new business space rapidly. *International Business Review, 13*, 555–571.

Ghauri, P., & Grønhaug, K. (2002). *Research methods in business studies.* London: Prentice Hall.

Ghemawat, P. (2003). Semiglobalization and international business strategy. *Journal of International Business Studies, 34*(2), 138–152.

Ghoshal, S., & Bartlett, C. (1990). The multinational corporation as an interorganizational network. *Academy of Management Review, 15*, 603–625.

Govindarajan, V., & Ramamurti, R. (2011). Reverse innovation, emerging markets, and global strategy. *Global Strategy Journal, 1*, 191–205.

Granovetter, M. (1973). The strength of weak ties. *American Journal of Sociology, 78*, 1360–1380.

Granovetter, M. (1985). Economic action and social structure: The problem of embeddedness. *American Journal of Sociology, 91*, 481–510.

Greve, H. R. (2003). *Organizational learning from performance feedback: A behavioral perspective on innovation and change.* New York: Cambridge University Press.

Gulati, R. (1995). Does familiarity breed trust? The implications of repeated ties for contractual choices. *Academy of Management Journal, 35*, 85–112.

Gulati, R. (1999). Network location and learning: The influence of network resources and firm capabilities on alliance formation. *Strategic Management Journal, 20*, 397–420.

Gulati, R. (2007). *Managing network resources: Alliances, affiliations and other relational assets.* New York: Oxford University Press.

Gulati, R., & Sytch, M. (2007). Dependence asymmetry and joint dependence in interorganizational relationships: Effects of embeddedness on a manufacturer's performance in procurement relationships. *Administrative Science Quarterly, 52*(3), 32–69.

Gupta, A. K., & Govindarajan, V. (2002). Cultivating a global mindset. *Academy of Management Executive, 16*, 116–126.

Hagedoorn, J., & Narula, R. (1996). Choosing organizational modes of strategic technology partnering: International and sectoral differences. *Journal of International Business Studies, 27*(2), 265–284.

Hair, J. F., Anderson, R. E., Tatham, R. L., & Black, W. C. (1998). *Multivariate data analysis.* Upper Saddle River, NJ: Prentice-Hall.

Håkansson, H., & Snehota, I. (1995). (Eds.), *Developing relationships in business networks.* London: Routledge.

Halinen, A., Salmi, A., & Havila, V. (1999). From dyadic change to changing business networks: An analytical framework. *Journal of Management Studies, 36*, 779–794.

Hallen, B. L., Katila, R., & Rosenberger, J. D. (2014). Unpacking social defenses: A resource-dependence lens on technology ventures, venture capital, and corporate relationships. *Academy of Management Journal 57*(4), 1078–1101.

Hargrave, T. J., & Van de Ven, A. H. (2009). Institutional work as the creative embrace of contradiction. In T. B. Lawrence, R. Suddaby, & B. Leca (Eds.), *Institutional work: Actors and agency in institutional studies of organizations* (pp. 120–140). Cambridge: Cambridge University Press.

Hennart, J.-F. (2009). Down with MNE-centric theories! Market entry and expansion as the bundling of MNE and local assets. *Journal of International Business Studies, 40*(9), 1432–1454.

Hitt, M. A., Bierman, L., Uhlenbruck, K., & Shimizu, K. (2006). The importance of resources in the internationalization of professional service firms: The good, the bad, and the ugly. *Academy of Management Journal, 49*(6), 1137–1157.

Hitt, M. A., Ireland, R. D., Camp, S. M., & Sexton, D. L. (2001). Strategic entrepreneurship: Entrepreneurial strategies for wealth creation. *Strategic Management Journal, 22*, 479–491.

Inkpen, A. C., & Tsang, E. W. K. (2005). Social capital, networks, and knowledge transfer. *Academy of Management Review, 30*, 146–165.

Johanson, J., & Mattsson, L.-G. (1988). Internationalisation in industrial systems: A network approach. In D. Ford (Ed.), *Understanding business markets: Interaction, relationships and networks* (2nd edn, pp. 194–213). London: Dryden Press. (Reprinted from N. Hood & J.-E. Vahlne (Eds.), *Strategies in global competition* (pp. 287–314). New York: Croom Helm.)

Johanson, J., & Vahlne, J.-E. (1977). The internationalization process of the firm: A model of knowledge development and increasing foreign market commitments. *Journal of International Business Studies, 8,* 23–32.

Johanson, J., & Vahlne, J.-E. (1990). The mechanism of internationalization. *International Marketing Review, 7*(4), 11–24.

Johanson, J., & Vahlne, J.-E. (1992). Management of foreign market entry. *Scandinavian International Business Review, 1*(3): 9–27.

Johanson, J., & Vahlne, J.-E. (2003). Business relationship learning and commitment in the internationalization process. *Journal of International Entrepreneurship, 1,* 83–102.

Johanson, J., & Vahlne, J.-E. (2006). Commitment and opportunity development in the internationalization process: A note on the Uppsala internationalization process model. *Management International Review, 46,* 165–178.

Johanson, J., & Vahlne, J.-E. (2009). The Uppsala internationalization process model revisited: From liability of foreignness to liability of outsidership. *Journal of International Business Studies, 40,* 1411–1431.

Johanson, J., & Vahlne, J.-E. (2011). Markets as networks: Implications for strategy-making. *Journal of the Academy of Marketing Science, 39*(4): 484–491.

Johanson, J., & Vahlne, J.-E. (2014). Replacing traditional economics with behavioral assumptions in constructing the Uppsala model: Toward a theory on the evolution of the multinational business enterprise. *Research in Global Strategic Management, 16,* 159–176.

Johanson, J., & Wiedersheim-Paul, F. (1975). The internationalization of the firm: Four Swedish cases. *Journal of Management Studies, 12,* 305–322.

Johnson, G., & Huff, A. (1998), Everyday innovation/everyday strategy. In G. Hamel, C. K. Prahalad, H. Thomas, & D. O'Neal (Eds.), *Strategic flexibility: Managing in a turbulent economy* (pp. 13–27). Chichester: Wiley.

Jones, M. V. (1999). The internationalization of small high-technology firms. *Journal of International Marketing, 7*(4), 15–41.

Jones, M., & Coviello, N. (2005). Internationalisation: Conceptualising an entrepreneurial process of behaviour in time. *Journal of International Business Studies, 36* (3), pp. 284–303.

Jones, M. V., Coviello, N. E., & Tang, Y. K. (2011). International entrepreneurship research (1989–2009): A domain ontology and thematic analysis. *Journal of Business Venturing, 26,* 632–659.

Kale, P., Dyer, J. H., & Singh, H. (2002). Alliance capability, stock market response, and long-term alliance success: The role of the alliance function. *Strategic Management Journal, 23,* 747–767.

Kale, P., Singh, H., & Perlmutter, H. (2000). Learning and protection of proprietary assets in strategic alliances: Building relational capital. *Strategic Management Journal, 21,* 217–237.

Katila, R., Rosenberger, J. D., & Eisenhardt, K. M. (2008). Swimming with sharks: Technology ventures and corporate relationships. *Administrative Science Quarterly, 53,* 295–332.

Keupp, M. M., & Gassmann, O. (2009). The past and the future of international entrepreneurship: A review and suggestions for developing the field. *Journal of Management, 35,* 600–633.

Kiss, A. N., Danis, W. M., & Cavusgil, S. T. (2012). International entrepreneurship research in emerging economies: A critical review and research agenda. *Journal of Business Venturing, 27*(2), 266–290.

Knight, G. A., & Cavusgil, S. T. (1996). The born global firm: A challenge to traditional internationalisation theory. *Advances in International Marketing, 8,* 11–26.

Knight, G. A., & Cavusgil, S. T. (2004). Innovation, organizational capabilities, and the born-global firm. *Journal of International Business Studies, 35,* 124–141.

Kogut, B., & Zander, U. (1992). Knowledge of the firm, combinative capabilities, and the replication of technology. *Organization Science, 3,* 383–397.

Kogut, B., & Zander, U. (1993). Knowledge of the firm and the evolutionary theory of the multinational corporation. *Journal of International Business Studies, 24,* 625–645.

Kostova, T., & Roth, K. (2003). Social capital in multinational corporations and a micro–macro model of its formation. *Academy of Management Review, 28,* 297–317.

Krackhardt, D. (1992). The strength of strong ties: The importance of philos in organizations. In N. Nohria & R. G. Eccles (Eds.), *Networks and organizations: Structure, form and action* (pp. 216–239). Boston: Harvard Business School Press.

Krishnan, R. T. (2010). *From jugaad to systematic innovation.* Bangalore: Utpreraka Foundation.

Kumar, K. (2009). The role of local entrepreneurship and multinational firms in the growth of IT sector: An exploratory study of Bangalore. *South Asian Journal of Management, 16*(3), 24–42.

Kumar, K., & Krishnan, R. T. (2003a). Growth challenges of software SMITs: A strategic analysis. *IIMB Management Review, 15,* 112–118.

Kumar, K., & Krishnan, R. T. (2003b). *Emerging market companies ascending the value curve: rationale, motivation and strategies.* Paper presented at the Strategic Management Society Mini-Conference on Emerging Economies, Hong Kong.

Kumar, N., Mohapatra, P. K., & Chandrasekhar, S. (2009). *India's global powerhouses: How they are taking on the world.* Boston: Harvard Business School Press.

Kumar, N., Stern, L. W., & Anderson, J. C. (1993). Conducting interorganizational research using key informants. *Academy of Management Journal, 36,* 1633–1651.

Kumaraswamy, A., Mudambi, R., Saranga, H., & Tripathy, A. (2012). Catch-up strategies in the Indian auto components industry: Domestic firms' responses to market liberalization. *Journal of International Business Studies, 43,* 368–395.

Kundu, S. K., & Katz, J. (2003). Born-international SMEs: BI-level impacts of resources and intentions. *Small Business Economics, 20,* 25–47.

Lane, P. J., & Lubatkin, M. (1998). Relative absorptive capacity and interorganizational learning. *Strategic Management Journal, 19,* 461–477.

Latour, B. (1987). *Science in action.* Milton Keynes: Open University Press.

Lavie, D. (2006). The competitive advantage of interconnected firms: An extension of the resource-based view. *Academy of Management Review, 31*(3), 638–658.

Lavie, D., & Rosenkopf, L. (2006). Balancing exploration and exploitation in alliance formation, *Academy of Management Journal, 49,* 797–818.

Lawrence, T. B., & Suddaby, R. (2006). Institutions and institutional work. In S. Clegg, C. Hardy, W. Nord, & T. B. Lawrence (Eds.), *Handbook of organization studies* (pp. 215–254). London: Sage.

Lawrence, T. B., Leca, B., & Zilber, T. B. (2013). Institutional work: Current research, new directions and overlooked issues. *Organization Studies, 34*(8), 1023–1033.

Lawrence, T. B., Suddaby, R., & Leca, B. (2011). Institutional work: Refocusing institutional studies of organization. *Journal of Management Inquiry, 20*(1), 52–58.

Lee, C., Lee, K., & Pennings, J. M. (2001). Internal capabilities, external networks, and performance: A study on technology-based ventures. *Strategic Management Journal, 22*, 615–640.

Levinthal, D. A., & March, J. G. (1993). The myopia of learning. *Strategic Management Journal, 14*, 95–112.

Lewicki, R. J., & Bunker, B. B. (1996). Developing and maintaining trust in work relationships. In R. M. Kramer & T. R. Tyler (Eds.), *Trust in organizations: Frontiers of theory and research* (pp. 114–139). Thousand Oaks, CA: Sage.

Lewis, M. W. (2000). Exploring paradox: Toward a more comprehensive guide. *Academy of Management Review, 25*, 760–776.

Lorenzen, M., & Mudambi, R. (2013). Clusters, connectivity and catch-up: Bollywood and Bangalore in the global economy. *Journal of Economic Geography, 13*(3), 501–534.

Lorenzoni, G., & Lipparini, A. (1999). The leveraging of interfirm relationships as a distinctive capability: A longitudinal study. *Strategic Management Journal, 20*, 317–338.

Lu, J. W., & Beamish, P. W. (2001). The internationalization and performance of SMEs. *Strategic Management Journal, 22*, 565–586.

Lubatkin, M. F., Simsek, Z., Ling, Y., & Veiga, J. F. (2006). Ambidexterity and performance in small- to medium-sized firms: The pivotal role of top management team behavioral integration. *Journal of Management, 32*, 646–672.

Luo, Y., & Tung, R. L. (2007). International expansion of emerging market enterprises: A springboard perspective. *Journal of International Business Studies, 38*(4), 481–498.

Madhok, A. (1995). Revisiting multinational firms' tolerance for joint ventures: A trust-based approach. *Journal of International Business Studies, 26*, 117–138.

Madhok, A. (2006). How much does ownership really matter? Equity and trust relations in joint venture relationships. *Journal of International Business Studies, 37*, 4–11.

March, J. G. (1991). Exploration and exploitation in organizational learning. *Organization Science, 2*, 71–87.

March, J. G. (2006). Rationality, foolishness and adaptive intelligence. *Strategic Management Journal, 27*, 201–214.

McDougall, P. P., & Oviatt, B. M. (2000). International entrepreneurship: The intersection of two research paths. *Academy of Management Journal, 43*, 902–908.

McDougall, P. P., Shane, S., & Oviatt, B. M. (1994). Explaining the formation of international new ventures: The limits of theories from international business research. *Journal of Business Venturing, 9*, 469–487.

McDougall-Covin, P., Jones, M. V., & Serapio, M. G. (2014). High-potential concepts, phenomena and theories for the advancement of international entrepreneurship research. *Entrepreneurship Theory and Practice, 38*, 1–10.

McEvily, B., & Marcus, A. (2005). Embeddedness and the acquisition of competitive capabilities. *Strategic Management Journal, 26*, 1033–1055.

McEvily, B., & Zaheer, A. (1999). Bridging ties: A source of firm heterogeneity in competitive capabilities. *Strategic Management Journal, 20*, 1133–1156.

McGrath, R. G., & MacMillan, I. (2000). *The entrepreneurial mindset*. Boston: Harvard Business School Press.

McNaughton, R. B., & Bell, J. D. (1999). Brokering networks of small firms to generate social capital for growth and internationalization. *Research in Global Strategic Management, 7*, 63–82.

McNaughton, R. B., & Pellegrino, J. (2015). Policy implications of international entrepreneurship. In S. A. Fernhaber & S. Prashantham (Eds.), *Routledge companion to international entrepreneurship* (pp. 235–244). London: Routledge.

McPherson, M., Smith-Lovin, L., & Cook, J. M. (2001). Birds of a feather: Homophily in social networks. *Annual Review of Sociology, 27*, 415–444.

Meyer, K. E., Mudambi, R., & Narula, R. (2011). Multinational enterprises and local contexts: The opportunities and challenges of multiple embeddedness. *Journal of Management Studies, 48*(2), 235–252.

Milanov, H., & Fernhaber, S. A. (2014). When do domestic alliances help ventures abroad? Direct and moderating effects from a learning perspective. *Journal of Business Venturing, 29*, 377–391.

Miles, M. B., & Huberman, A. M. (1994), *Qualitative data analysis*. London: Sage.

Mills, J. S. (1848). *Principles of political economy with some of their applications to social philosophy*. London: Longmans, Green and Co.

Mudambi, R., & Navarra, P. (2004). Is knowledge power? Knowledge flows, subsidiary power and rent-seeking within MNCs. *Journal of International Business Studies, 35*, 385–406.

Mudambi, R., Schründer, C. P., & Mongar, A. (2004). How co-operative is co-operative purchasing in smaller firms?: Evidence from UK engineering SMEs. *Long Range Planning, 37*(1), 85–102.

Nahapiet, J., & Ghoshal, S. (1998). Social capital, intellectual capital, and the organizational advantage. *Academy of Management Review, 23*(2), 242–266.

Nambisan, S., & Sawhney, M. (2011). Orchestration processes in network-centric innovation: Evidence from the field. *Academy of Management Perspectives, 25*(3), 40–57.

Nanda, R., & Khanna, T. (2010). Diasporas and domestic entrepreneurs: Evidence from the Indian software industry. *Journal of Economics and Management Strategy, 19*(4), 991–1012.

Nasra, R., & Dacin, M. T. (2010). Institutional arrangements and international entrepreneurship: The state as institutional entrepreneur. *Entrepreneurship Theory and Practice, 34*(3), 583–609.

Nasscom. (2014). *India: Software product hotbed*. Retrieved November 11, 2014, from www.nasscom.in/software-products.

Nebus, J. (2006). Building collegial information networks: A theory of advice network generation. *Academy of Management Journal, 31*, 615–637.

Ocasio, W. (1997). Towards an attention-based view of the firm. *Strategic Management Journal, 18*, 187–206.

O'Mahony, S., & Bechky, B. A. (2008). Boundary organizations: Enabling collaboration among unexpected allies. *Administrative Science Quarterly, 53*(3), 422–459.

Orton, J. D. (1997). From inductive to iterative grounded theory: Zipping the gap between process theory and process data. *Scandinavian Journal of Management, 13*, 419–438.

Oviatt, B. M., & McDougall, P. P. (1994). Toward a theory of new international ventures. *Journal of International Business Studies, 25*, 45–64.

Oviatt, B. M., & McDougall, P. P. (2005). Defining international entrepreneurship and modeling the speed of internationalization. *Entrepreneurship Theory and Practice, 29*(5), 537–554.

Ozcan, P., & Eisenhardt, K. M. (2009). Origin of alliance portfolios: Entrepreneurs, network strategies and performance. *Academy of Management Journal, 52*, 246–279.

Patibandla, M., & Petersen, B. (2002). Role of transnational corporations in the evolution of a high-tech industry: The case of India's software industry. *World Development, 30*(9), 1561–1577.

Penrose, E. T. (1959). *The theory of the growth of the firm*. Oxford: Basil Blackwell.

Phelps, R., Adams, R., & Bessant, J. (2007). Life cycles of growing organizations: A review with implications for knowledge and learning. *International Journal of Management Reviews, 9*: 1–30.

Phene, A., & Almeida, A. (2008). Innovation in multinational subsidiaries: The role of knowledge assimilation and subsidiary capabilities. *Journal of International Business Studies, 39*, 901–919.

Phillips, N., & Lawrence, T. B. (2012). The turn to work in organization and management theory: Some implications for strategic organization. *Strategic Organization, 10*, 223–230.

Portes, A. (1998). Social capital: Its origins and applications in modern sociology. *Annual Review of Sociology, 24*, 1–24.

Portes, A., & Sensenbrenner, J. (1993). Embeddedness and immigration: Notes on the social determinants of economic action. *American Journal of Sociology, 98*(6), 1320–1350.

Prahalad, C. K. (2004). *The fortune at the bottom of the pyramid: Eradicating poverty through profits.* Philadelphia: Wharton School Publishing.

Prashantham, S. (2005). Toward a knowledge-based conceptualization of internationalization. *Journal of International Entrepreneurship, 3*(1), 37–52.

Prashantham, S. (2008). New venture internationalization as strategic renewal. *European Management Journal, 26*(6), 378–387.

Prashantham, S. (2011). Social capital and Indian micromultinationals. *British Journal of Management, 22*(1), 4–20.

Prashantham, S., & Berry, M. M. (2004). The small knowledge-intensive firm: A conceptual discussion of its characteristics and internationalisation. *International Journal of Entrepreneurship and Innovation Management, 4*(2), 150–158.

Prashantham, S., & Birkinshaw, J. (2008). Dancing with gorillas: How small companies can partner effectively with MNCs. *California Management Review, 51*(1), 6–23.

Prashantham, S., & Birkinshaw, J. (2015). Choose your friends carefully: Home-country ties and new venture internationalization. *Management International Review*, in press.

Prashantham, S., & Dhanaraj, C. (2010). The dynamic influence of social capital on the international growth of new ventures. *Journal of Management Studies, 47*(6), 967–994.

Prashantham, S., & Dhanaraj, C. (2015). MNE ties and new venture internationalization: Exploratory insights from India. *Asia Pacific Journal of Management*, in press.

Prashantham, S., Dhanaraj, C., & Kumar, K. (2015). Ties that bind: Ethnic ties and new venture internationalization. *Long Range Planning*, in press.

Prashantham, S., & Floyd, S. W. (2012). Routine microprocesses and capability learning in international new ventures. *Journal of International Business Studies, 43*(6), 544–562.

Prashantham, S., & McNaughton, R. B. (2006). Facilitating links between MNC subsidiaries and SMEs: The Scottish Technology and Collaboration (STAC) initiative. *International Business Review, 15*, 447–462.

Prashantham, S., & Young, S. (2011). Post-entry speed of international new ventures. *Entrepreneurship Theory and Practice, 35*(2), 275–292.

ProductNation, 2014. *Tracking the size of the Indian B2B software product industry.* Retrieved November 11, 2014 from http://pn.ispirt.in/ispirt-size-growth-b2b-software-products-india-index-ispixb2b/.

Putnam, R. D. (2000). *Bowling alone: The collapse and revival of American community.* New York: Simon and Schuster.

Putnam, R. D., & Goss, K. (2002). Introduction. In R. D. Putnam (Ed.), *Democracies in flux: The evolution of social capital in contemporary society* (pp. 3–20). New York: Oxford University Press.

Ramamurti, R. (2004). Developing countries and MNEs: Extending and enriching the research agenda. *Journal of International Business Studies, 35*(4), 277–283.

Reuber, A. R., & Fischer, E. (1997). The influence of the management team's international experience on the internationalization. *Journal of International Business, 28*, 807–825.

Rindfleisch, A., & Moorman, C. (2001). The acquisition and utilization of information in new product alliances: A strength-of-ties perspective. *Journal of Marketing, 65*, 1–18.

Ring, P. S., & Van de Ven, A. H. (1994). Developmental processes of cooperative interorganizational relationships. *Academy of Management Review, 19*, 90–118.

Rugman, A. M., & D'Cruz, J. R. (1997). The theory of the flagship firm. *European Management Journal, 15*(4), 403–412.

Rugman, A. M., & D'Cruz, J. R. (2000). *Multinationals as flagship firms.* New York: Oxford University Press.

Rugman, A. M., & Verbeke, A. (2001). Subsidiary-specific advantages in multinational enterprises. *Strategic Management Journal, 22*, 237–250.

Sapienza, H. J., Autio, E., George, G., & Zahra, S. A. (2006). A capabilities perspective on the effects of new venture internationalization on survival and growth. *Academy of Management Review, 31*, 914–933.

Sapienza, H. J., De Clercq, D., & Sandberg, W. R. (2005). Antecedents of international and domestic learning effort. *Journal of Business Venturing, 20*, 437–457.

Sarkar, M. B., Echambadi, R. A. J., & Harrison, J. S. (2001). Alliance entrepreneurship and firm market performance. *Strategic Management Journal, 22*, 701–711.

Saxenian, A. (2006). *The new argonauts: Regional advantage in a global economy.* Cambridge, MA: Harvard University Press.

Schulz, M. (2001). The uncertain relevance of newness: Organizational learning and knowledge flows. *Academy of Management Journal, 44*(4), 661–681.

Scott, W. R. (2001). *Institutions and organizations.* Thousand Oaks, CA: Sage.

Shane, S. (2003). *A general theory of entrepreneurship: The individual–opportunity nexus.* Northampton, MA: Edward Elgar.

Shipilov, A. V., Li, S. X., & Greve, H. R. (2011). The prince and the pauper: Search and brokerage in the initiation of status-heterophilous ties. *Organization Science, 22*(6), 1418–1434.

Simsek, Z., Lubatkin, M. H., & Floyd, S. W. (2003). How networks influence entrepreneurial behavior: A structural embeddedness perspective. *Journal of Management, 29*, 427–442.

Slotte-Kock, S., & Coviello, N. (2010). Entrepreneurship research on network processes: A review and ways forward. *Entrepreneurship Theory and Practice, 34*, 31–57.

Smith, W. K., & Lewis, M. W. (2011). Toward a theory of paradox: A dynamic equilibrium model of organizing. *Academy of Management Review, 36*(2), 381–403.

Smith, W. K., & Tushman, M. L. (2005). Managing strategic contradictions: A top management model for managing innovation streams. *Organization Science, 16*, 522–536.

Stuart, T. B., & Sorenson, O. (2007). Strategic networks and entrepreneurial ventures. *Strategic Entrepreneurship Journal, 1*, 211–227.

Terjesen, S., O'Gorman, C., & Acs, Z. J. (2008). Intermediated mode of internationalization: New software ventures in Ireland and India. *Entrepreneurship and Regional Development, 20*(1), 89–109.

Tolbert, P. S., & Zucker, L. G. (1983). Institutional sources of change in the formal structure of organizations: The diffusion of civil service reform, 1880–1935. *Administrative Science Quarterly, 28*, 22–39.

Turnbull, P., Ford, D., & Cunningham, M. (1996). Interaction, relationships and networks in business markets: An evolving perspective. *Journal of Business and Industrial Marketing, 11*(3/4), 44–62.

University of Cambridge (2007). *Cavendish spawns the future of reading.* Retrieved on November 11, 2014, from www.cam.ac.uk/news/cavendish-spawns-the-future-of-reading.

Uzzi, B. (1997). Social structure and competition in interfirm networks: The paradox of embeddedness. *Administrative Science Quarterly, 42,* 36–67.

Uzzi, B., & Gillespie, J. J. (2002). Knowledge spillover in corporate financing networks: Embeddedness and the firm's debt performance. *Strategic Management Journal, 23,* 595–618.

Uzzi, B., & Lancaster, R. (2003). Relational embeddedness and learning: The case of bank loan managers and their clients. *Management Science, 49,* 383–399.

Vandaie, R., & Zaheer, A. (2014). Surviving bear hugs: Firm capability, large partner alliances, and growth. *Strategic Management Journal, 35,* 566–577.

Vapola, T. J. (2011). The laws of attraction: Start-up firm's drivers for multinational partner selection. *Journal of International Entrepreneurship, 9,* 39–61.

Vapola, T. J., Tossavainen, P., & Gabrielsson, M. (2008). The battleship strategy: The complementing role of born globals in MNC's new opportunity creation. *Journal of International Entrepreneurship, 6*(1), 1–21.

Venkataraman, S., & Sarasvathy, S. D. (2001). Strategy and entrepreneurship: Outlines of an untold story. In M. A. Hitt, E. Freeman, and J. S. Harrison (Eds.), *Handbook of strategic management* (pp. 650–668). Oxford: Blackwell.

Wang, J., Cheng, S., & Ganapati, S. (2012). Path dependence in regional ICT innovation: Differential evolution of Zhongguancun and Bangalore. *Regional Science Policy and Practice, 4*(3), 231–245.

Welch, C., & Wilkinson, I. (2004). The political embeddedness of international business networks. *International Marketing Review, 21*(2), 216–231.

Welch, D. E., & Welch, L. S. (1996). The internationalization process and networks: A strategic management perspective. *Journal of International Marketing, 4*(3), 11–28.

Wiklund, J., & Shepherd, S. (2003). Knowledge-based resources, entrepreneurial orientation, and the performance of small and medium-sized businesses. *Strategic Management Journal, 24,* 1307–1314.

Wright, M., Filatotchev, I., Hoskisson, R., & Peng, M. (2005). Strategy research in emerging economies: Challenging the conventional wisdom. *Journal of Management Studies, 42,* 1–34.

Wright, M., Lockett, A., Clarysse, B., & Binks, M. (2006). University spin-out companies and venture capital. *Research Policy, 35,* 481–501.

Wright, M., Westhead, P., & Ucbasaran, D. (2007). The internationalization of SMEs and international entrepreneurship: A critique and policy implications. *Regional Studies, 41,* 1013–1029.

Xu, D., & Meyer, K. E. (2013). Linking theory and context: Strategy research in emerging economies after Wright et al. (2005). *Journal of Management Studies, 50,* 1322–1346.

Yang, Q., Mudambi, R., & Meyer, K. E. (2008). Conventional and reverse knowledge flows in multinational corporations. *Journal of Management, 34*(5), 882–902.

Yin, R. K. (1994). *Case study research: Design and methods.* London: Sage.

Yli-Renko, H., Autio, E., & Sapienza, H. J. (2001). Social capital, knowledge acquisition, and knowledge exploitation in young technology-based firms. *Strategic Management Journal, 22,* 587–613.

Yli-Renko, H., Autio, E., & Tontti, V. (2002). Social capital, knowledge, and the international growth of technology-based new firms. *International Business Review, 11*(3), 279–304.

Yli-Renko, H., & Janakiraman, R. (2008). How customer portfolio affects new product development in technology-based entrepreneurial firms. *Journal of Marketing, 72,* 131–148.

Young, S., Hood, N., & Peters, E. (1994). Multinational enterprise and regional development. *Regional Studies, 28,* 657–677.

Young, S., & Tavares, A. T. (2004). Centralization and autonomy: Back to the future. *International Business Review, 13,* 215–237.

Yu, J., Gilbert, B. A., & Oviatt, B. M. (2011). Effects of alliances, time, and network cohesion on the initiation of foreign sales by new ventures. *Strategic Management Journal, 32,* 424–446.

Zaheer, S. (1995). Overcoming the liability of foreignness. *Academic Management Journal, 38,* 341–363.

Zahra, S. A. (1996). Technology strategy and new venture performance: A study of corporate-sponsored and independent biotechnology ventures. *Journal of Business Venturing, 11,* 289–321.

Zahra, S. A. (2005). A theory of international new ventures: A decade of research. *Journal of International Business Studies, 36,* 20–28.

Zahra, S. A., & Dess, G. (2001). Defining entrepreneurship as a scholarly field. *Academy of Management Review, 26,* 8–10.

Zahra, S. A., Ireland, R. D., & Hitt, M. A. (2000). International expansion by new venture firms: International diversity, mode of market entry, technological learning, and performance. *Academy of Management Journal, 43,* 925–950.

Zhou, L., Wu, W., & Luo, X. (2007). Internationalization and the performance of born-global SMEs: The mediating role of social networks. *Journal of International Business Studies, 38,* 673–690.

Zietsma, C., & Lawrence, T. B. (2010). Institutional work in the transformation of an organizational field: The interplay of boundary work and practice work. *Administrative Science Quarterly, 55*(2), 189–221.

Zeitsma, C., & McKnight, B. (2009). Building the iron cage: Institutional creation work in the context of competing proto-institutions. In T. B. Lawrence, R. Suddaby, & B. Leca (Eds.), *Institutional work: Actors and agency in institutional studies of organizations* (pp. 143–175). Cambridge: Cambridge University Press.

Index

Page numbers in *italics* denote tables, those in **bold** denote figures.

156   *Index*

market knowledge 6, 23, 50
markets-as-networks approach 19
market segments 122, 128, 135
market selection 6, 50–1
Mason, Dwayne 117
Microsoft 61, 128; alliance with Nokia 118; business and technology processes 132; cross-border partner program 134–5; engagement with start-ups 138–9; Gridsum–Microsoft relationship 91; knowledge-base 65; MVP Global Summit 125; .NET platform 130; Office Business Applications unit 133; Open Borders program 87, 134; quality-certification program for ISVs 131; Skelta–Microsoft relationship 61–2, 85–7, 127–39; software ecosystem event 133; summit in Seoul, Korea 87; Vista operating system 133; Worldwide Partner Conference 62, 132, 134
Microsoft China 91
Microsoft ecosystem 87, 125, 133–4
Microsoft India 57, 62, 85–8, 130, 132–3, 135
Milgram, Jason 125
Mitoken 73
MNE–INV engagement 24–6, 99, 106; adding value to the social capital 38–42; ambidexterity challenge 39–40; attention deficiency 40; balancing tensions 38; effects of MNE networks on 102–3; Invensys–Skelta 47–8; on knowledge transfer and joint innovation 108; overembeddedness trap 38–9; phenomenon of 104; relevance of 55; research agenda 102–4; research on coevolutionary dynamics between 104–5; rising innovation and 47–52; Skelta–Microsoft relationship 61–2
MNE–NV relationships: architecting 113; brokering 113; challenge associated with 109; coaching 114; consolidation of 119; extension of 119–21; feasibility of 113; formation of 119; institutional barriers dividing 109; institutional work of facilitating 111, 112–14; interfirm asymmetry 109; on knowledge transfer and joint innovation 108; management innovations to facilitate 109; Ningbo Smart City Initiative, China 114; on social interaction 109
mobile Internet services 49
mobile telephony 122
motivation, to collaborate with MNEs 114
Motorola 52, 73, 133
multinational enterprise (MNE) networks 3–4; alliance-forming behaviors of 24, *29,* 30; arbitraging goodwill 88–9; bargaining power 25; battleship strategy 25; cultivating coethnic internal champions 89; development of ties 28–30; effects on international new ventures 27; embedded 19–20; engagement patterns with small/ medium and large companies *54;* formation of 119; geography-spanning relationships 42; gravitational pull, to the home market 87, 90, 94; influence on new venture internationalization 15; in-house competency centers 41; internationalization outcomes 87–90; knowledge-seeking actions in host markets 104; leveraging of ties 30–3; marketing capabilities 119; need for partnering proactiveness 28–30; network relationships **101**; new venture ties with *37;* orchestration 22–4; outsourcing strategy *53;* partnering with partners of 89–90; potential and motivation to engage with new ventures 26; research on constraining effects of 103–4; role in new venture internationalization 102; role of bridging social capital 32–3, 40–2; significance of 23; *versus* SME partners 71–6; as source of social capital 4; strategic renewal 30–2; subsidiary entrepreneurship 4, 20–2; as substitute for voids in entrepreneurial system 67–9; *versus* venture capitalist ties 59–60
multi-unit organizations 31, 88
Munro, H. 14

Nahapiet, J. 8, 36
Nasscom 46, 48, 54, 62, 76, 131, 133; Innovation Award 133
NetGalactic Internet Solutions 47, 128
.NET software 130
network-based internationalization 16
networking organization, cross-border 77
network orchestration, notion of 89
network relationships 7, 75, 116–17; benefits of 14; Indian software ventures 46; in international markets 58; local 13; overseas (host-market) 9, 13; portfolio of 12, 14; role of 9; of small internationalizing venture 11; Uppsala approach to 15–17; utilization of 12
networks intermediaries 34
network theory in sociology, principle of 108
new venture internationalization *see* international new ventures (INVs)
new ventures (NVs) 108; international *see* international new ventures (INVs); internationalization-seeking 118;